CAPTAIN O'BANION AND THE CHINESE TROOPS ON MANEUVERS AT EAGLE ROCK, CALIFORNIA

DOUBLE TEN

Captain O'Banion's Story of the Chinese Revolution

BY

C A R L   G L I C K

Author of "Shake Hands with the Dragon"

雙
十

WHITTLESEY HOUSE

M C G R A W - H I L L   B O O K   C O M P A N Y ,   I N C .

London   -   -   -   -   -   New York

DOUBLE TEN

Copyright, 1945, *by* CARL GLICK

SECOND PRINTING

PUBLISHED BY WHITTLESEY HOUSE
A division of the McGraw-Hill Book Company, Inc.

Printed in the United States of America

TO

AL POWERS,

GRATEFULLY FOR INTRODUCING ME TO CAPTAIN O'BANION

AND

MY CHINESE FRIENDS,

SOME OF WHOM ARE THE SONS AND GRANDSONS OF THE
REVOLUTIONISTS OF 1911

Contents

Illustrations

DOUBLE TEN

*Captain O'Banion's Story
of the Chinese Revolution*

CHAPTER ONE

Forty Years Later

THE Captain, now retired, and I stood on the street corner in front of the Union Station in Los Angeles looking at a map he had drawn. A couple of marines passed by and, hearing a word or two of what we were saying, paused a moment and gave us suspicious looks. After all this was America in wartime—October of 1943—and what kind of funny business was this?

Who were these two elderly civilians? And what were they up to, standing on this spot looking at a hand-drawn map and whispering about drilling soldiers in the waiting room yonder, meeting and bribing Japs in the USO Club, and discussing an attempted assassination?

Probably if they hadn't been in such a hurry to catch their train the marines would have stopped and investigated. Maybe they reported us to the Federal Bureau of Investigation . . . I don't know for certain.

But it wouldn't have bothered the Captain. There had been a time when he was accustomed to that sort of thing— and always had an answer up his sleeve. Then, too, years ago hadn't he walked brazenly and openly into Los Angeles with the stolen war plans of Japan in his coat pocket?

Today the Captain is in his late sixties, straight as an arrow with a proud military carriage, a stubborn bulldog chin, yet a friendly twinkle in his honest Irish eyes. Not much of a talker; yet, what he says he means. If you want to start an argument with him, go ahead. That's your business. But first take a second look at the Captain and see for yourself his confident air of a champion.

This afternoon he said with a dry chuckle, "Damn funny, but I don't think some of my neighbors in Sierra Madre even know of the part I played in the Chinese Revolution of 1911. I've never mentioned it—kept it under my hat all these years. I was sworn to secrecy. And I haven't talked—until now. A lot of people in the old days guessed something was going on, but just exactly what it was all about, and what General Homer Lea and I were up to, they didn't know for certain. How surprised they would have been had we told them the real truth. It was all what we call today very hush-hush!"

The Captain lighted his pipe. Then he said, "Where we're standing now used to be the heart of Chinatown. They tore it down some years ago—except for those few blocks across the street—to make way for this new Union Station. The old landmarks I knew so well forty years ago are now gone forever. Here was Marchessault Street. On this corner was the banquet hall where that night they tried to assassinate Dr. Sun Yat-sen."

I put on my glasses and peered over his shoulder at the map.

"The armory where we drilled the soldiers secretly was down the street a block—about where the waiting room now is. And the stockade was beyond that on Juan Street—where the tracks are."

He turned and pointed to the USO Club at the right of the station.

"About there was the Japanese bathhouse where I met

and bribed the Jap who helped me steal the plans," said the Captain.

Then he indicated some old buildings on the other side of Alameda Street.

"All that's left of the old Chinatown as I knew it is over there," he said.

He handed me the map, and I put it carefully away in my pocket for future reference. Then we crossed over and he led me up what is known as Ferguson's Alley, dismal, dingy, and narrow, and only a block long. At one side were the back doors of restaurants and shops, and on the other was a long row of dilapidated, tottering old buildings; some empty, the others quiet and deserted looking.

"Hasn't changed a bit in forty years," smiled the Captain. "But not so many people about. In the old days this was one of the busiest streets in Chinatown."

He indicated a doorway, halfway below the surface of the street, and partly concealed by a balcony.

"That's where the highbinders' hideout used to be. In that building Soo Hu-hem destroyed the White Man after he had stolen him."

"Pretty obvious place for a hideout," I said.

The Captain grinned as he replied, "One door to get in by, but half a dozen exits that not even the police knew about."

We climbed the short hill and came out on North Los Angeles Street. When old Chinatown was torn down, many of the merchants and restaurant owners moved some blocks away and built what is called China Village and New Chinatown. Their new shops and restaurants were designed in the approved Chinese style. Colorful and attractive, these two places are today popular playgrounds for sightseeing tourists.

But on North Los Angeles Street is a bit of the old Chinatown as it used to be. Here are the stores and shops of the elders who cling to the old Chinese ways. Here stubborn old China still does business in the old-fashioned manner—even as they did in those days when China had an empress on the Dragon Throne, and in Los Angeles they were plotting a revolution to overthrow her. In the dimly lighted stores are precious antiques, Chinese herbs and medicines, and imported dried foods from China. Here at night the elders sit and gossip, play mah-jongg and fan-tan, and relax as they smoke their water pipes after the day's work is done.

"It was on this corner that I saved the life of the Chinese hatchetman whom I nicknamed Duke," said the Captain. "As I told you, he became my chief operative. Did a lot of undercover work for me. Nobody—not even Homer Lea— knew about him. Duke was a great help!"

We stopped and looked into one of the windows. Among a lot of cheap gimcracks to tempt the souvenir hunter were a number of rare old pieces. The Captain pointed to a large, round brass bowl.

"It's a bowl like that the revolutionists, members of the Po Wong Wui, used. It was filled with blood. I dipped the Chinese brush in and signed the oath of that secret society. For all I know this might even be the very same bowl. If I'm not mistaken this is George Chun's store. Let's find out."

I hadn't as yet heard the Captain speak of George Chun, so I had no idea who he was.

"Hasn't changed a bit," whispered the Captain as we

went in. At the back was an old man bending over a book. He looked up as we entered, and seemed annoyed at our intrusion.

"Isn't this George Chun's store?" asked the Captain.

The merchant nodded, but made no spoken reply.

"Is George Chun still alive?" asked the Captain.

"He's still alive," answered the merchant.

"Is he around now?"

"No. He's just gone home," said the merchant. "He's getting to be an old man and so leaves early these days."

"Live far from here?" persisted the Captain.

"Why do you ask?" inquired the merchant, suspiciously.

"I'd like to see him. Could we send for him?"

"I don't know," said the merchant, displaying the typical Chinese caution when talking to a stranger. It is wisest, so they reason, to find out all you can about a man's business and the purpose of his call before you answer too many questions.

"Who shall I say wants to see him?" asked the merchant, peering over his glasses.

"An old friend."

"And the name, please?"

"Ansel O'Banion," said the Captain softly.

The merchant rose and came out from behind his desk. For a moment he stared at the Captain. Then a smile swept over his face, and he held out his hand.

"Captain O'Banion!" he exclaimed. "I didn't quite recognize you at first. Do please forgive me . . . I am George Chun."

The two men shook hands.

Then Chun said, "It's been a long time since I've seen you, my friend."

"Yes; over thirty years."

"Why haven't you been around?"

"I don't go many places these days," said the Captain. "Rarely get into Los Angeles even. I built myself a home at the foot of the mountains in Sierra Madre. I've got a garden, some chickens, and a good wife who is topside mess sergeant. I sort of live the life of Riley in retirement. I'm not a young man any more. I'll be sixty-eight my next birthday."

"I'll be eighty-one," smiled Chun. "After some of the things we've done, men our age are entitled to a little peace and quiet."

"That's it exactly," said the Captain.

For a moment they stood silently. Then Chun smiled again and said, "Well, we succeeded, didn't we, Captain?"

"Yes. We succeeded," smiled O'Banion.

Then Captain O'Banion introduced me. He told Chun that he was telling me the story and that I was planning to write a book about it.

Chun eyed me soberly. "Good," he said. "Now it can be told. So many of the old-timers are dead. Others never came back from China. But there are some still around, like myself, who remember. Yes, now it can be told!" And he wished me good luck.

"I've been showing Carl around Chinatown," said O'Banion.

"It's not like what it was in the old days," said Chun.

The two men smiled as if they shared a secret together.

"Now our sons and grandsons are off to war," said Chun. "Perhaps the story isn't finished. Perhaps it's still a part of the same revolution."

"Perhaps," said O'Banion.

"Come and see me again, Captain. Come soon and let's have a long talk about the old days—and those to come, too."

They shook hands and we went on our way.

"He's one of the old-timers who remember," said O'Banion. "Quite a revolutionist in his younger days. Made speeches and gave a lot of money to the cause."

It now being time for dinner, we walked over to the New China Village and sat down at a table in a bright, gay, and modernistic restaurant. As a middle-aged Chinese woman came over to the table to get our order, the Captain took a silver star from his pocket. He laid it on the table. The Chinese woman started to hand us menus, then stopped as she saw the star. She picked it up without a word and looked at it carefully. Then she handed it to O'Banion and smiled.

"That's the decoration Prime Minister Kang Yu-wei gave you from the Boy Emperor, isn't it, Captain O'Banion?" she said.

"Yes," he answered.

"Long time no see." She smiled.

"Thirty years," answered the Captain.

"Nearer forty," she said. "I was a little girl then. Do you remember me?"

"I certainly do," said O'Banion.

She put the menus aside. "Please let me order your dinner, Captain," she said. "I remember what you used to like. I am working here now. We are short of help. This is my eldest son's place. He's a lieutenant in the Air Corps, and my baby—he'll be nineteen in January—will be going soon. You'll have chopsticks, of course?"

"It's been a long time since I've used them," said O'Banion.

"One never really forgets. You were quite an expert in the old days."

As she went away to order our dinner, the Captain said, "Well, I fancy we're her guests tonight. Just like the Chinese. When I used to be around Chinatown, never once did they let me pay for my dinner!"

"Did she have anything to do with the revolution?" I asked.

"Oh, yes, certainly, in a way. I'll tell you about her—and all the others, too."

And he did. So here's the story of the part Captain Ansel E. O'Banion played in the Chinese Revolution of 1911 as he told it to me. It is, as he carefully explained, only a chapter in the whole story. But it is an important chapter in the great revolution of our century, which toppled an empress from her throne, freed the people of China from tyranny and oppression, and helped start China on the way toward being the ideal republic she is trying to achieve today. Just as we, too, in the United States of America are working toward that goal.

It's not a story so much of what took place in China as it is the story of the revolutionary movement here in the United States. It's really the story of Americans of Chinese descent in this country who plotted and planned, sacrificed and suffered in order that their native land might become like the America of their adoption—a democracy of free men and women.

That now and then, although not often, I have not given the real names of certain persons mentioned must obviously be pardoned. As a matter of fact, I don't know the names of some few of these Chinese. The Captain never told me. And wisely. For the end is not yet—and no revolution is ever brought to a final and complete victory. The foes of a democratic form of government are ever active, and the struggle for freedom and the rights of man is a new battle for each succeeding generation.

The struggle in China had been going on for over three hundred years when Ansel O'Banion, a young man of twenty-seven, a romantic, lusty, fighting Irishman got involved in the Chinese revolutionary movement. It happened in Los Angeles, and was something of a surprise even to him. It's doubtful that he really knew exactly what he was getting into. But he had a flair for adventure and wasn't afraid of man or devil.

It really started one morning at Fort Riley, Kansas, when he was handed a letter of introduction to Lieutenant General Homer Lea from The Adjutant General's Office of the War Department in Washington.

CHAPTER TWO

The War Department Recommends a Sergeant

ON THAT particular June morning First Sergeant O'Banion of Troop A was going about his regular duties when an orderly from headquarters appeared on the scene with the request that Sergeant O'Banion report immediately to Colonel C. C. Carr, Commanding Officer of the 4th United States Cavalry.

This well-known outfit, famous as the Gray Horse Troop, had served with distinction in the Philippine Insurrection. Only the previous September, the insurrection being over and peace declared, they had returned to the United States and were now stationed at Fort Riley, Kansas. Those who had enlisted for a period of three years—and among them was O'Banion—were expecting this month of June to receive their honorable discharge from the United States Army. Their record in the Philippines as soldiers and fighters was clean.

Just why Colonel Carr should send for him Sergeant O'Banion had no idea. But he dusted off his shoes, buttoned up his coat, put his hat on at the proper angle, squared his shoulders, and marched off to headquarters.

When he arrived at the colonel's office, he was shown in immediately. The colonel requested his aide to step outside, close the door, and see to it that he wasn't disturbed, as he wished to have a long talk with Sergeant O'Banion.

When they were alone, Colonel Carr said, "Sit down, sergeant."

O'Banion, being a good soldier, sat down.

This was, so O'Banion felt, going to be an interview out of the ordinary. Colonel Carr fumbled with some papers on his desk a moment, and pulling out a memorandum, laid it before him.

Then he said, "Sergeant, do you mind telling me something about yourself? I am not asking this because of any personal curiosity. But there have been inquiries concerning you from the War Department in Washington. Your service record says you were born in Norfolk, Nebr., on Feb. 11, 1876—but it doesn't tell me anything about your early youth, and why you enlisted in the Cavalry."

This was a rather unusual request, and it was all too obvious to O'Banion that the colonel was checking up on him. Although why the War Department should be interested in him, O'Banion couldn't even hazard a guess. But since they were making inquiries, he thought the wisest thing for him to do was to tell the truth—and tell it with a flourish.

So he said, "That's right, sir. It was in Nebraska I started to see the world. My mother had eleven children, and my father always said I was the meanest, the liveliest, and the orneriest of the lot, but I never gave him any trouble to speak of—much. We lived on a stock farm four miles from town, and as a kid I was practically raised on a horse."

In fact, as he went on to tell the colonel, it was said of the O'Banion children that their cradle was a western saddle. So young Ansel was an efficient horseman at an age when most boys are just learning to ride.

The O'Banions were hardy pioneers, restless and adventurous. Each succeeding generation had moved a little farther west from Kentucky, where they had originally settled in this country. And Ansel was no exception. As a lad he had often heard tales of the Pacific coast, and as he grew older he had but one ambition, to go west and see for himself what the land of the forty-niners was like. So when he was sixteen, and big for his age, husky and self-reliant, his father gave him permission to start out in the world seeking his fortunes.

"And," as he said to Colonel Carr, "I'm twenty-seven now—and still seeking 'em."

"Twenty-seven's a good age," said the colonel. "By that time a man, if he's worth his salt, should have some sense and should know what he wants to do with his life, and recognize an opportunity—should one come his way."

"Yes, sir," agreed O'Banion, wondering just what the colonel was driving at.

But he continued with his story. In November of 1891, riding his favorite horse, Randy, he set out from home and headed west. It was, however, three years before he finally arrived in California. His first stop was at Sheridan, Wyo., where he worked for a time herding mules in a lumber camp. From there, going by way of Yellowstone Park, he came to Billings, Mont. Here he landed a job riding the ranges as a cattle locator, and it was here, too, that he first met Captain George H. Cameron.

Captain Cameron at that time was in command of Company A of the 4th United States Cavalry, stationed at the Crow Indian Reservation. Their duty was to keep an eye on the Indians, and to be prepared to nip any possible uprisings. O'Banion hadn't been riding the ranges long before he became acquainted with the officers and cavalrymen at this army post. One day Captain Cameron, observing that O'Banion was an alert, quick-witted, and fearless youth, called him into his office and asked him if he'd like to do some undercover work for him among the Indians. It was his first experience at that sort of thing, and O'Banion welcomed the opportunity with enthusiasm.

All he had to do was to watch the Indians, keep track of their movements, and try to discover what they might be planning to do next. But it was dull and uninteresting, for the Indians were so damned well-behaved that he rarely ran into anything that was even worth reporting. However, it was good training, and he learned a great deal from Captain Cameron that proved of value later.

But a year of riding the range in Montana was enough. The call of the open road was in O'Banion's blood, and so in July of 1893 he packed up and moved on. From Washington he continued down the coast, working his way as he went, and finally landed in Southern California. First one job and then another came his way, and finally he became superintendent of a ranch at Orange owned by A. H. Bibber, a retired cavalry officer.

Then the Philippine Insurrection broke out. War was declared. One morning O'Banion read in the newspaper that Troop A of the 4th United States Cavalry was leaving for the Philippines, and was now at San Francisco, its port of embarkation. This was the outfit he had known in Montana. Without waiting to change his clothes or shave, O'Banion went into Los Angeles and enlisted. He was sworn into the service on June 19, 1899.

But, such being the ways of the army, he was kept in San Francisco for three months. Troop A sailed without him, and Private O'Banion was left behind to fuss and grouse and gripe and fume in the approved soldierly manner. Finally, however, his orders came, and he sailed for the Philippines. Thirty-two days after leaving San Francisco he landed in Manila. And around the last of September caught up with Troop A at San Fernando, Luzon Island, some sixty miles north of Manila. Three days later the invasion was on.

"And so," as he said to Colonel Carr that morning at Fort Riley, "that's about the way it was. I think, sir, the rest of it is all there on my service record."

"Yes," said Colonel Carr. "Fine record, sergeant. I see here you have had seven citations given you for bravery and efficiency in action. Captain Cameron says that you attracted his attention by coolness and gallantry under fire in the Philippine service, and afterwards demonstrated that you possessed all the qualities sought in the senior non-commissioned officer. He also says that you reached your position as first sergeant in one enlistment, and that you are an exceptional horseman. In conclusion he says—and I am quoting—'His services would be of great value in any position requiring close attention to business, determination, control of men, intelligence and absolute sobriety.'"

Hearing this last, O'Banion scratched his chin in an embarrassed manner and said, with a sheepish grin, "I never let him catch me taking a drink."

The colonel didn't seem to hear this, for he continued, "I have also here comments upon your service in the Philippines by the generals under whom you served; first when you were chief scout with General Young's Provisional Brigade. Then later with General Swan's expedition in January of 1900, and also with General Lawton and General Funston. They have all written to the War Department—praising you highly. Your term of enlistment is up this month, sergeant. Would you like to reenlist and be a Regular Army man? You'll be promoted to the rank of squadron sergeant major. The army needs men like you."

O'Banion thought a moment, and then said, honestly, "Got no complaints about army life, colonel. But what the hell? The war's over, so why stick around? Think I'd like to try ranching again for a change. I'll be crawling out of bed at dawn—just the same as in the army. Thanks, colonel, but home in California looks good to me right now."

The colonel smiled as he replied, "Good luck, sergeant. But my guess is you like adventure and enjoy a good fight too much to settle down quietly on a ranch for the rest of your life. You're not made that way. No romantic, fighting, adventurous Irishman ever is."

"It's worth a try, sir," said O'Banion, thoughtfully.

Then the colonel suddenly asked a question that seemingly had nothing whatever to do with what they had been discussing.

"Have you ever met any Chinese, sergeant, or ever had any dealings or experiences with the Chinese people?"

O'Banion hesitated a moment before answering. The first thought to cross his mind was just how much, if anything at all, did the colonel know about Two Thumbs? He had never discussed with anyone his secret dealings with this Chinese agent who had worked with him in the Philippines and succeeded so cleverly in every mission he had undertaken. There was just the possibility that the colonel didn't know. But what was the harm in telling him? It was a thing of the past, and the Philippines were thousands of miles away.

So he said, "Yes, sir. I met one in the Nueva Ecija Province. This Chinese was bootlegging a native liquor called Vino to our soldiers. Damnedest tasting stuff—flavor of sweet coal oil. A Philippine drink made out of rice—and wasn't intended for a white man. Yet this Chinese was selling it to the soldiers at five cents for a pop bottle full. On one bottle a soldier would get so cussed drunk he'd fight snakes. Then he'd begin to laugh. It's the original giggle-water. I've seen some men so drunk they'd go around laughing like idiots, and then start in fighting or doing mean things to helpless natives. Two or three drunks on this stuff and a man would have softening of the brain. Funny thing about Vino—if you sobered up after a drunk and stubbed your toe, you'd get drunk all over again. I caught this Chinese selling this poison to our boys, and I told him that if I caught him at it again I'd kill him."

"What did he say to that?" asked Colonel Carr.

"Just grinned at me, and said he had to make a living some way or other," replied O'Banion. "And so that gave me an idea."

As he went on to tell the colonel, on this particular campaign in the Nueva Ecija Province the fighting was largely guerrilla warfare. And often they didn't know who the enemy were. The villages seemed filled with friendly natives. Certainly they were on good terms with the soldiers and, to all appearances, unarmed. Yet at night there would be surprise attacks upon the camp. But the next day, when the villages would be searched, no trace of any guns could be found.

Orders came from headquarters that for anyone who located a gun among the natives and brought it in, the army would pay a bounty of $30 mex, or $15 in American

1ST SERGEANT O'BANION AT FT. RILEY, KANSAS

money. Now this Chinese came and went freely in and out of the villages and was on good terms with the natives.

So O'Banion said to him, "I think I can use you. If you throw away those damn five-cent pop bottles, I'll make you a Filipino millionaire."

"Okay. How?"

"What's your name?" asked O'Banion.

"Everybody call me Two Thumbs," and he held up his right hand. To O'Banion's surprise he really did have two thumbs.

"Good name, and it fits in more ways than one," said O'Banion. "Now here's the idea."

And then he told him his scheme. O'Banion had observed that in the Philippine Islands, among the villages, the men were either soldiers or gamblers. It was the women who did the buying and selling; they traded and bartered, and were ambitious "someday to have a little business of their own." O'Banion felt that from these women, if approached in the right way, Two Thumbs would be able to discover where the guns were hidden.

The quickest and surest approach was to marry the women. They all wanted Chinese husbands, as the Chinese had the deserved reputation of being good merchants. Two Thumbs nodded agreement to the plan.

After all, in the island marriage among the natives at that time was not binding between the two parties forever. It was more a matter of temporary expediency. In those days the man with the bank roll made the best husband—until the bank roll was spent. So, being supplied with money, Two Thumbs, with genial good humor, started out marrying all the women who could be persuaded.

Then the procedure in each case was simple. After the

wedding ceremony as such—there must have been some sort of ceremony, O'Banion always thought, although he was never invited—the bride would tell Two Thumbs where her former husband hid his gun.

Two Thumbs had been instructed by O'Banion never to approach him in the daytime, and under no consideration to come up and speak to him when there was anyone else around. After obtaining his information, he'd slip up to the edge of the camp in the early evening. Just as soon as he knew that O'Banion had seen him, he'd walk into the jungle. When O'Banion could get away without arousing suspicion, he'd join Two Thumbs. Then Two Thumbs would tell him where the guns were and give him a map indicating the exact spot, invariably in a rice stack. In the Philippines rice is cut and stacked, as we handle wheat.

The next day O'Banion would take a detail of soldiers, go to the spot, tear down the rice stack, and find the guns. In one haul alone, he obtained 132.

Then, as the army advanced, Two Thumbs would go into the next village and find himself another bride; and the same performance would be repeated.

Hundreds of guns were seized in this fashion. O'Banion was commended by his commanding officer, and Two Thumbs made a lot of money—and had a little fun besides.

This taught O'Banion two things that were to prove valuable later. One was that there's always someone around to do whatever needs to be done, provided they get paid for it. The other thing he learned was that when working undercover—as long as you get results—keep mum, and don't let your right hand know what your left hand is doing.

As a debt of gratitude to O'Banion for throwing him this

chance to make money, Two Thumbs often came to him with information he had obtained in the villages. He was probably the first, if not the only, unofficial Chinese secret agent who has ever worked for the United States Army. He often warned O'Banion of impending raids and would inform him, too, when the enemy was preparing to send diseased women into the camps. They would come sneaking in at night and could cause as much damage and havoc to the lives and health of the soldiers as bullets. But when O'Banion was prepared for their coming, he knew what to do, and was therefore able to prevent illness and disease.

For all this information he was grateful to Two Thumbs and never begrudged him the money he earned. By the time the insurrection was over and peace declared, Two Thumbs was a rich man. The last O'Banion heard of him he had gone to Manila, married a Chinese wife in the orthodox Chinese manner, and opened an antique shop.

When O'Banion had finished telling this story to Colonel Carr, the colonel said, "Good work, sergeant. I am quite convinced you are the type of man the War Department is seeking. One more question. Have you ever heard of Homer Lea?"

"No, sir, not to my knowledge. Should I know of him?"

"Not necessarily," answered Colonel Carr. Then he added, "But I've been instructed to give you a letter of introduction to him on the day of your discharge. Should ranching bore you, take this letter to Homer Lea. It is strictly confidential and not to be shown to anyone but Homer Lea. Should you decide not to present it, destroy the letter and forget all about it."

"Yes, sir," said O'Banion.

"Whatever you decide to do, sergeant, good luck!"

"Thank you, sir," replied O'Banion. He saluted and walked out of the office, somewhat puzzled.

As he went back to the barracks he thought to himself, "The colonel went to a hell of a lot of bother telling me about this letter of introduction to some—what's-his-name? Nuts to it. Sounds screwy to me."

He was even more surprised, on his day of discharge, when he saw by whom the letter was signed.

CHAPTER THREE

Background for a Revolution

ON JUNE 18, 1902, Sergeant O'Banion received his honorable discharge from the United States Army. The next day he was on the train bound for home in California. Tucked away in his inside pocket was the letter Colonel Carr had given him. It read as follows:

Lieutenant General Homer Lea,
South Bonnie Brae Street,
Los Angeles, California.

The bearer of this letter is A. E. O'Banion, former 1st Sergeant of Troop A, 4th United States Cavalry, of whom I have previously written you. Without question he has all the qualifications you mentioned in your letter to the Auditor of the War Department.

Yours respectfully,
Adna R. Chaffee,
Major General, United States Army.

If it hadn't been for the fact that the letter was addressed to a lieutenant general, O'Banion might have been more interested. But for the present he had seen enough of war and bloodshed, of agony and suffering, of violence and destruction.

He knew, however, who Major General Chaffee was. While he had not served under him in the Philippines while Chaffee was there, he had heard stories of this soldier and humanitarian. He knew that General Chaffee, a Regular Army man, had been in command of all the Allied forces during the Boxer Rebellion in Peking in 1900. It is a matter of historical record that, after the capture of Peking, General Chaffee's consideration and just treatment of the residents of that city during the occupation won the respect and admiration not only of the members of the invading forces but of the Chinese as well.

With this background of service in China, Chaffee's letter to Homer Lea had more than ordinary significance. Especially, too, when we know that in January of 1904 Chaffee was made a lieutenant general and appointed Chief of Staff of the United States Army in Washington.

But implications such as this did not bother O'Banion as he got off the train at Orange, Calif., and made his way along the country road to the Bibber ranch. He whooped for joy at being home again and forgot all about the letter to Homer Lea. It was possible, of course, that General Chaffee was acting in an unofficial capacity.

A whole year passed. As June of 1903 rolled around, the restlessness of spring came to O'Banion. He had now had twelve months of farming. The army life belonged to the "good old days"—just as in the army he had often said, "When I get home again—oh, boy—I stay there!" It wasn't that ranch life was dull—but the thought kept recurring to him that from now on, for the rest of his life, he would be doing this sort of thing. And for an adventurous young man who, on his own, had come halfway across the continent and had seen action on the battlefields of the Philippines, the idea wasn't too appealing.

He said since that if it hadn't been for the fact that he

had a cold that June morning things might have been different. It wasn't that his resistance was low; it was merely that having the sniffles made him a little more bored than usual with farming. He went into town to get some medicine from Dr. A. J. Scott and, while sitting in the doctor's office, unburdened himself.

"So it's dull for you here in Orange," said the doctor. Then he added, with a twinkle in his eye, "I know it's confidential, and you aren't supposed to mention it. So you don't need to make a reply to what I'm going to say. But when you were discharged from the army a year ago you were given a letter of introduction to Homer Lea."

"Who told you that?" asked O'Banion, being cagey.

"Homer Lea. He's an old friend."

"Who is he, anyway?"

"A young fellow—about your age, I fancy," replied Dr. Scott. "Some people think he's something of a genius; others say he's a crackpot. No two people agree, yet everybody who knows him likes him. Why don't you go and meet him, then form your own opinion?"

"He's a lieutenant general, isn't he?" asked O'Banion.

"Yes."

"I don't want to get into the service again," said O'Banion. "I'm planning to be married in August, and if I got into the army, God knows where I might be shipped. I'm perfectly content to stay right here in the good old U.S.A."

"You probably would."

"What's this Homer Lea got up his sleeve, anyway?" was the next question O'Banion asked.

"I'll give you a hint, but it's strictly confidential," said the doctor.

"I've learned to keep my mouth shut," replied O'Banion.

"So I've heard," smiled the doctor. "That's another one of the reasons why Homer Lea thinks you're the right man. Between you and me, in strict confidence, he's planning a revolution."

O'Banion's eyes stuck out of his head. "A revolution— here in the United States?" he exclaimed.

"Partly, sort of, in a way," answered the doctor evasively. "More I can't tell you. That's up to Homer. Go see him, even if nothing comes of it."

"You've sold me a bill of goods, doctor. A revolution here in the U.S. sounds like dirty work at the crossroads to me. I'll see him, if only to find out what in hell it's all about."

"There's the telephone; here's his number," said Dr. Scott. "Phone him now and ask for an appointment."

The voice that answered O'Banion was a pleasant one, and when he gave his name, the reply came, "I'd be delighted to see you this afternoon at three o'clock. Please meet me in the lobby of the Angelus Hotel on South Spring Street."

When O'Banion arrived at the appointed hour, there was no mistaking the man he had come to see. Over in a corner, not far from the windows, sat a smiling young man. He was dressed in a blue uniform unlike any O'Banion had ever seen. He was later to learn that it was the dress uniform of the Chinese Imperial Reform Army. But O'Banion's first thought was that he didn't look much like a general. A slight, slender, almost frail-looking youngster, he had keen, piercing eyes and the sensitive pale face of a scholar. He had more the appearance of a poet than a soldier and, physically, certainly was quite the opposite type from broad-shouldered, husky O'Banion, tanned and rugged from his days spent in the open on the ranch. O'Banion was not par-

GENERAL HOMER LEA IN DRESS UNIFORM

ticularly impressed. Whatever proposition this frail-looking youngster had to offer had better be good!

He introduced himself. Homer Lea smiled, invited him to sit down, and said, "For some months now I've been anticipating your coming to see me."

The two men shook hands, and O'Banion pulled up a chair. He handed Homer Lea the letter from General Chaffee.

Homer Lea glanced at it quickly and then said, "I knew General Chaffee during the Boxer Rebellion. When I returned to this country two years ago—after my escape from China—I wrote to him. I needed someone to assist me, a man of certain definite qualifications."

"What were they?" inquired O'Banion, bluntly.

"Someone who has seen active service, a senior noncommissioned officer, preferably one with scout experience. Also discreet, not too talkative, and who—should I make a suggestion—would be intelligent enough to take hold of that idea and go ahead on his own."

"And General Chaffee recommended me?" O'Banion was still suspicious.

"Here you are, at any rate." Homer Lea smiled. "I had one chap—a former West Pointer—but he wouldn't use chopsticks and ate rice with his fingers. The Chinese didn't like him." O'Banion blinked, but Homer Lea continued, "How much did Dr. Scott tell you?"

"Not much—something about a revolution."

"Yes. To me the only justified wars are revolutions—the revolt of an oppressed nation. The American Revolution was unique in history—the first time a whole people rose to defend their rights and declare their freedom. The French Revolution was next—inspired by our Declaration of Independence. Now we are planning the third—the Chinese Revolution. We shall so plan it and perfect our schemes that, unlike those others, when it occurs it will be bloodless. Would you like to join forces with me on this?"

O'Banion started to speak, but Homer Lea held up a restraining hand as he continued: "Please wait before you give your answer. What I'm going to offer you is a dangerous proposition. There are great risks to be taken. We are playing a hide-and-seek game with governments—and the secret controlling forces behind those governments. There may be times when we do not know exactly who are our friends—or who our enemies. We may ultimately land in jail, or even be murdered. So I don't want you to give me a definite answer until you know the risks involved."

"I've been in tight spots before," murmured O'Banion, beginning to be intrigued.

"I know. First I should like to explain why I feel this revolution is justified. In the first place, the Chinese people have always interested me. I knew a Chinese cook when I was a boy in Los Angeles. What he told me of China, its philosophy and ways of life fascinated me. I wanted to know more.

"When I went to Stanford University I met two Chinese students, and began asking them questions. They often took me to Chinatown in San Francisco. They even taught me to speak some Chinese. It was through these two friends that I learned of the underground revolutionary movement —the sole purpose of which is to overthrow the present corrupt government of China. This revolution has been going on now for over two hundred and fifty years.

"So far there have been two open, but unsuccessful, attempts to rid China of domination by the Manchus. This time we shall work secretly, and we do not want to fail. We cannot afford to fail!"

Then he went on to tell O'Banion that the trouble really started in 1644. That was the year the Manchus, wild Tartar horsemen who lived north of the Great Wall, came galloping across the plains. With fire and sword they swept south and conquered the peace-loving people of China proper, or what is known as the Middle Kingdom. The Mings, who had sat upon the Dragon Throne and ruled China for over two hundred years, were overthrown. When the conquering army descended upon Peking, the Emperor committed suicide.

Yet some of his generals sought vainly to stem the oncoming hordes. For seven long and bitter years, battles were fought and all the horrors of war inflicted upon an innocent people. In the end the Mings who rebelled against the Manchus were crushed, and a Manchu Emperor sat upon the Dragon Throne and began to rule China.

Because of this warfare and the resistance offered by those loyal to the Mings, the Manchus saw the necessity of maintaining a large standing army. They established camps all over the country. To support this army, large sums of money were needed. Therefore, heavy taxes were levied, and the people of China paid dearly for the privilege of having their foreign conquerors maintain their rule.

"Even today, in 1903, the Royal Manchu Army controls China," Homer Lea said. "This is an important point to remember. To rid China of this large standing army is one of the very first steps in our plan. We hope it can be done peacefully. We want to avoid as much bloodshed as possible. Rather than cut off heads, we'd prefer to cut off queues."

The queue, he went on to explain to O'Banion, was

really a badge of servitude. The Manchus were horsemen.
They wore their hair long, done up in braids on the top
of their heads. And they forced the conquered men of
China to shave the forepart of their heads and wear their
hair in queues hanging down their backs. There was a purpose in this: a Manchu horseman could easily capture a
fleeing Chinese by grabbing his queue and, with a swift
stroke of the sword, cut off his head. And they made the
women bind their feet. It was so much simpler for a soldier
bent on rape to seize a woman who could not run away.

Centuries passed and the injustices increased. The cor-
ruption of the officials knew no bounds. Lands were seized
for nonpayment of taxes. Small independent merchants had
their shops taken away from them. The poor became
poorer, while the rich rulers waxed fat. What laws were
passed were all in favor of the mandarins. The culture of
the Mings was swept away.

The love of scholarship still remained, however. But it
was only the classics—and the approved classics—that were
studied. Politics and the discussion of politics were forbidden in the schools. The less the people knew about government, so thought the Manchus, the easier it was to rule and
govern them in their own Manchu way. So, should there be
an inquiring scholar who dared to ask questions, the sen-
tence was "Off with his head." And the execution grounds
ran red with blood.

But as Homer Lea said, "To silence an entire people does
but one thing—it drives all political thought underground.
And since political ideas could be exchanged only in secret,
all over China secret societies grew and flourished. There
are more secret societies in China today than you can shake
a stick at. I've been in touch with at least a dozen or more.

The more important of these is the San Ho Wui, or, as it is better known, 'The Triad Society.' It is Cantonese in origin. The Cantonese, you know, have always been the group most rebellious against the Manchu rule. For all I know, this Triad Society may have been formed by the surviving Mings following the seven years' war. Or it may have its roots deep in the past of China. But I do know its motto today is 'Fan Tsing Fuk Ming,' which means 'Destroy Tsing —the Manchus—Restore Ming.' These secret societies are the hidden unknown strength of China today."

They were so strong in 1850, he told O'Banion, that they burst into the open and the Taiping Rebellion occurred. For fourteen years this rebellion raged. It was one of the bloodiest revolutions in the history of the world. Over thirty million people were slain before the rebels were finally subdued in 1864. And it would have succeeded if it hadn't been for foreign assistance given to the Manchus.

Commanding the Royal Manchu Army was a British officer, often called Chinese Gordon. There is some debate among historians as to whether he was a soldier of fortune on his own or was actually backed and supported by the British government.

Yet this Taiping Rebellion, even though suppressed, almost brought about the end of the Manchus. There was dry rot in the palace of the Emperor, and the Dynasty might have fallen if it hadn't been for one of the most remarkable women of history, the Empress Dowager Tsu Hsi. For over fifty years she ruled China and held the tottering Manchu Dynasty together.

She was a stubborn old lady, wanting her way—and getting it. She increased the strength of the army following the

Taiping Rebellion. She levied heavier taxes, until China was almost bankrupt. Anyone who dared oppose her wishes was murdered, and his bleeding, grinless head was hung by its queue outside the palace walls. A reign of terror swept China.

Her spies were everywhere: in the teahouses, on the streets, and even behind closed doors in the home of patriots where it was hoped the unsuspecting would destroy themselves by some carelessly spoken word. Those who opposed her had one of two courses open to them: either to keep silent and work undercover and in secret, trusting not to be caught, or else to flee the country. And the latter course appealed to many of the revolutionists.

They came to America, and here they lived, patiently biding their time, waiting for the hour of freedom. They had their secret societies in this country. There were Manchu spies here, too. So in secluded rooms in the Chinatowns of this country plots were formed and plans laid—all neatly hidden from our police and Secret Service.

Now and then a murdered Chinese would be found in a dark alley or basement. Was he a revolutionist or a Manchu spy? The police didn't know enough to ask. To them he was merely another dead Chinese. And if there was mention of the killing in the newspapers it was said to be due to another of those tong wars.

Then, in 1900, the issues in China became even more confused when the Boxer Rebellion burst into the open. This was the second open revolt against the Manchus. But it, too, failed.

"I know the reasons for its failure," Homer Lea told O'Banion. "I was in China at the time. I had a hand in the

Boxer Rebellion and shall tell you about it. While I went to China as a private citizen, however," he added smilingly, "I came home as a lieutenant general in the Chinese Reform Army. To explain how all this happened, I must tell you something about myself."

CHAPTER FOUR

Escape from China

SINCE his death, over thirty years ago, Homer Lea has become something of a legendary figure. A colorful, mysterious, and unusual personality, there have been many conflicting stories told about him. This is obviously bound to happen to any man who does most of his work in secret.

Even the writer of the sketch of his life in *The Dictionary of American Biography* was somewhat puzzled. He says in conclusion, "He has been hailed as one of the great military geniuses of history, and he unquestionably impressed some observers with the right to this title. No one can doubt his uncanny skill in organizing and leading the forces of the Chinese people. Opinions as to his motives differ, and it is not easy to determine whether he was an unselfish enthusiast fascinated by the cause of Chinese freedom, or whether he seized an opportunity to satisfy his passion for military experience. At all events he is one of the most picturesque personalities of his generation and, perhaps, the most gifted American who ever joined a foreign legion."

As Homer Lea told O'Banion, he was born in Denver, Colo., on Nov. 17, 1876. When he was sixteen his father moved his family to Los Angeles, where Homer attended high school and was graduated in 1896.

His ambition was to become a lawyer. There was no thought in his mind of a military career. That was an impossibility, for he had a slight curvature of the spine, was a small man, five feet four in height, and weighed about 120 pounds. But despite his physical handicap and his inability to take part in school athletics, he liked to go on long hunting trips, was an expert fencer, and never once said, "Quits."

The fact that he was slightly hunchbacked was one of the things that so endeared him to the Chinese. Now, in the Chinese social scheme, the scholar is given first place and highly honored. And obviously, in China as elsewhere, a man who bends over his books all day becomes in time stoop-shouldered. So the Chinese scholar who hasn't a stoop can't be—as the Chinese reason—much of a scholar. And consequently it is often said in China that a man's brains are in his back.

Then, too, Homer Lea had a broad, powerful chest— something unusual in scholars, who are invariably thin-chested. The Chinese honor a man with a deep chest. He has strength. So the rare combination of scholarly stoop and strong chest made him popular with the Chinese.

Since he had piercing, keen blue eyes, the Chinese used to say of him, "General Lea can see fifteen feet into the ground." This was a compliment, for it meant he was far-sighted.

They liked him, too, for his sense of humor. He was courteous, quick-witted, an excellent public speaker, kindly and friendly, and above all else, courageous. No wonder the Chinese—and everybody who knew him—liked him.

The year after he graduated from high school he attended Occidental College, studying history and other subjects required for his entrance into Stanford University, where he went in 1897 to study law. He would put maps upon the walls of his room and fight out the battles of the world which he was studying in his history classes. In this way campaigns became more vivid, and it was a great help in understanding the course of events and in interpreting the causes that led to the rise and fall of nations. In time, military tactics became his hobby—just as some men play chess or collect postage stamps.

At Stanford he became acquainted with two Chinese students and because of them found his lifework. Allen Chung was a handsome, heavy-set youth, always calm and collected in manner, and a few years older than Homer Lea. Lou Hoy was quite the opposite, a high-strung, nervous, but forceful chap. Their parents lived in China and were reputed to be wealthy. At least, these two young men always had plenty of spending money. They made a good team.

When they learned that Homer Lea had a friendly interest in things Chinese, they took him often to Chinatown to enjoy Chinese food. Through them Homer Lea quite naturally met other Chinese. And it wasn't long until he began to hear about the Empress Dowager Tsu Hsi and the unsuccessful attempts to drive her from the Dragon Throne.

Back in his room at Stanford a new map went up on the wall—a map of China. And now this college freshman had an unsolved military problem to tackle, a new war of his own—a war to remove the enslaved people of China from the tyranny of a murderous old woman.

Some of his ideas, which he often discussed when in Chinatown, impressed the Chinese. It wasn't long before Allen Chung and Lou Hoy confessed the truth about themselves—they were revolutionists, members of a secret society whose purpose it was to overthrow the Manchus. Homer Lea pledged his support and one night in Chinatown was secretly initiated into this undercover society.

To the annoyance of his family, he quit college, gave up all thought of a legal career, and announced his intention of going to China. If a revolution was to take place there, he wanted to be in the thick of it.

He tried to secure official standing. His first wish was to travel as an envoy of the United States government, to observe what was going on, and have the backing of our government so that he could go and come freely in all camps.

But he didn't succeed with this idea. The United States government wasn't sending—or so they said—an unknown twenty-three-year-old youth to China to make observations on the internal troubles of that country. But he did obtain a passport from the State Department and the unofficial blessing of President McKinley. He was told to be a good boy and not get into trouble. If he did, the United States government wouldn't take any responsibility for what might happen to him.

With the help of Allen Chung and Lou Hoy, the Chinese Chamber of Commerce gave him his ticket to China. The elders of Chinatown were wise enough to realize that the idealistic youth of today is the man who will do battles tomorrow. Through the secret society of which he was a member in good standing, he was given directions about making contact with the revolutionary leaders in China.

In June, 1900, he set sail from San Francisco. He arrived safe in Canton. From there he went to Hong Kong, where he had a long talk with a then unknown, but now world-famous, revolutionist. Then he started on his way to Peking. There he met Kang Yu-wei, Prime Minister to the imprisoned Boy Emperor, Kuang Hsu. And soon Homer Lea was up to his neck in the intrigue that was going on in the Forbidden City of the Empress Dowager Tsu Hsi.

Now at this time the Empress Dowager, while unquestionably the ironhanded ruler of China, was not the lawful head of the state. The power behind the throne, yes; but Kuang Hsu, her nephew, was legally emperor. She would have liked to get rid of him—if she only dared.

From the moment when, as a girl of sixteen, she had been brought into the palace as one of the twenty-eight Manchu virgins honored by heaven as the Emperor's concubines, she had slowly but surely fought her way, by all sorts of trickery and murder, closer and closer to the throne upon which, someday, she intended to sit.

There were so many concubines at court that the Emperor never became fully acquainted with them all. But he came to know Tsu Hsi. She bribed a eunuch to carry her, wrapped in a red silk shawl, into the Emperor's bedchamber one night and to lay her, blushing modestly, but quite naked, at the foot of the royal bed. She bore him a son. That was her first step to power.

But the son died under mysterious circumstances; so did the Emperor. And other members of the royal household who stood in the way of Tsu Hsi, or who disobeyed her commands, met death in strange ways. Did she really murder them? Or is that only gossip? Let historians quarrel over the right answer. We only know that one by one heirs to the throne disappeared until only the child Kuang Hsu was left.

As a small boy he was obedient to the wishes of his aunt. He even allowed her to sign all royal edicts with the Great Seal of China, which some people say she had stolen anyway, and kept hidden for only herself to use. But when he grew to manhood Kuang Hsu began to think for himself, and then the trouble started. Without consulting his aunt, he appointed as his prime minister Kang Yu-wei—one of the important persons in our story.

Kang Yu-wei was a Cantonese. He was, undoubtedly, a great man. Besides being an eminent scholar, famous for his advanced ideas on national and international questions, he was also a student of foreign governments. There is some academic debate concerning him, of course, for like all men of decided political opinions he had his supporters and also his enemies. Some writers have considered him an impractical idealist who had the welfare of China at heart; others have said he was only an ambitious, vainglorious man, seeking personal power. However that may be, certainly his ideas for the future of China did not coincide with those of the Empress Dowager. And when he was summoned to the Forbidden City, to serve as adviser to the then reigning Emperor Kuang Hsu, there was the devil to pay.

Kang Yu-wei was convinced that, if China was to progress and take her rightful place among the great nations of the world, she must step out of her shell. She must no longer be isolated. China had goods to sell the world; her inner resources had as yet not been tapped. She could grow as rich as other nations. But first she must put her own house in order. She must become a modern nation at home before she could properly deal with other great world powers.

Other ministers of state in the royal palace felt as he did. They managed to bring about what is known in history as the Hundred Days' Reform. The Emperor Kuang Hsu issued a series of edicts which, had they gone into full effect, would have transformed China—and very possibly might have prevented, or at least delayed, the present World War.

But the Empress Dowager objected. She was opposed to "reforms" of any kind. She wanted to keep China for herself and her dynasty and saw no reason for ever doing business with foreign powers. The word "isolationist" was not in use then, but it fitted her perfectly.

She forced the abdication of Kuang Hsu as emperor, made him a prisoner in his own palace, and assumed the throne. She was now, in fact, Empress of China—and nothing stood in her way.

She quickly put an end to all reforms. She even beheaded six of those in the plot with Kang Yu-wei. But she didn't stop the revolutionists altogether. Some of them hurried underground and worked in secret. Others fled the country.

Then came the Boxer Rebellion. At that time the world thought this was the Empress Dowager's defiance of the "foreign devils" in her kingdom and an attempt to get rid of them. Today, we know it was but the second revolt—like the Taiping Rebellion—against the Manchus.

The Boxers were members of a secret society organized in Shantung and had as their original name I-Ho-Tuan, which means "Band of Patriotic Union." When, now and then, the Manchu spies got wind of their secret activities, they changed their name and went on with their underground revolutionary work. They were known sometimes as the Plum Blossom Fists and also as the Society of the Righteous Fists.

By 1900, when they came out into the open, it was customary to speak of them as Chuen-fei, which means "Bandits of the Fists" or more simply and briefly "Boxers." And it was known that their aim was to rid the country of foreign devils—referring, of course, to the Manchus.

But the Empress Dowager, by lies, intrigue, and all the underhanded tricks of subtle diplomacy, managed to turn the Boxers away from the Manchus and against what she considered the foreign devils—meaning, of course, representatives of other nations. Some of the Boxers threw in their lot with her. Others remained true to their original purpose.

So, when the fighting started in Peking and the Foreign Legations were besieged, it wasn't always easy to tell friend from foe. While the Manchu soldiers were firing on American troops and the soldiers of other nations, Chinese troops were fighting Chinese soldiers. It was, in fact, a rebellion within a rebellion.

And in the midst of it was Homer Lea. He was in command of Chinese troops who fought against the Royal Manchu Army and who, when the rebellion was finally put down and the Siege of Peking was over, marched into the city alongside the Americans. His commission as lieutenant general in what was known as the Chinese Reform Army had been given him by the imprisoned Boy Emperor!

When the Empress Dowager fled from Peking, it was this little army of loyal Boxers, commanded by General Lea, who went in pursuit. Had they captured her, there would have been no Chinese Revolution of 1911. But they were doomed to failure.

The Royal Manchu Army attacked them in the rear. Homer Lea's ragged army of Chinese volunteers were outnumbered and beaten. Those who were not killed fled to the hills. Homer Lea was left a general without an army.

But he did not surrender, nor did the defeated soldiers. Those who fled became brigands and waited patiently for another hour to strike and overthrow the Empress Dowager.

Although the Empress Dowager made peace with the Allied Powers, against whom she had waged a losing war, and returned to her palace in Peking, the revolutionists, in the days of turmoil that followed, made yet another attempt. They felt that if they could free the Boy Emperor and put him back upon the throne, they could through him reform the government and bring about the liberation of China. Even though he was emperor—without a throne, however— he must definitely be considered one of the revolutionists. And so Homer Lea and the Boy Emperor worked hand in glove.

One thing Homer Lea did was to organized what he later would smilingly refer to as his Pai, meaning "private army intelligence." (Now, *pai* is a Chinese word and, depending upon how you say it, can have several meanings. One is "to worship," another is "to pay one's respect." Still another is "white," but the one he probably meant was "hundred." This had for him, as we shall see, a very special significance.)

The very first thing he did in China was to select carefully the men who were to act as his secret agents. He even placed some in the palace, right under the very nose of the Empress Dowager. These were, in a few instances, court doctors, men who could come and go as they pleased.

All through the years, after his return to the United States, he was in constant touch with these agents and was kept informed of all that was going on. In fact he knew, day by day, just what was happening to the imprisoned Boy Emperor. But there was never any direct correspondence between them. The agents sent their reports to certain Chinese in this country, who passed the word along to General Lea. Certainly it was due to these agents in the Forbidden City that his life was saved in China.

The revolutionists, led by Kang Yu-wei, continued their plotting and planning to oust the Empress Dowager from the Dragon Throne. There was, among the other members of the Reform party, one man whom Kang Yu-wei respected. This was his friend and pupil, Liang Chi-chao, a learned scholar of the old school. One by one, Liang Chi-chao succeeded in getting important cabinet officers of the Empress Dowager on the side of the revolutionists. Their plans were perfected in secret. A date was set to free the Boy Emperor.

But, on the evening before, the Empress Dowager swooped down upon the revolutionists. She, too, had her spies, and they had got wind of what was going on.

But Homer Lea's counter-intelligence also had been at work. He learned that the Empress Dowager was wide-awake. He had even been told the exact hour of the day when all those in the plot would be seized and arrested. He informed the revolutionists. Most of them believed him. The others, not fully convinced that this American boy of twenty-three knew what he was talking about, scoffed and said there was no danger. He offered them a way to escape, but they declined.

In the meantime Homer Lea had talked now and then with some high-ranking Japanese naval officers. They were very polite, these officers, very suave, and, oh, so very, very friendly. They believed, too, in the overthrow of the Empress Dowager, so they said, and were willing to do all they could to help.

"Should you ever need to leave China in a hurry," they told Homer Lea, "come to us. We will get you out. Come to Japan—there will be a haven for you. In Japan, in peace and quiet—and like gentlemen, you can go ahead with your plans for a revolution."

Knowing the Empress Dowager was going to strike, he took advantage of this offer of the Japanese Navy. Kang

Yu-wei and Liang Chi-chao felt the same way. They fled to Hong Kong. There a Japanese battleship was waiting for them, and aboard this ship the three men sailed for Tokyo.

The revolutionists who remained behind didn't have long to regret their indecision. They were caught—and sixteen of them promptly put to death. Some were beheaded; others, because of their rank and high standing, were cordially invited by the Empress Dowager to commit suicide. They accepted her invitation with dignity. Thus, the plot to liberate the Boy Emperor came to nothing, and he remained a lonely prisoner within his palace. A reign of terror now started in China that spread even to the Chinatowns of America.

But for three months Homer Lea was safe in Japan, together with Kang Yu-wei and Liang Chi-chao. They were treated royally. The Japanese gave them the keys to their island kingdom, took them everywhere to see the sights, gave banquets in their honor, and did everything in their power to make them happy. And the three exiles responded like gentlemen. They made many expressions of their gratitude and said many complimentary things about their new-found Japanese friends.

The Japanese said they regretted deeply that all the other members of the Reform party hadn't come to Japan along with Kang Yu-wei and Liang Chi-chao. Japan was very sympathetic toward a revolution in China, and would do all she could to help when the proper time came. But it made Homer Lea suspicious. Somehow, it didn't sound quite right. Just exactly what were Japan's intentions?

He played along with the Japanese, trying to find out all he could. He also discussed the matter carefully with Kang Yu-wei and Liang Chi-chao. They felt that the best thing for young Homer Lea to do at this time was to return to the United States. They would remain in Japan.

"But they had no intention of joining up with the Japanese or enlisting their help," Homer Lea told O'Banion. "They were loyal to their native country, if not to the Empress Dowager and the government in power. So we spent long hours together, talking and planning what we would—or could—do next. We came to one conclusion—the revolution must go on. Even though in exile—and not daring to return to China to continue the fight—yet fight we would. And so we made our plans. Should you join up with us, I'll tell you what those plans are. We haven't even an army as yet. But that, Mr. O'Banion, is where you fit into the picture."

He didn't explain at the moment, but went on:

"For years all revolutionary movements in China to overthrow the Manchus have failed. Since the Taiping Rebellion, there has been constant bloodshed. If the suffering people of China are to be freed, we must not fail this time. We have but one chance left—it may be a desperate chance, but we are taking it. Perhaps if we can enlist the aid and support of the Chinese living in America—there is some hope. Here, we think, if we work secretly and cautiously—and wisely—we have a chance. We must work in America; there is no other place to go." He paused a moment. "It will be dangerous. There are forces here opposed to us—not only among the Chinese who are still loyal to the Manchus, but among our own people. Should we be caught, we may have to pay for it with our lives. But unless we succeed this time—" He shrugged his shoulders with a gesture of futility.

"Am I understanding you correctly?" asked O'Banion.

"Are you planning to cause a revolution in China by doing all your work here in the United States?"

"That's the idea in a nutshell, Mr. O'Banion," replied Homer Lea.

O'Banion looked about him. The lobby of the Angelus Hotel was crowded. People were constantly coming and going. Then he glanced at Homer Lea seated calmly in a chair at his side.

From what stories he had read, he had always pictured revolutions as being planned in dark cellars, with flickering candles on the tables and guards standing at the doors fully armed and prepared to shoot any inquisitive stranger on sight. If he ever got mixed up in a revolution, that's the way he'd like to discuss the plans. But to sit in a crowded hotel lobby and hear a man make the statement that he intended to overthrow a government—start a revolution—and that it might result in his death—was beyond his experience.

"Just what is it you want of me?" he asked cautiously.

"Should you decide to join with us, I'll tell you our plans in detail. This afternoon I've only told you the background—the reasons why a revolution is necessary. How we intend to go about it is another story."

Homer Lea rose and held out his hand. "I know," he said, "you will want to consider this before you give your answer. If you say, 'Yes,' that's final. There's no turning back. Suppose you take two or three days to think about it, and then get in touch with me again."

"I've thought!" said O'Banion, then, with the reckless impetuosity of a foolhardy twenty-seven-year-old youth who loved a good fight, added, "When do we start?"

"Tomorrow!" smiled Homer Lea.

"Good. What do I do first?"

"Take the oath of allegiance to our secret society. In three days we'll have a banquet in Chinatown and swear you in. So tomorrow, if you'll meet me again at this time, I'll tell you something about the Po Wong Wui. I'm very glad, Mr. O'Banion, that you are going to be with us."

"Thanks," replied O'Banion. "Same with me."

"Until tomorrow then."

They shook hands, stood and grinned at each other for a moment, and then went their separate ways.

CHAPTER FIVE

An Oath Signed in Blood

AS HOMER LEA told O'Banion the next day, the Po Wong Wui was a secret society founded in Japan by Kang Yu-wei, Liang Chi-chao, and himself. Literally translated it means "Protect Emperor Society" or, as it might be said, "Free and Liberate the Boy Emperor."

Kang Yu-wei was elected not only vice-president and secretary, but also treasurer. The position of president was left open until such time later on when the right leader might be found to head the revolutionary movement. But in the meantime the only officeholder was Kang Yu-wei, and it made him very happy. In letting him hold all the offices, so Homer Lea explained—and it was typically Chinese—Liang Chi-chao and himself were freer to make suggestions and also have more personal liberty. They could come and go as they pleased, say what they liked, and no one could accuse them of seeking or obtaining undue power.

In all, Homer Lea spent three months in Japan. By the time he returned to the United States, plans for the organization of the Po Wong Wui had been perfected. Now, fine ideals are one thing and high-sounding words may arouse men to action, but for a successful revolution more than ideals and words are needed. Much more important are money and an army! And so the plan for the Po Wong Wui was simply to do what could be done among the Chinese in America toward raising money and enlisting an army.

Upon Homer Lea's arrival in San Francisco, he was met at the boat by Allen Chung and Lou Hoy. They went immediately to Chinatown and there Homer told them of the new secret society to overthrow the Empress Dowager.

"What, another?" said Allen Chung. "I belong to four already!"

Clenching his hand and pointing his thumb up, he shook his fist in the air. Homer Lea and Lou Hoy knew what he meant, and responded by making the same gesture. It was one of the secret signs of the Boxers—now used by the soldiers of the United Nations everywhere—"Thumbs Up for Victory!"

"I know," said Homer Lea. Then he told them briefly the purpose of the Po Wong Wui. Other secret societies seemed negative in their approach. They all wanted to overthrow the Empress Dowager. But the Po Wong Wui was positive. "Do something," it seemed to say. "Liberate the Boy Emperor. Take action. March forward!"

That very night Homer Lea initiated Allen Chung and Lou Hoy into the secret society. Then, like the Three Musketeers, these young crusaders and bright-eyed idealists started out to gain other members. One of the first important Chinese in this country to join was a newspaper publisher in Fresno. Ben Young was his name. Ultimately he gave his whole fortune and all his time to the movement. All over the United States went Homer Lea, Allen Chung, and Lou Hoy.

They visited every Chinatown in the country. They even went to small towns where there were only twenty or even fewer Chinese. It took them many months. Usually the first man they approached in every city was the secretary of the Chinese Chamber of Commerce. Once persuaded—and it wasn't always easy—he became secretary of the society in his city, and also subtreasurer. Then he promoted membership in his community and swore others in.

As Homer Lea told O'Banion, he thought one of the reasons for their success was the fact that the dues of this secret society were placed so low it really wasn't much of a risk. Each member paid only 50 cents a month. Practically anyone could afford that. Each man also took an oath that he would pay this of his own volition without ever having to be asked for it.

That angle particularly pleased the elders. It seemed so fair and such an honest way of collecting money. No force, no coercion, no "pay up or else" sort of thing. Then, too, they were quite willing to risk only 50 cents a month. Should these young men fail, it was very little to lose. But should they succeed, how very smart of them!

Also each member who paid in his 50 cents appointed himself a committee of one to talk it over with his acquaintances and persuade them to join also. Like a mushroom, the Po Wong Wui grew all over the United States.

Later Chinese in Mexico and Canada were approached. And in time revolutionists in China were initiated. They did not, however, pay dues. It seemed too dangerous for money to be passed among them. Also, their brothers, cousins, and friends in America preferred to bear the whole financial burden. It was such a polite gesture. Ultimately this Po Wong Wui became the most powerful and influential Chinese secret society in this country.

O'Banion was initiated into the Po Wong Wui on June 27, 1903. At that time there were chapters all over the United States, and money in the treasury. The next step was raising an army. It was for this that O'Banion had been selected.

Before the night of the banquet, O'Banion didn't really know quite what to expect. He had never set foot in Chinatown, and certainly had never been at a Chinese banquet. Almost anything might happen.

At six o'clock that evening, Lou Hoy called for him at Homer Lea's home. Save for the fact that Lou Hoy wore his queue knotted around the back of his head, he did not differ from any other American youth of overseas extraction. He was dressed conventionally in a well-tailored suit and spoke perfect English.

O'Banion couldn't help liking him. He was quite a different sort of man than Two Thumbs, whom he had known in the Philippines: keener, more alert, and vastly more intelligent, although Two Thumbs was by no means stupid. Lou Hoy, O'Banion found, was as Homer Lea had described him: a slight, slender youth, with snappy black eyes, quick nervous gestures, and an infectious smile.

As they made their way into Chinatown, Lou Hoy pointed out various shops and restaurants and told O'Banion the names of the owners. O'Banion was intrigued by what he saw in the windows: strange-looking foodstuffs piled high in large baskets and bowls, alongside of imported Chinese curios; bronze and porcelain statues of gods and goddesses; vases of delicate designs and colors, rich, embroidered tapestries, fanciful headdresses, and jewelry of jade and hammered gold. From an open window came the sound of music; a vague, unusual melody, and a rhythm unlike any he had ever heard. Pleasing, but a trifle "spooky."

As they walked along, Chinese loitering in the doorways

all nodded briefly to Lou Hoy. O'Banion had the feeling that they were looking him over carefully, that his walk through the streets at this hour of the evening was really a tour of inspection—and he was the one being inspected. He had the thought that a hundred curious eyes were staring at his back. And he was right. It rather amused him, for he was doing some looking over, too, as they strolled along.

Lou Hoy led him down Marchessault Street until they came to number 416. Here was a large brick building. It was what Lou Hoy called the Armory.

"We're having the banquet here tonight," he said, in explanation. "They've set up tables, and the food will be brought in. But we thought it fitting to start where we hope to do most of our training. This will be our headquarters, you know."

As the crowd began to gather, O'Banion saw that the only men present who were not Chinese were Homer Lea and himself. Homer Lea took pains to introduce him to everyone, and mentioned briefly who he was. This man was a merchant, that one owned a restaurant, here was the son of a merchant, and so on, and so on. A few old men, clad in long Chinese gowns, bowed and smiled as they were introduced and, instead of conventionally shaking O'Banion by the hand, shook their own hands.

"It's a Chinese custom," whispered Lou Hoy. "These are the elders, the leaders of Chinatown. Some of them cling stubbornly to the old ways, and at formal banquets such as this observe carefully all the rules of good manners. We young men respect them highly."

Others present had on silk blouses worn outside their loose, baggy trousers, their queues braided with black silk hanging down their backs. A great many were wearing thick-soled Chinese slippers. Some few had on little, black, round caps with red buttons on the top. These, so Lou Hoy told O'Banion, were mandarins, graduates of colleges in China. The young men present, however, were without exception as conventionally dressed in American clothes as was O'Banion. Homer Lea wore his uniform.

In all, there were about 150 men present. When they had finally all assembled, the doors were locked and the banquet was ready to start.

As Homer Lea whispered to O'Banion, "They are all, without exception, members of the Po Wong Wui. And I think ninety-nine per cent can be fully trusted. One or two may possibly be Manchu spies. I have no way of knowing for certain. Perhaps we may be able to find out, or maybe swing them over to our side."

They sat down. There was one long table in the Armory, with the speaker's table at the end. Homer Lea sat at the head. At his left he placed O'Banion. Next to him was Lou Hoy. Others at this table were Allen Chung and several of the elders of Chinatown.

Before the food was served, Homer Lea rose and for about forty minutes spoke in Chinese. O'Banion didn't know a thing he was saying, but later he learned that Homer gave him a glowing and proper introduction and said, among other things, that after careful investigation they had found in O'Banion a man to be trusted. And he asked that from now on they accept him as their friend.

In response to this speech, Allen Chung, who was acting as sort of host, rose and thanked Homer Lea, not only for all he was doing and had done but also for bringing O'Banion to Chinatown. He then said they were now going to swear O'Banion into the Po Wong Wui.

The only preparation given to O'Banion for this ceremony had been an hour before the banquet started. Lou Hoy had carefully instructed him how to sign his name in Chinese—a few strokes of the brush. O'Banion had carefully memorized each stroke, and he wouldn't forget.

On the table next to the speaker's table, directly in front of Homer Lea, was placed a large, round bowl. Those near by moved back. A long carving knife was laid beside the bowl. Then a live chicken, held by the feet, the wings locked together, was brought in. Its neck was wrung.

"Merciful to kill it first," said Lou Hoy.

The man holding the chicken placed it on top of the bowl. Another man seized the carving knife. With one swift stroke he cut the chicken open from the neck on down. The bottom of the bowl was quickly filled with blood.

By the bowl was laid, written in Chinese, the secret oath of the Po Wong Wui. O'Banion stepped to the bowl, dipped his finger in the blood, and signed his name.

The bowl was removed. Not a drop of blood had been spilled on the table.

Everybody jumped to their feet, held up their wineglasses, and cried, "Ho sai gui!" This is a Chinese toast and means, "May all the world be good to you."

"Ho sai gui!" echoed O'Banion.

The banquet had started. As O'Banion sat down at his place he said to Lou Hoy, "Tell me again just what it is I signed."

"It's really rather simple," replied Lou Hoy. "Allen Chung and General Lea and I thought it up in San Francisco. It says, briefly, 'I do solemnly swear that I will support the Po Wong Wui, both financially and morally, and will not at any time divulge any of the secrets pertaining to the Po Wong Wui, nor the names of any of the officers thereof, on pain of death.' "

"Fine!" said O'Banion, grimly. "Now I know where I stand!"

One more detail of the ceremony had to be gone through, but first the banquet was served. Dish after dish was brought to the table in true Chinese banquet style—one at a time. After the eighteenth dish O'Banion lost count. General Lea and Lou Hoy kept telling him what he was eating: shark's fin soup, roast squab, turtle, boneless duck and pineapple, and so on through the whole range of Chinese delicacies. Between courses toasts were drunk, and the waiters were kept busy filling up the wineglasses.

The banquet had been going on for two hours, when one by one the young men present rose and left the room. What was being planned was a surprise for the elders. It was Lou Hoy's idea—he enjoyed a little show now and then and liked a bit of the dramatic mixed up in whatever he was doing.

Soon came a signal from the door. General Lea rose. O'Banion stood by his side. Into the banquet hall marched forty Chinese in new military uniforms. They had been purchased a week before by General Lea from a wholesale costume house in Cincinnati, Ohio, and were especially designed with blue trousers, blouses, and caps on which was the insignia of the Imperial Dragon of China. This was the symbol of the Manchus, but it had been thought best to use it. To the curious outsider it would seem they were loyal to the Empress. There also were dragons on the buttons. The leggings were of brown canvas. Later, when the cavalry was organized, they wore yellow stripes on their trousers. Those of the infantry were white, an inch and a half wide.

Seeing them, the thought that flashed through O'Banion's mind was, "Just like raw recruits the world over—not a uniform fits!"

And they didn't. Later, however, each man had his uniform tailored. But tonight, putting them on for the first time, what did it matter? The look of pride in their eyes and the determined lift to their chins were what counted. Even if they appeared most unsoldierly in their ill-fitting uniforms with their queues hanging down their backs, they were, from this moment on, soldiers—and damned proud of it!

The elders were delighted. So this was one of the ways their money was being spent. Good!

"Ho! Ho!" they cried, and applauded.

General Lea turned to O'Banion and said in English, "Before you stands the first group of volunteers for the Chinese Imperial Reform Army. You are their captain! There is, however, no written commission—you can well understand why. But the Po Wong Wui confirms in words this appointment. From now on, Captain O'Banion, these soldiers are in your hands."

Captain O'Banion smartly saluted General Lea.

The Chinese waited silently for O'Banion to say something. He faced them and made one of the shortest, simplest, and yet most effective speeches of his life: "Soldiers, you are magnificent! Tomorrow we start training. But tonight let us enjoy ourselves. Do please sit down and go on eating!"

Pleased and delighted, for at this propitious moment he had said exactly the right thing, they cheered, broke ranks, and did as he ordered. The banquet lasted until two o'clock in the morning.

And that's how it started. A twenty-seven-year-old lieutenant general, an Irish captain, forty untrained soldiers—this was the entire Chinese Imperial Reform Army that planned to topple an empress from her throne and free far-off China!

CHAPTER SIX

The Western Military Academy

PERHAPS the whole scheme might have failed completely if it had not been for the careful planning of Homer Lea. Every move he made, every step he took, was carefully thought out in advance. He balanced the possibilities of failure against the possibilities of success, and knew for a certainty at all times just exactly what he was doing. Nothing was left to chance.

On the surface everything seemed quite innocent. It was a beautifully confusing setup, really. Only the members of the Po Wong Wui knew the truth. To all others, including the merely curious, the potential enemies, and inquiring newspaper reporters seeking a story, the answer was simple. Homer Lea and Ansel O'Banion were conducting a military academy for young Chinese students.

It was Homer Lea's brain child. He had a friend in Los Angeles, a young attorney just starting to practice law. And so, quite legally and aboveboard, this attorney obtained a charter for the school. It was called the Western Military Academy, and all during the years soldiers were being trained to take part in a revolution, the charter hung in a prominent place in the Armory. All who wished could look and see for themselves that here, indeed, was an orthodox military academy, approved by the state of California and subject to its laws. And the laws were never really broken, though they may have been twisted and bent a little now and then.

As directors of this school, five prominent citizens of Los Angeles consented to serve. Three of these men were bankers, the fourth was an attorney, and the other was president of the Board of Trade. But they didn't know at the time the real purpose of this school. Only General Lea and Captain O'Banion knew that secret.

Others interested in the school—but unofficially, of course —were Major General Adna R. Chaffee, General Harrison Gray Otis, former governor general of the Philippines and founder and owner of the *Los Angeles Times,* Major General J. P. Story, Captain D. P. Quillin, and the Hon. Elihu Root, Secretary of State—to mention a few.

So the five directors of the school were only too glad to lend their names and give their support. They thought it was purely educational and their interest was a humanitarian one. Lending a helping hand to the education of young Chinese was a worthy cause. And perhaps, too, through these young men and their connections in their native land, they might obtain a banking concession or two in China.

Their names were on the charter, of course, and that helped a lot when busybodies began snooping around. Of course, too, there were a lot of books in evidence at the school. Plenty of them—on all subjects. Nobody ever read them, but they came in handy when a raid was expected.

When that happened, the rifles vanished quickly, and the soldiers were discovered, each surrounded by books, intent upon their studies. They had all been carefully instructed never to hold a book upside down.

From time to time reports on the progress of the school

were made to the directors. They were pleased at this thoughtfulness. Since they had not been asked for money, there were no meetings of the board of directors, no conferences, and no wranglings over the policy to be pursued.

"Just give us your moral support," Homer Lea had said. "The Chinese will finance the school and run it in their own manner. I'm afraid if anybody interfered, we might get into difficulties."

"Yes, yes, of course," said one director. "The Chinese have their own peculiar way of doing things. I see no reason to poke my nose into their affairs. It's a fine work you are doing with these young Chinese lads, Homer, a fine work. They'll be educated to become good citizens. Congratulations—and keep it up."

"Yes, sir, and thank you, sir," replied Homer Lea, modestly.

However, as becomes all properly conducted schools, including military academies, a definite course of study was outlined. Little folders were printed—not many of them, but enough—with the announcements of the courses, subjects, and hours of credit—just like the Stanford catalogue, which had served as a model. Not so many courses, naturally, but those listed had a familiar look. It was a neat case of harmless academic plagiarism.

The subjects to be taught were the obvious: beginning English, M.W.F. at eight o'clock; advanced English, T.Th. at seven o'clock; algebra, chemistry, and so forth, and so forth. There were enough courses for any school. But no one ever got around to teaching any of these subjects. The students were all too busy learning other things, like the manual of arms, for instance.

The key to the school—or rather, the Armory—was given

to O'Banion by Homer Lea on the night of the banquet of the Po Wong Wui. From then on he was in complete charge; he was in fact the whole faculty: the dean of men, professor of this, and professor of that, and the teacher for every subject listed in the catalogue. He was the head of every department, including the graduate school. But he never once called a faculty meeting. Had he done so he would have had to talk to himself. Nor was he ever called Professor either. His official title was Captain.

There were really two rooms to this Armory; one in front, where the books were kept and the charter was hung, and another room at the back, large enough for drilling the men. To make certain no one ever poked his unwelcome nose into this Armory, the doors were kept locked. And certainly no one but O'Banion and Homer Lea and the Chinese ever stepped into the military drill room. There were guns in this room—7-millimeter Mauser rifles with dagger bayonets.

The first thing O'Banion did on his initial meeting with his army was to talk over with them definitely what they were going to do. Then each recruit, for the sake of the records, put down a name—not always the real one—on specially prepared slips of paper, and added his age, profession, and other such necessary information. These young men were from all walks of life: merchants, clerks in stores, farmers, and others. During the day they were busy at their various occupations. It was only in the evening that they attended the military academy and drilled. The hour set each night was for eight o'clock. Those who had to get to work early in the morning would be dismissed at midnight. The others would stay on until one or two o'clock.

That first evening there were about 60 present. But as

time went on more recruits joined up, until finally the number was limited to 120. Before O'Banion appeared on the scene, not one of them had ever had any military training. He had to start from scratch.

He lined them up and looked them over carefully. Never before in his army career had he seen such raw recruits. They knew nothing about drilling. They were there to learn. So, being Chinese, they not only acted dumb, but they were dumb, in a military sense. The blank expression of their faces, O'Banion felt, was not unlike that of a stale mince pie. Some of them didn't even speak English. But he had an interpreter at his elbow. Never at any time were commands given in Chinese.

Undaunted, he started in. First of all, he showed them how to stand: stomach in, chins up, shoulders back. No doubt anyone looking in on the scene as O'Banion put them through their paces, showing them "right dress" and all the other elements of what today is called "basic training," might have thought it amusing. But not the Chinese. Nobody ever thought of laughing at another man's mistakes. It was a serious business with them.

However, as time went on, and they began to learn what it was all about and the way a good soldier carried himself and drilled, their expressions changed. That first look of blank bewilderment gave way to a smiling but grim determination. Their eyes began to sparkle with enthusiasm, and they had that snappy, authoritative air of willing and well-trained soldiers.

Roll call was always at eight o'clock in the evening. No one missed. The only times a man was absent was when illness prevented his coming. They were serious-minded young men, bent upon doing their work well. "Goldbricking" was not in their scheme of things. Sober and intent, they wanted hard work and more of it. Nor were salaries of any sort paid to them. Volunteers all, they were the ones who paid to be trained.

Willingly each month and without waiting to be asked, they paid their 50 cents into the treasury of the Po Wong Wui. And so, night after night, their training as soldiers went on in secret. Sundays and holidays were all the same to them. The only time taken off was a week during Chinese New Year.

The troop was organized exactly like a regular company. Allen Chung was made a captain; Lou Hoy became a first lieutenant; Hom Toy was second lieutenant, and Soo Huking, first sergeant.

Now and then, while the drilling was going on, General Lea would come to the Armory. Satisfied with what was going on, and delighted with the progress being made, he then suggested to Captain O'Banion the next step to be taken.

He showed O'Banion a map of the United States. Around certain cities he had drawn a red circle.

"In these cities there are active and flourishing chapters of the Po Wong Wui," he said. "Let us start training soldiers in these spots exactly as we are doing in Los Angeles."

"Who'll we get?" asked O'Banion.

"What about some of the discharged noncommissioned officers you served with in the Philippines? Can they be trusted?" inquired Homer Lea.

"Some damn well can," replied O'Banion. "When you've been in a battle side by side with a man, you know!"

The next day he wrote a letter to former Sergeant Lawrence Meece of Troop A, 4th United States Cavalry. Meece was one of the best soldiers O'Banion had known in the Philippines.

In his letter O'Banion was somewhat cagey. He merely stated that he knew of several openings for some good men who might once again want to see some action. He hinted of the danger involved, the risks to be taken, but he promised a certain amount of adventure and implied it would be a unique experience. Would Meece like to get in on this? And did he know where some of the other men from Troop A were now located? Who among them did he think might be interested?

The reply from Meece was disappointing. Meece said that he was now engaged in business in Hutchinson, Kans.; if there was anything he could do in Hutchinson to help O'Banion he would be only too glad, but his soldiering days were a thing of the past. He did, however, give O'Banion the names and addresses of a number of former cavalrymen. In checking over this list, O'Banion saw that some of them were now living in the cities Homer Lea had marked on his map with a red circle.

Feeling that he must proceed carefully, he wrote a second letter to Meece, in which he asked that Meece write to some of these men for him. He suggested that Meece inquire; and if they were looking for a sort of part-time job, to write O'Banion.

Letters began coming in. Carefully O'Banion checked them over. He selected only the best men. He wrote, pledging them to secrecy, and asked that they say nothing whatever until such time as he had the opportunity of meeting and talking with them. He could not, he felt, be too cautious.

However, the grapevine among former comrades-in-arms

being what it is, several heard that something was in the
wind and, as O'Banion has often said, "tried to horn in."
But their services were declined. Years later some of these
men talked and claimed to have been in on this revolutionary movement. But they weren't. At the time, they didn't
even know the real purpose or exactly what was going on.
They did guess that something was on foot—and it has been
suspected that among them were those who later caused
trouble.

Those chosen were all picked men and, as O'Banion well
knew, to be thoroughly trusted. Four months after the training started in Los Angeles, another company was organized
in San Francisco, with former Corporal John Collins in
charge. Their headquarters were in a brick building on
Jackson Street in Chinatown and became one of the most
important "branches" of the Western Military Academy.

Corporal Collins was a born soldier, a tough fighter, and
had served in the United States Army for more than seventeen years. Later Collins went to China and was made a
captain in the Chinese Army there; when the revolution
broke out, he was in the thick of it.

Sacramento was next on the list. In this city, former Duty
Sergeant Pete MacDonald, a professional soldier of fortune,
was made drillmaster. A redheaded man about fifty, he had
served in the Colonial British troops in the Boer War as
well as in the Philippines.

And then O'Banion, with General Lea, Lou Hoy, and
Allen Chung, began making "business trips" about the
country. During his absences from Los Angeles, the drilling
of the troops was in charge of a former army officer. But
he was not told the real purpose back of the military academy. He may have guessed something, but he was a per-

sonal friend and kept his mouth shut. Today he is a high-ranking peace officer in the state of California.

Within a year companies of the Chinese Imperial Reform Army were being trained secretly in twenty-one cities of the United States. In St. Louis, Sergeant Francis Drischler, an architect by profession, was in charge. In Chicago was Sergeant William Donohue, a two-fisted, fighting Irishman. In New York City, the troops were trained on Canal Street by Sergeant Jim Bradley, a cool, calm, typical New Yorker. Boston had Sergeant Jim Littleton, precise in manner, a fine dresser, and a great stickler for discipline. In Denver was Corporal Frank C. Hardy, a slim, blond, good-looking young fellow. Others were Corporal William Grady in Portland, Ore., a man of fifty with a rumbling bass voice; Sergeant Joe Miller in Spokane, Wash., who had seen twenty years of service; Sergeant Jim Healy in Seattle, an old China hand, speaking their language and popular with the Chinese; and Sergeant William English in Hanford, Calif., an old army man, every inch a soldier. There was a company in Philadelphia, too—that caused a lot of trouble later.

In some cities and towns on the west coast, Chinese were in charge. In Fresno was thirty-five-year-old Ben Young, owner of the Chinese newspaper there, a college man who had had military training while in school. Several Chinese from other cities came to Los Angeles for special instruction from O'Banion. They then went back to their homes and organized companies. Among them were Wing Lee, a merchant, from Phoenix, Ariz.; Wah Gee, a laundryman from San Bernardino, who ran his outfit so well that after a year the thirty-one soldiers in his command sold their businesses and came to Los Angeles to devote their entire time and savings to the revolution; Suey Wing, from Santa

Barbara, where they had a building of their own, and never once did the residents of this city guess that a revolutionary army was being trained behind closed doors not far from the City Hall; Lou Mon, from Oxnard, who brought his company of fifteen men from this town and Ventura to Los Angeles, and they were among the first to go to China when the time came; and Tom Lee, a merchant from Bakersfield, who had some sixty men in his company. All these Chinese drillmasters were made first lieutenants.

The procedure in every city was about the same. General Lea's idea at first was to have in each of the twenty-one cities one hundred men, making in all a total of 2,100 soldiers. But that scheme did not quite work out. In some towns only fifteen or twenty men were available, while in the larger cities there were many more than one hundred volunteers. At one time in Los Angeles the full strength was 120. While in Philadelphia, where Neely Darr helped now and then, over 150 were trained.

All the men from the United States Army selected by O'Banion were made captains and initiated into the Po Wong Wui. The ceremony of signing their names in blood preceded the banquet given in their honor. The matter of their pay was settled completely to their satisfaction—and as it happened was the result of a conversation held one evening at one of these banquets in an Eastern city.

Among the Chinese present that night was a curious, elderly man. Not only had he been one of the first to join the Po Wong Wui in this city, but he was heart and soul in sympathy with the movement. He paid his 50 cents monthly and wanted to do more. Seated next to the captain who was to drill the troops, he asked him many questions about the United States Army: the duties of a sergeant, and why a corporal was of different rank than a captain, and so on.

Now, the pay for these drillmasters had previously been decided upon as $150 a month. But in the course of conversation, the captain let fall the remark that in the cavalry each man was allotted an extra ten dollars a month for the use of his horse.

"You are all former cavalrymen?" asked the Chinese.

"Oh, yes, every one of us," was the reply.

"Then you are entitled to an extra ten dollars a month for the care of your horse."

"But we don't need horses in this work."

"That does not matter," said the Chinese. "Horses or no horses—it is the custom. You are cavalrymen. And what the United States Army does—so shall the Chinese Imperial Reform Army do. Each month you will receive ten dollars for the care of your horses—whether you have horses or not. I shall see to it myself. But please do not thank me. I am doing only what is fair and right!"

And the money was paid into the treasury out of the pocket of this elderly Chinese every month on the dot!

These drillmasters were always paid in cash—never by check. The money was kept in the custody of the subtreasurer of the Po Wong Wui in each city, and the captains had only to go to this man to receive their pay when it was due. It was only the cavalrymen, however, who received the extra ten dollars.

Each captain, of course, had another job in the city where he was doing his drilling. This served as a front; if he wanted to go to Chinatown evenings, that was his own business.

O'Banion, of course, was ranking captain. And while all

reports were sent directly to General Lea, he, too, knew exactly what was going on in every city. He often went about the country visiting the various companies and watching the progress they were making. Since he fully trusted all these men, he did not—as is sometimes done—have his own private intelligence. If he had, his men would have, as he has said, "gone sour on me."

However, every Chinese was an intelligence officer on his own. They were always on the lookout for anyone unduly curious. And should they suspect that someone was against them, it was reported immediately; as were rumors, statements, or anything of a suspicious nature. These reports, like all secret orders of a confidential nature, were always written in Chinese. The first sergeant in every company was the man selected to handle all such reports and see that they were delivered into the hands of General Lea.

What conclusions could be drawn from these reports were made only by General Lea, Captain O'Banion, Allen Chung, and Lou Hoy. He had planned from the beginning that the fewer the men who knew the inside of what was happening the better it would be for all concerned. He made it a rule that was followed carefully: "Don't let anyone know any more than what he is supposed to know!"

To the various captains throughout the country, O'Banion wrote ordinary letters now and then.

Occasionally one of the men he had appointed might display a little healthy curiosity.

"How many men have you got in Los Angeles?" he would ask.

"Never mind," O'Banion would reply. "Don't ask questions. It isn't permitted. You can be assured we are doing all right."

A smart soldier knows exactly what that means and minds his own business.

For two years everything ran smoothly. Fully organized and under complete control from headquarters in Los Angeles, 2,100 Chinese were drilling secretly in this country.

And then in 1905, despite all the precautions taken, somehow or other the U. S. Secret Service got wind of what was going on. An investigation was started—and trouble was deposited on the doorsteps of the Chinese Imperial Reform Army.

However, anticipating that perhaps someday something like this might happen, General Lea and Captain O'Banion were not wholly unprepared.

CHAPTER SEVEN

The Children of Chinatown

BOTH Homer Lea and O'Banion hoped, of course, to avoid suspicion as much as possible. Certainly the Western Military Academy, on the surface, was open and aboveboard. Yet it wasn't quite so simple as all that. Even as they moved toward their goal, step by step, it was also important for them to be fully aware that their enemies—whoever they might be—also were making plans and were not inactive. They felt they must anticipate the pitfalls and the dangers, and if possible spike the enemy's guns before they went into action.

Consequently, whatever Homer Lea might be doing secretly—and doing it efficiently and well—he must have a reason for his behavior and an explanation to make to his friends should questions be asked. So he deliberately set about acquiring, in certain circles, a reputation as a mild eccentric. He let it be known he was writing a novel and a play. The play, called *The Crimson Spider,* is still unproduced. But the novel, *The Vermilion Pencil,* a melodramatic story about the secret society of the Boxers, was ultimately published by the McClure Company in 1908. On the surface, therefore, his activities invited scrutiny. And since it was known he was writing a book about the Chinese, there was nothing much that could be said.

O'Banion had to have a reason, too, for people were certain to ask what this former army man was doing in Chinatown. And how did he make a living? Certainly there weren't enough students at the military academy to pay him a decent wage.

The matter was discussed with Homer Lea, and it was decided that O'Banion must, also, have a front of some sort. It should be, they felt, one that would explain not only his frequent trips about the country, but also the long hours he spent teaching English to young Chinese men.

Through a friend, Walter Pixley, a merchant in Orange, he obtained a job as salesman and also out-of-town buyer for the William H. Hoegee Company, a sporting goods store in Los Angeles. Then, when he boarded a train and found his old friend Homer Lea in the same coach, it was merely a coincidence.

Even this blind was not enough, however. Then the Chinese had an idea. It was so pat that it worked beautifully and later proved advantageous in more ways than one.

Chinatown at that time was not, it must be admitted in all fairness, a safe place in which to roam about at night. However, it was not entirely the fault of the Chinese. They were an inarticulate minority and minded their own business. As far as possible they administered their own justice in their own way, and among themselves they maintained order. But they could not control the outside rowdy elements, nor defend themselves against the petty thieves and the plain drunken bullies of Los Angeles who thought the proper way to wind up a night's spree was to go to Chinatown and wreck the place.

Chinatown was a veritable haven for crooks, criminals, and thugs of all types and classes. There were, for example, the petty pickpockets and cheap sneaks who specialized in "rolling a drunk." More formidable types to handle were the genuine professional holdup men with criminal records. Many crooks of this sort preyed on Chinatown because there they were comparatively safe from prosecution.

They could—and often did—walk into a shop and intimidate the peace-loving owner, take his cash, and walk out. They knew the Chinese would seldom resist. If one did, and was found dead the next day, the police called it another example of "lawlessness in this hotbed of crime." And if a Chinese merchant was beaten up for attempting to protect his property—well, what's against beating up a "Chinaman"?

The Chinese, particularly the elderly merchants, became incensed at this state of affairs. They knew the crime wave of Chinatown—with all the implications in the newspapers about the so-called "Yellow Peril"—was not due to the Chinese, but largely to outside elements. Finally in desperation they petitioned the city of Los Angeles to permit them to appoint a special police officer for their protection. Here was something unique in American police history. Imagine a small group of people asking to be allowed to provide their own police protection and, furthermore, being perfectly willing to bear all expenses!

The man they wished appointed was Ansel E. O'Banion. Who could be better suited? Broad-shouldered, proud, but not boastful of his youthful strength, he had a quick Irish wit, and a quicker fist should trouble occur. In their petition they agreed that all factions in Chinatown would cooperate fully with him and also promised that O'Banion in turn would show no partiality of any sort to the Chinese. So one day, in company with the attorney for the Western Military Academy, O'Banion was sworn in as a special deputy sheriff. Later, in 1905, under Mayor Harper and Chief of

Police Hammel, he was made a special police officer. During all the years he was in Chinatown, that was his official position with the city of Los Angeles.

In the beginning he faced the problem of cleaning up Chinatown alone and singlehanded. But after a time he organized what he called his "amateur police force." These were willing volunteers, utterly without any previous police training. And they were paid by O'Banion out of his own pocket. Some received ice-cream sodas; others, cigars. To the children of Chinatown—his best helpers—went, now and then, the ice-cream sodas. Typical of the kind of men to whom cigars were given occasionally was Tony Poledo, a professional boxer. O'Banion became acquainted with him under rather unusual circumstances.

One day Suey Wing opened a barbershop on Alameda Street. He fitted it up in fine style—even with shutters on the windows, which were his pride and joy. Every morning before he opened up for business, he'd take the shutters down and put them inside. Then one morning, to his dismay and annoyance, he found that someone had spit tobacco juice on his bright, new shutters.

He hoped it wouldn't happen again. But it did—day after day—always the tobacco juice in exactly the same spot.

Suey Wing reported the matter to the police, and they promised to help. They stationed a man across the street to see if he could catch the mischiefmaker. But the policeman didn't succeed, and every morning the shutters were ruined as before. O'Banion himself spent a couple of nights shuffling in and out of doorways, but had no luck whatever, even though he waited until the last noisy sight-seer had gone home in the early morning hours. He began to think that standing around the streets waiting to find the offender was not the best method in the world. So he tried another trick—and caught his man.

"How did you do it?" asked Suey Wing, pleased and grateful.

O'Banion told him it was very simple. He got himself a blanket, wrapped up in it and laid down on the porch over the shop. But he didn't sleep. He kept an eye open for every bum that came along. And sure enough, along toward morning the offender appeared. He was Tony Poledo, the boxer. Tony was in training for a fight and came out early, running along the street doing his shadow boxing and limbering-up exercises.

As he passed the shop he spat straight at the shutters. O'Banion slid down from the porch in a flash and nailed him on the spot. He gave him the hip-lock, grabbed him, and threw him into the gutter. By the time Tony was on his feet, O'Banion had the handcuffs on him. He took him to the police station and had him locked up. Tony was fined $10 in Judge Austin's court.

A few days later a chastened and apologetic Tony came to see O'Banion. He confessed that what he had done had been a lousy, thoughtless trick, and that someday he'd prove to O'Banion he was truly sorry. And he did. He appeared unexpectedly one morning about five o'clock in just the nick of time. O'Banion was in the thick of one of the most rousing fights of his life—and if ever a man needed help, he did.

He was having a one-man battle with the Coyote gang. These young ruffians were notorious sneak thieves and pickpockets. Singly, and sometimes in pairs, they'd find a drunk sleeping in a doorway and proceed to "roll him." Whenever O'Banion caught them at this, he'd beat them up and literally kick them out of Chinatown. After several run-ins with O'Banion and resenting the full force of his two fists, they decided to gang up on him.

Early one morning O'Banion came upon a couple of them rolling a drunk on the east side of the plaza. He went into action. The two weren't so hard to handle, but the drunk—who was merely pretending—jumped to his feet and joined in the fight. And others, who had been waiting around the corner and in the dark spots in the park for just this opportunity, came up on the run.

It was one against many. And O'Banion was alone. He squared off, tried to handle them one at a time, but others would rush up. The fight was going against him. He was getting tired. How much longer he could hold out, he didn't know.

Then down the street came Tony Poledo, skipping along to limber up his muscles. He saw immediately what was going on, paused a moment with his fists clenched in the air, and then cried, "Boy, this looks like the real thing!"

He plunged into the fight on O'Banion's side. It wasn't long until, with his expert and professional help, the gang took to their heels.

"Thanks, Tony," said O'Banion. "I've never been so damn glad to see anybody in my life!"

"I guess that squares me now, doesn't it?" grinned Tony.

From that time on they were friends.

It was the last he ever heard of the Coyote gang, too. And soon it was the same story with the other cheap crooks and pickpockets who infested Chinatown. Word spread through the underworld that there was a two-fisted fighting Irishman in that district, administering justice in his own way. And a broken nose or a black eye, or both, would be harder to take than a few free meals in a police station. It was the same with the thoughtless drunks, who thought they'd have some good, innocent fun in Chinatown.

His strong-arm treatment worked. Chinatown was a large district to cover, but he covered it by degrees. He worked on the theory that, if you give a man enough physical punishment once, threaten him with the same dose if you ever see him again, and then repeat the dose at the first opportunity, you seem to curb the criminal instincts of a lot of people.

It wasn't always easy, of course. Sometimes O'Banion got a beating himself, but he always came back for more. And in time the rowdies, the drunks, and the pickpockets learned to stay away from Chinatown.

Handling the thieves who not only broke into the Chinese stores, but often in broad daylight walked in and helped themselves, was yet another matter. His greatest help in handling this problem came from the children of Chinatown.

Captain O'Banion early discovered that the due process of law wouldn't work, as far as Chinatown was concerned. If he took a man to jail for robbing a Chinese shop, the proprietor would not appear to testify in the case. The Chinese merchants had had previous experience of Los Angeles justice as applied to the Chinese, with often disastrous results. So O'Banion would find himself with a guilty man and no one to appear against him. The case would be dismissed for lack of evidence. But later the merchant would be robbed again, sometimes his place wrecked and himself manhandled in the bargain. Knowing the Chinese would seldom resist, the thieves were bold and brazen.

But with the help of the children of Chinatown, O'Banion

put a stop to this. His best helper was a little eight-year-old girl named Wong. She lived in Ferguson Alley, where her mother, a widow, had a small shop.

She was a tiny girl, demure and quiet—yet she played a part in the revolution, too. O'Banion first became acquainted with her when she used to come to the Armory evenings to watch the soldiers drill. She'd never stay long, just an hour or so early in the evening. She was so quiet, so small and mouselike, that often when he was busy drilling the soldiers he wasn't even aware she was present. She never said a word—just sat quietly looking on. If anyone tried to talk with her, she would pretend she hadn't heard. So, instead of scolding her and sending her home, in time the troops accepted her as their mascot.

She was a great admirer of General Lea and always smiled and spoke to him whenever he came around. She was fond of big Captain O'Banion too and, like the soldiers, was eager and willing to accept any command he might wish to give. Her mother had often been a victim of thieves at her store, so when O'Banion asked the little Wong girl if she would like to help him put an end to this abuse, she quickly nodded her assent.

And when he told her from now on she was his first lieutenant and in command of the children of Chinatown, she was the happiest girl on earth. He asked her to bring her little friends—all of them—to the Armory one night for a special meeting. Carefully he instructed them in what they were to do.

Now, a thief, intent on robbing a store, never paid any attention to these children. They were always underfoot, playing in the shops or on the streets. The thief would enter a store, intimidate the owner, help himself, and walk out—

sometimes bold enough even to raid the cash register. Quickly the merchant would speak to one of the children, who would hurry off to find O'Banion.

Other children would trail the thief, keeping up their innocent pretense of playing games. They would point out the offender to O'Banion. And how startled the thief would be when O'Banion tapped him on the shoulder, told him exactly what he had stolen, and led him off to the nearest patrol box to telephone the police.

The children would tag behind, crying, "Loy coya—loy coya," meaning "Come along." The thief never suspected the part they had played in his capture.

However, it wasn't always O'Banion's purpose to have the man arrested and sent to jail. It was difficult, as has been said, to get the Chinese merchant to appear in court and testify against the thief. But there was a way out.

Near the patrol box was a wooden culvert. O'Banion did not search the thief on the spot. That wasn't in his line of duty, anyway. He would tell the culprit to sit down on the curb near the culvert. He'd then turn his back and pick up the telephone. Seeing the hiding place, the thief would invariably slip his loot into the wooden culvert. Whereupon the children—who had been pretending not to be watching —would speak a few words in Chinese to O'Banion.

He would pick up the thief by his shoulders, stand him on his feet, and give him what he called the "cure"—a good beating. He'd then boot him out of Chinatown with the warning not to come back. It was good advice and readily accepted. Robbing a Chinese store was not, as these petty thieves began to discover, so easy as it appeared. And soon— as with the pickpockets and the drunks—they learned to stay away from Chinatown.

Of course, as soon as the thief ran off, the children would retrieve the stolen property and return it to its rightful owner. It made the children happy to do this. The merchants were pleased, too. There was no trouble in the law courts—yet justice had been administered.

The gratitude of the Chinese to O'Banion was unbounded. He was known and respected all over Chinatown. To his great embarrassment, merchants, standing in the doorway of their stores or passing him on the street, would salute and call him Captain. He tried to make them stop this, saying that only soldiers saluted. But knowing the salute was a mark of respect, why shouldn't the merchants do as the soldiers did? It was a great nuisance, but there was nothing he could do to stop it. Even years afterward, now and then walking down the streets of Los Angeles, he would be recognized by one of the old-timers, and the greeting was a formal military salute.

It was being called Captain that he was afraid would be open to misinterpretation in some quarters. But there was a way around that. He joined the California National Guard, and on Nov. 24, 1905, was commissioned captain of Troop D, 1st Squadron, California Cavalry, by Governor George C. Pardee. From then on, everything was perfectly all right.

The Chinese had other ways of showing their gratitude, too. One day a wealthy Chinese druggist came to see O'Banion. He was one of the most prominent elders of Chinatown, and heart and soul devoted to the revolutionary movement.

After the proper exchange of courtesies, he said to O'Banion, "You are often in Chinatown very late at night— sometimes drilling the soldiers—other times chasing home disorderly and overly drunk drunkards. So I know that after a long day's work, and before going peacefully home,

you may perhaps, now and then, wish a little drink yourself. So, do please come with me. I want to show you what
I have named the Mousetrap."

He led the way to the Armory, and there on the side wall
showed O'Banion a small cabinet, which had been built and
put up by a Chinese carpenter. It was about two feet high,
one foot wide and one deep, and was firmly and securely
locked.

The key was produced and the door opened. Inside
O'Banion saw four bottles—one each of brandy, whisky, gin,
and rum—and five glasses.

"This is yours," said the elder. "And here's the key. The
only other key to this I shall keep myself. Please do not
thank me. It is you I have to thank for all you are doing."

And there was the Mousetrap all during the years
O'Banion spent in Chinatown. An empty bottle was always
replenished, and the glasses washed and cleaned every morning by the elder himself.

Other merchants showed their appreciation in different
ways. It was an unwritten rule in every restaurant that if
O'Banion came in for dinner, no matter whether alone or
with friends, he was never allowed to pay. Should he pro-
test, the answer would be, "Come in tomorrow. I don't
know how much it is. I'll have to ask the cook—and he's
gone home."

When he dropped in the following day and asked for the
bill, the cashier would look surprised, shake his head in
dismay as if he were worried over O'Banion's failing memory, and say, "But you forget—it's all been taken care of.
I can't allow you to pay me twice!"

The Chinese even thought up another scheme to make
his way easier in Chinatown. One night he was invited to

a banquet. The hosts this evening were the Chinese Chamber of Commerce and the vegetable farmers and hucksters. After they had been eating for over two hours, Ho Lee, of the Chamber of Commerce, rose and made a speech. On behalf of all the Chinese, he said that the farmers and hucksters were having troubles and difficulties of their own. They were being swindled when buying horses and feed.

There were, he said, some four hundred hucksters who had their horses stabled in Chinatown. Many of these horses were thin, ill-fed, scrawny animals. Often they were sick—and who was there among the Chinese to take care of them? Now Captain O'Banion was a former cavalryman. He knew horses, how they should be handled, their proper care and feeding. Would it be possible, therefore, asked Mr. Lee, smiling, for the Captain to open a horse market and feed store in Chinatown for the exclusive use of the Chinese?

O'Banion replied that it would. This would give him a perfect excuse for being in Chinatown all day long. So, shortly after that, at 742 North Alameda Street—right in the very heart of Chinatown, and next door to a Japanese bath-house—the Hay and Feed Market was opened.

O'Banion's business methods with the Chinese were very clean-cut. First of all, he bought some fine horses, trained and broke them—and then was ready for a little expert trading. A huckster with a scrawny horse would see one of O'Banion's fine animals and politely ask, "How much?"

O'Banion would tell him $275, or whatever the price might be. The Chinese would shrug his shoulders and say he would like to buy the horse, but how did he know its value?

"How much did you pay for that nag of yours?" O'Banion would ask.

CAPTAIN O'BANION

"Twenty-five dollars from Dutch Charlie—but I got cheated."

"Needs fattening up," O'Banion would suggest.

Whereupon the Chinese would ask that O'Banion take care of the horse for one week and see what could be done. In the meantime, since he had his business as usual, he would borrow one of O'Banion's plump, well-fed horses. If, at the end of the week, he found he liked the horse, he would come back and pay O'Banion $250, and leave with him the old nag. And back to Dutch Charlie went this spavined animal.

Of course, the Chinese bought all the feed for their horses from O'Banion. Books were kept for the business in an unorthodox, but very Chinese manner. Every morning O'Banion would ride on his horse to the stables of the Chinese hucksters. He had keys to all of them, for by the time he got around in the morning the hucksters were off on their daily rounds with their wagons. O'Banion would unlock the door, ride in, look at the supply of hay and grain, and see for himself what was needed. No Chinese ever gave him an order. He was supposed to see to it that feed was always on hand. When he got back to the Hay and Feed Market, he would tell his helpers what to deliver and where.

Now each huckster had a room where he slept in the stable. Often several men shared the same stable. They would put their wagons in front, and the horses lined up in a row in the middle. And on every Sunday morning O'Banion went to these stables to collect.

During the week, of course, with each lot of feed delivered he had left a slip on which the amount due was listed. The hucksters kept these slips religiously, and on Sunday morning, when O'Banion appeared, they had the exact amount ready for him. They handed him the money with the slip. He dropped the cash into a buckskin bag hanging from his saddlehorn, tore up the slip—and that's the way he kept his books.

Once when he was out of town for three weeks the book-keeping, as he said, "got all messed up." His helpers didn't know how much was due each week. They didn't even know how much feed had been delivered. But O'Banion didn't worry. He had told the Chinese he would be away. When he got back they came, one by one, to the Hay and Feed Market and paid exactly what was due. That's just how honest they were!

Obviously, being so closely connected with the Chinese, he could not avoid, now and then, becoming embroiled in one of their tong wars. When one broke out, he was on the scene. The first night he spent at the headquarters of one of the quarreling tongs, and the next with the opposing faction. When he was appointed a special police officer, he had promised not to show any partiality—and he didn't.

Apart from political quarrels, there were usually four reasons for tong wars. One very good reason—and in this respect the Chinese are not different from all men every-where, regardless of race, nationality, or creed—would be an argument over a woman. Another reason would be the be-trayal of an oath. The Chinese heartily dislike a "squealer." Should a Chinese once pledged to secrecy break his promise, he'd ultimately be caught, no matter where in the world he might try to hide.

The other two reasons were purely economic. Should a thief abscond with money belonging to others, he as good as signed his death warrant. That was also true of the man who failed to pay his honest debts.

More often than not there were more threats of tong wars than actual wars. A guilty man was always given a chance to redeem himself. But if he persisted in his dishonesty and stubbornness, death was the penalty.

Whenever a shooting occurred, it was done by one of the "bow how doy"—sometimes poetically called hatchetmen, which is a misnomer, as they invariably used revolvers. They have also been called highbinders. Far from being professional killers or even criminals murderously inclined, these highbinders of the tongs were volunteers, public-spirited men, who considered the keeping of the law and order their first duty to their fellow men and their community. They were really not unlike our vigilantes.

Ordinarily they were well-behaved members of the community. They all joined missions, went regularly to Sunday school—even signed the pledge not to drink or smoke any more—and some sported white ribbons in their buttonholes, proving they kept their word. It was a wise precaution, for in case they ever should get into trouble with the police, they had a good record behind them.

No man was ever condemned to death until—after all ordinary methods of persuasion for him to lead a moral life had failed—the leaders of the tong were in unanimous agreement as to his guilt. Then the highbinders of the tong were called in. They would be told the name of the man who was to die. The headman of the tong would get five or more broom straws—depending upon the number of hatchetmen in the tong. Each would draw a straw. The man who got the shortest was the man to do the job—whether he wanted to or not. If he needed someone to help him on this particular assignment, he would select that man himself. In any event, the price paid by the tong for the fulfillment of justice was usually $400. If a man had a helper, he paid him out of the money received.

Promptly after the deed was done, the killer would be hidden away by the tong. After the trouble was finally settled to everyone's satisfaction, the police would often be tipped off as to where the highbinder could be found. But, of course, there would never be any witnesses to testify against him. Often the police were frantic, and the unsolved murder of another Chinese was entered in the police registers.

Quite naturally, O'Banion became acquainted in time with many of the highbinders of the various tongs. It was during what might have turned out to be a vicious tong war that he saved the life of one of these highbinders. This man became one of the leading revolutionists and O'Banion's most trusted friend and undercover agent.

CHAPTER EIGHT

The Feast of the Dead

ONE evening, after the drilling at the Armory was over, Soo Hu-hem, whom O'Banion had made quartermaster sergeant, said to him, "In a few days now I'm going to be a rich man. I'll have $5,000 of easy money in my pocket."

"That's fine," exclaimed O'Banion. "How'll you get it?"

"I shall play the lottery—and hold the winning ticket."

"Don't be too damned certain," warned O'Banion.

"Why not? The scheme I'm cooking up can't fail."

"Sounds to me like the lottery isn't on the up-and-up," said O'Banion, skeptically.

Soo Hu-hem looked grieved. "Captain, surely you aren't doubting my honesty?"

It wasn't that he was doubting his honesty, O'Banion told him, but merely how could any man be certain he was going to hold the winning ticket in a lottery?

Now, Soo Hu-hem was O'Banion's right-hand man. The drilling hadn't been going on for long when O'Banion discovered in him a natural born leader. Soo Hu-hem was the oldest man in the outfit, thirty-five at the time. He was American-born and had been raised on the Bixby Horse Ranch near Long Beach. The cowboys on this ranch were all Mexicans, and Soo Hu-hem grew up with them. Rawboned, and six feet tall, he had all the characteristics of a Mexican cowboy: a good fighter, a daredevil, and a man among men wherever he might happen to be.

When he was twenty-five he came to Los Angeles and opened a laundry. The building where he had it is still standing, incidentally, at 215 North San Pedro Street. In his laundry he had about twenty Chinese working for him, older men who were not in the troop. But they were loyal to Soo Hu-hem and did their share in furthering the cause of the revolution.

If Soo Hu-hem is alive today, he is an old man. What ultimately happened to him, O'Banion never knew. He was one of the first to go to China, and one of the most active of the revolutionists. O'Banion had found him not only a man to be relied upon, but one whom he could trust completely. So, obviously, he was puzzled over Soo Hu-hem's statement that he intended holding the winning lottery ticket.

But, as Soo Hu-hem told him, the answer was easy—he planned to steal Yim Lo Wang, known as the White Man.

They stopped at a restaurant to get a bite to eat, and over the teacups Soo Hu-hem told O'Banion what it was all about.

Now, the most important festival among the Chinese is the celebration of the New Year. This usually comes sometime around the first of February, depending upon the behavior of the moon. Next in importance is the Feast of the Dead or, as it is sometimes called, the "Feast of the Hungry Ghosts." This occurs every four years in April.

On this day honor and respect are paid to those silent kinsmen who now dwell in that land from which no traveler ever returns. Joss is burned before the altars of the family gods, and obeisance is made to the memory of one's ancestors. It is not unlike our own Memorial Day.

While this Feast of the Dead is still observed among the

Chinese in this country, in the old days there was much more public observance. At the time of our story it was customary to erect a shrine, or altar, near the plaza at North Los Angeles Street just opposite one of the tong headquarters. On this shrine—placed on a platform built especially for it—were the images of the Five Gods who rule the destiny of man. Now the principal figure is Yim Lo Wang, known as the White Man. For this particular shrine he was made of white crepe paper and strung onto a wire frame.

White is the color always worn at Chinese funerals. Red—symbolizing good luck—is worn by the bride at her wedding. But white—being all colors and yet no color—belongs to the dead.

Yim Lo Wang, since he is the Ruler of the Other World, is always represented as wearing white. He sits at the Pearly Gates and passes judgment on the men who come before him. However, to the Chinese, there is only one other world —heaven and hell are the same place. And beyond the Pearly Gates a man always gets exactly what he deserves, according to the way he has behaved in this world. Good, bad, or indifferent, it is Yim Lo Wang who knows more about you than your own family—and when you stand before him, it is he who decides what you are going to be in your next incarnation.

And, as Soo Hu-hem told O'Banion, "He's a hard man to get by. He knows everything—by far too much. If only he would disappear—think what a good time we'd all have down here below—knowing that we'd not have to face him when we die."

He shook his head sadly and then smiled. By this time O'Banion was well enough acquainted with the Chinese and their philosophical approach to life to know that even in their most solemn moments they have a touch of merriment and good humor. Whether they took Yim Lo Wang seriously was not the point. The idea was that he symbolized a certain thing—man's inner conscience, if you like—and what fun to be conscience-free for a time.

And so, as Soo Hu-hem went on, it was always a great temptation to steal the White Man. Moreover, it was a tradition among the Chinese that, if anyone was clever enough to steal him—and wasn't caught within twenty-four hours—the thief would receive a Chinese lottery ticket worth $5,000.

"But it's not easy to steal him," said Soo Hu-hem. "He's well-guarded, night and day, during the Feast of the Dead. That's why the shrine is put up in public—on the street—where everyone can see. It will be there for three full days. And two policemen—off duty—have been hired for $5 a day to stand guard. It will be very difficult to steal the White Man from under their very noses. However—" he paused, looked sober a moment, then shook his head doubtfully—"I have announced to everyone that I intend to make him vanish—and win the $5,000."

O'Banion said, "What'll you use—hocus-pocus or some Chinese magic?"

"No," replied Soo Hu-hem seriously, "not magic. Not magic at all. . . . But I boast too much. Tomorrow the shrine will be put up in the street by the plaza. Go take a look—and wish me luck!"

The next day O'Banion went around to North Los Angeles Street and saw for himself. There was a platform about six by ten feet and some three feet high—and on it was the shrine with the five images. In the center was Yim Lo Wang, a large image made of wire and covered with white paper. Seated on the platform, twirling his stick, was a burly policeman. There would be another there to take his place when night fell. How Soo Hu-hem would get by these two watchful eyes of the law was beyond O'Banion. It wasn't possible, he felt, to bribe those policemen.

All that day and that night Yim Lo Wang sat enthroned —reminding everyone to watch his step. The next afternoon he was still there, and O'Banion, meeting Soo Hu-hem, shook his head doubtfully.

Soo Hu-hem sighed and said unhappily, "What a boastful fool I've been. If I don't steal him, I'll never hear the last of this!"

"Right you are!" said O'Banion.

Then Soo Hu-hem brightened, as he added, "However, there's this to my advantage—if the White Man does vanish —by now everybody knows, or should know, that I am the man who stole him. In the meantime, all I can be is patient. Perhaps tonight something will happen."

And that very evening something did!

The policeman was on guard as usual. There were even quite a number of people standing about looking at the shrine—and perhaps in their hearts asking a prayer for forgiveness from stern-featured Yim Lo Wang. But there he sat, bland and indifferent. Then suddenly he rose straight into the air. As if blown along by a puff of wind, over the heads of the crowd he flew, and vanished through the open window of the tong headquarters. The crowd stared in open-mouthed wonder.

"Wow-ee!" cried the policeman. And letting out a dismayed cry of similar inexplicable words, jumped from the stand, and ran up the stairs to the tong rooms. The crowd, collecting their scattered wits, followed.

The door was unlocked and, not standing on ceremony, the policeman pushed it open and rushed into the front room. Six elderly Chinese playing mah-jongg looked up, surprised and startled.

"Where did it go to?" asked the policeman.

"Where did what go?" was the answer.

"The White Man."

"What white man?"

Like the statues of the three monkeys who see no evil, hear no evil, and speak no evil, the mah-jongg players confessed they had been here quietly all evening and had seen nothing, heard nothing, and consequently, could say nothing!

The White Man had vanished into thin air. He couldn't be found anywhere—although the tong headquarters were searched, the hallways, and the alley at the back. And he never was found. Yim Lo Wang was gone forever.

Soo Hu-hem was missing, too. He was probably, so O'Banion thought, someplace or other having a merry time without his conscience bothering him. Or else he was in hiding with Yim Lo Wang, confessing everything.

A whole day passed. Late that afternoon O'Banion got word that trouble was brewing. There were the threats of an impending tong war. Now, the lottery was conducted by a rival tong—and they had $5,000 at stake. They openly accused Soo Hu-hem of bribing the police. The policeman vigorously denied this, of course. But rumors flew thick and fast. And the merchants in Chinatown, as evening came, pulled down their shutters, locked their doors, and were prepared for the worst.

At exactly the same hour, to the very minute, that Yim Lo Wang had vanished, Soo Hu-hem appeared on the scene. As blandly indifferent as the god himself, he announced to

O'Banion that he was anticipating a very pleasant evening.

"I have had a very busy day doing nothing," said Soo Hu-hem. "I need a little amusement, so I thought tonight I'd play the lottery."

"Think you'll be safe?" asked O'Banion, and told him the rumors he had heard.

"How stupid to accuse a well-meaning and harmless policeman," said Soo Hu-hem. "He is quite innocent. I humbly confess that I—and I alone—am guilty!"

"But if you go to the lottery game, something may happen to you!"

"Oh, no. I'll be quite safe. Because if you went along with me, nothing would happen. You only need to wait outside and, when I have won, see that I get safely home with the money. What happens after that is my own business!"

"Okay!" said O'Banion. "I'll go, on one condition. Tell me how you stole the White Man."

"I intend to tell everybody," replied Soo Hu-hem. "There was no hocus-pocus, magic, or anything so obvious."

As he went on to inform O'Banion, the White Man was very light, weighing less than five pounds. A few days earlier, Soo Hu-hem had strung a wire from the peak of the roof of the tong over to a palm tree on the plaza. He put a ring onto that wire with another wire that had a hook on it. Yim Lo Wang was directly beneath this hook, in exactly the spot he'd always been in. Soo Hu-hem noticed this very carefully on the former Feast of the Dead when he had thought up this scheme. So all he did was to catch the White Man on the hook as one does a fish. It was ninety per cent luck—but it worked!

"But how did it vanish from the tong headquarters?" asked O'Banion.

"This much of the truth is between you and me only," said Soo Hu-hem. "I had a helper—a cousin of mine from San Francisco. I also had another wire from the back door of the tong. So when Yim Lo Wang appeared—he was fastened onto this wire—slid down into the alley—and suddenly vanished without anyone seen leaving the tong. I was on the roof—lying flat on my stomach. I've been there all day. No one thought of looking for me on the roof. In the alley my cousin grabbed Yim Lo Wang, bent the wire, wadded him up—thrust him inside his shirt—and walked out onto the street and started helping the policemen search."

"Where is he now?" asked O'Banion.

Soo Hu-hem shrugged his shoulders. "I know you won't tell—so here's the answer. My cousin—when he found he was of no help to the police—rambled off and went to the place on Ferguson Alley, where we sometimes go when we don't want to be found—or want to walk in one door and out another and make good our escape. I've just come from there. The White Man is no more. . . . So now to play the lottery!"

"Sure you'll win?" asked O'Banion.

"Positive. They are very angry at me—but they are honest men."

O'Banion went with Soo Hu-hem to the headquarters of the rival tong where the lottery was being played. He hung around outside. Along about two o'clock in the morning, while waiting on the corner of North Los Angeles and Marchessault streets, he noticed eight city plain-clothes detectives stalk out into the plaza. Expecting a tong war to break out at any moment now, they were prepared for any emergency.

When Soo Hu-hem finally came around the corner, he was accompanied by twelve members of his tong. The detectives, seeing this group of Chinese, and believing they were about to start trouble, rushed across the street and quickly grabbed as many Chinese as they could.

O'Banion noticed one slender, small Chinese who was a stranger to him. He moved into the crowd and rubbed against him to see if he was armed. He was. If he were taken to police headquarters and searched, he would be in serious trouble. The corner was very dark at this hour of the morning, so it was an easy matter for O'Banion to transfer the gun quickly to his own pocket. Nobody saw him.

When the detectives found that the Chinese were not armed, they let them go. Soo Hu-hem joined O'Banion. The others quietly disappeared into the night.

"Let's have a nightcap," suggested O'Banion, and led the way to the Mousetrap.

"Here's luck!" toasted Soo Hu-hem. "And I've had it—all along the line. What wise precautions the city takes. Those detectives did quite right. But there will not be a tong war."

He went on to tell O'Banion that when he won the $5,000 he told the tong he was not keeping the money for himself but was giving it to the Po Wong Wui for the use of the Chinese Imperial Reform Army. All bets were off, and peace among the tongs was declared on the spot. Also, every man present put his winnings on the table, and that, too, went into the general fund. It was a very profitable evening for the Po Wong Wui.

"Who's that man carrying a gun?" asked O'Banion, grimly.

"Oh, him! He's my cousin. Why?"

"When you see him, tell him I have his gun. If he wants it back, have him come and see me."

"He'll be there tomorrow," replied Soo Hu-hem.

The next morning there strolled into the office at the Hay Market a young Chinese whom O'Banion recognized as the stranger he had seen with Soo Hu-hem the night before. He was apparently somewhere in his late twenties; slim, slight of build, and carried his shoulders high. A very flashy dresser, he wore conspicuously two diamonds: one on a stickpin in his tie, the other in a ring on his finger. He had a rather disconcerting way of looking at a person; a frank and honest appraisal as if he were saying to himself, "Here I am, now what in hell are you like?" If it hadn't been for the pleasant, friendly twinkle in his eye, this look might have been misinterpreted as impertinence. But this chap was obviously nobody's fool.

"Good morning," he said, smiling.

"Good morning," replied O'Banion.

"Nice city—Los Angeles. I like it here—my first visit."

"I thought I'd never seen you around."

"No, my home's in Frisco. I came down to help Soo Hu-hem. He's my cousin, you know."

"So he told me last night."

O'Banion pulled open the drawer of his desk so that this Chinese could see his gun. It was a German Luger automatic—a particularly vicious-looking revolver. The stranger smiled, picked up the gun, and slipped it into his pocket.

"Thanks," he said. "You saved my life. Should you ever need help—please call upon me."

"Where can I find you?" asked O'Banion.

"Oh, the next time you're in Frisco I'll look you up," was the evasive answer.

Then, after chatting a bit about the comparative climates of Los Angeles and San Francisco, he went his way. O'Banion's first impression of him was that he was a quick-witted, smart young man and knew his way around without asking too many questions. He later had plenty of opportunity to confirm that judgment. He also discovered this Chinese had one of the quickest fingers on the trigger of any man he had ever met. His marksmanship was unfailing and his aim never wavered.

Every time he went to San Francisco on business for the troops this young Chinese was always on hand. And O'Banion soon learned that he was one of the leaders in the Po Wong Wui, and contributed heavily. But he never joined the company drilling in San Francisco.

"There are other ways I can serve," he said.

He was a great spender and never lacked for money. He enjoyed nothing better than to invite a group of his friends to dinner, and since O'Banion was always included on these occasions he came to know him well. In time, too, he heard his story.

His papers were in perfect order. They said he had been born in this country. But it wasn't true. He had been born in Canton and was smuggled into America when he was a boy of twelve. Just how it had been done, O'Banion never knew. He was never told. But a great many Chinese came into this country illegally about that time.

As a boy he had a job in a restaurant as a cook's helper. Later he became an expert chef. He was a wonderful cook, so O'Banion discovered—and it didn't matter whether it was French, American, or Chinese style; a touch of this, a dash of that, and the sauces that he could prepare were tops! When he grew older and had saved enough money, he started a restaurant of his own. In time he owned several. He hired men to run them for him and paid them, not a regular salary, but on a sharing basis.

Like all enterprising young men, he had his troubles and his headaches. One of his restaurants was situated in a particularly choice location. His rivals tried to take it away from him and, to his dismay, shot one of his partners, an old man, a cousin, whom he always referred to as Honorable Uncle. This man had helped him get a start in America.

Immediately, for revenge, he joined a rival tong and started learning how to use a revolver. When he was confident that he was a dead shot and wouldn't miss, he paid his debt to Honorable Uncle and killed the man who had murdered him. Shortly after, he was sworn in as a "bow how doy." Fearless, and not liking to be pushed around or see other people pushed around, he let it be known he was a friend of the underdog. In time he became the chief highbinder of the tong.

His revolver—the one O'Banion had taken from him that night in Los Angeles—was his most prized possession. Just how many tong killings this gun had figured in, O'Banion never knew. There were no notches on it—such as the Western badmen used for decoration. The Chinese think it is impolite to boast. But O'Banion did know that, had the police in Los Angeles that night got hold of the gun and traced it back to its rightful owner—it would have been just too bad!

"So, when you took that gun from me you really saved my life!" he told O'Banion.

His real name O'Banion never knew. He did have several nicknames, however, and O'Banion thought up one of his own to call him. It was a code name, and only O'Banion ever used it. There was no particular meaning or reason for calling him Duke—but Duke was the name he gave him, and as Duke he will be known in this story from now on.

Seeing him around so much, and observing the high regard in which the Chinese held him, O'Banion had an idea one day. He felt that the time might come when he would need an undercover man to assist him. So one evening after the troops had been dismissed he asked Duke to have a bite to eat with him.

"There's something I'd like to discuss with you privately," he said.

"Then let us go to my home," said Duke.

O'Banion had never been there. Usually when they had their midnight suppers in Chinatown and had something to discuss concerning the Po Wong Wui, Duke would lead the way to an empty banquet hall in Chinatown. There'd be a table in the center of the room—with no other people present, so that nobody could listen to what was being said. It perhaps wasn't too strange—yet Duke always knew exactly what banquet hall would be vacant. But this evening, since it was only too evident that O'Banion had something he wished to discuss with him alone, Duke led the way to his own home.

It was up a side alley. They climbed a rickety flight of narrow stairs—made narrow for a purpose. Only one person could go up at a time. Duke paid a high rental for this place, but it was worth it. There were several exits, some of them secret. It was so contrived that, in case he might be trapped, he could make his escape. He was also very careful whom he admitted. There was a sliding panel on the door and, whenever there was a knock, Duke's wife would look through this peephole and see who was there before she let him in. All during the years that followed, whenever O'Banion went to see Duke at his home, he had to go through this inspection. But, as Duke often said, "The wise man in guarding his home cannot take too many precautions."

This evening, after they had had supper, which Duke cooked, O'Banion came quickly to the point.

"One of these days—the way things are beginning to develop—I shall need someone to work secretly with me," he said. "I don't want the troops to know about it. Certainly not the members of the Po Wong Wui. And not even Homer Lea. Nobody at all, in fact. Do you want to be that man?"

"Yes!" Duke smiled.

Then O'Banion went on to explain how they would work. In the first place, they must never be seen in public together. Nobody must ever know who Duke was or what business he had with O'Banion. Whenever they were to meet it must be done secretly, just as everything they did would be done in secret.

They planned carefully just how they would get in touch with each other, what devious ways they would take, and the secret signals to be passed between them. In the meantime they would wait, bide their time—but now O'Banion was prepared for anything that might happen.

CHAPTER NINE

Taps for the Manchus

AS TIME went on, it was found that the Armory was too small for the drilling of the troops. Since it was only two store buildings thrown into one, it wasn't possible to do much marching around in such a limited space. But on the corner of Apablasa and Juan streets stood the Stockade, a two and a half acre lot surrounded by a ten-foot board fence. It had once been used as a ball park. Anticipating, of course, that ultimately a drill ground would be needed, Homer Lea had made arrangements for the rental of this property even before O'Banion took over the drilling. It was lighted by electricity and kept locked during the day. And since it was used only at night, nobody really knew much about what went on there.

By the time they had drilled for a year, the company in Los Angeles was at its full strength, exactly 120 men. Should a man die or by force of circumstances move to another city—which was a rare occurrence—a new recruit came forward to take his place.

One of the soldiers, a lad of about eighteen at the time, had to go back to China with his family. He was grieved at leaving this country, and regretted having to sever his connection with the troop. But he told O'Banion that he would not soon forget all that he had learned. And he didn't.

Some time after he had been in China word came back

to O'Banion of what the boy was doing. In his village near
Canton he organized the young men into a company. With
wooden guns, they started drilling. This lad copied everything he had seen O'Banion do. The drilling was in the
open, where everybody could see. But because they had
all been raised in the village, nobody paid any attention to
them. They thought they were only "playing soldier." But
when the revolution came here was a well-formed and
trained company of soldiers to step in and do their part.

Years later this boy, now grown and with a family, came
back to the United States. He is now a prominent merchant
of Chinatown, and his sons today are serving in the United
States Army.

One day a prosperous merchant of Chinatown came to see
O'Banion, bringing with him his thirteen-year-old son,
Tommy Gun. The boy, so his father said, was most eager
to join the troop and become a soldier. But one look at
the youngster and O'Banion shook his head.

"He's much too young!" he said.

Tommy Gun looked disappointed. "But someday soon,
I shall be older!" he exclaimed.

O'Banion patted him on the head and told him to hurry
and grow up. He gave him a dime to buy some peanuts
and said to come around when he was eighteen. The merchant, shaking his head sadly, went on home.

But the next day he was back again, this time alone.
Again he asked O'Banion if he couldn't stretch a point and
allow the boy to join the troop. But again O'Banion answered, "No!"

"I understand, of course," said the merchant. "However,
he is most anxious to learn. Do you mind, if now and then,
when you are not busy, he comes here and asks you a few

questions about the proper conduct of an army? At home I try to teach him respect for his elders and the courtesy due them. But his education will not be complete, I feel, until he also knows the good manners of a soldier. Do you mind?"

"Not at all," replied O'Banion.

"Thank you, Captain," said the merchant, bowing.

So every once in a while Tommy Gun would drop around and talk with O'Banion. He was an intelligent youngster, and the questions he asked made sense.

One of the things that interested Tommy was the fact that on the drill ground the commanding officer usually had a trumpeter behind him, so that when he shouted out orders —and perhaps couldn't be heard—the trumpeter would blow the call. Little Tommy began asking what these calls sounded like. So O'Banion would whistle them for him and tell him whether it was "Column right," "Forward march," "Right oblique," "To the rear march," and so forth.

Tommy Gun would whistle the call after O'Banion had told it to him and would say, "Very nice. Very nice." Then when it was time for him to go home, O'Banion would give him a dime for peanuts—and off he'd scamper. This went on for several months.

One evening O'Banion was drilling the troops and gave the command, "Forward march!" Then he almost jumped out of his skin. Behind him, right in his ear, the notes of a bugle blew the call to perfection. He turned around. There, with a brand-new trumpet and grinning from ear to ear, stood Tommy Gun.

The soldiers, obeying the command, were marching straight toward the fence.

"Halt!" cried O'Banion.

"Halt!" went the notes of the command on the trumpet.

"At ease!" said O'Banion, and Tommy blew the call.

The soldiers broke ranks and crowded around. Discipline for the moment was completely forgotten. The little Wong girl, who as usual this evening was quietly watching the soldiers drill, entirely lost control of her emotions. She jumped up and down in her excitement and clapped her hands to show her approval.

"Now what is this?" asked O'Banion.

Tommy replied, beaming, "I no eat peanuts. I save money. My honorable father also give me money he save. And I buy trumpet and take lessons. See!"

And then and there he blew again every call, which he had memorized from the Captain's whistling. So Tommy was sworn into the company and made official trumpeter. His father later bought him a uniform—exactly like those of the soldiers. And from then on, whenever O'Banion gave a command, Tommy—without having to be told—blew the call on his bugle. He fastened a red tassel on it, too. That was for "good luck."

So the troop was now complete—trumpeter and all. The elders of Chinatown were pleased, and money poured into the treasury of the Po Wong Wui in a continuous stream. In the meantime, Homer Lea was writing glowing accounts of the progress of the movement in the United States to his two coconspirators, Kang Yu-wei and Liang Chi-chao, who were still in Japan. They wrote back saying it was hard to believe that in such a short time—little more than a year —so much had been accomplished. General Lea replied by inviting Liang Chi-chao to come to America and see for himself. Liang Chi-chao accepted the invitation. He arrived in San Francisco in the summer of 1904 and was met at

the boat by Allen Chung and Soo Hu-hem, who brought
him to Los Angeles.

Now Homer Lea wanted to make as great an impression
upon Liang Chi-chao as possible, but he had another reason for bringing him to this country. He felt that the time
was now ripe to make an open declaration, among the
Chinese at least, of their intentions and purpose. There
was nothing secret about Liang Chi-chao's visit. In fact,
Homer Lea had told some inquiring reporters that he was a
Manchu Prince. He really wasn't, but it made a good story,
and the newspapers fell for it hook, line, and sinker.

So when the Prince stepped off the train in Los Angeles,
he was met not only by General Lea in his full dress uniform, but also by the troops in command of Captain
O'Banion. Many prominent citizens of Los Angeles, including the directors of the Western Military Academy, had been
invited to meet the Prince. Wanting to make as good a
show as possible out of this, General Lea had arranged for
a band, a police escort, and had obtained permission to
parade through the streets to Chinatown.

Liang Chi-chao was clad in an elaborate Chinese gown,
his well-plaited queue nicely dressed and hanging down his
back, and on his head he wore a round black cap with the
jade button showing he was a mandarin of the highest rank.

"Present arms!" commanded O'Banion.

"Toot-toot-toot!" echoed Tommy Gun on his bugle.

General Lea greeted the Prince and then led him, to the
delight of the crowd, through the ranks of the soldiers
standing at attention. Liang Chi-chao was very much pleased
and said so, in Chinese. He was even more pleased when
they stepped into the waiting hack and the parade started.
Straight to a banquet hall in Chinatown on North Los An-

geles Street, Captain O'Banion and the soldiers led the way.

And then the speeches started. The address of welcome by Ho Lee was a masterpiece of polite utterance. In reply, Liang Chi-chao, who didn't know a word of English, spoke in Chinese and accepted graciously the hospitality and friendliness offered him. General Lea then spoke, and the exchange of courtesies might have gone on forever if Captain O'Banion hadn't signaled to Tommy Gun.

Tommy picked up his bugle and with gusto gave the mess call. It was the same as saying, "Let's eat!" Everyone laughed and applauded and the banquet was on.

During Liang Chi-chao's stay in Los Angeles he lived with Homer Lea. He visited the Armory on several occasions and inspected the troops. He was pleased and delighted with all that was being done. Almost every evening there was a banquet, and Liang Chi-chao always spoke. Every faction in Chinatown did its best to do him honor.

During the day he and General Lea held long conferences. He was shown the reports from the various companies throughout the United States.

And then one morning Homer Lea causually mentioned that in Hong Kong he had met a Chinese doctor who, declaring openly his rebellion at the Empress Dowager, had cut his queue.

"I know—Sun Yat-sen—that madman!" exclaimed Liang Chi-chao. "He has no dignity. He now looks like a Japanese."

"But why do not all Chinese in revolt against the Empress declare their independence and cut their queues?" asked Homer Lea.

"Someday, yes. But the time is not now!"

"There is no time like the present!"

Liang Chi-chao smiled blandly and shrugged his shoulders.

To some Chinese—especially the revolutionists in America—the queue was a badge of servitude, indicating their subservience to the Manchus, who had forced the wearing of queues upon conquered China. Yet to others, the stubborn elders who clung to the habits of two centuries, the queue was their most prized possession and an indication of a man's social standing. To call an elder "Mo-pien"—which translated means "tailless"—was as neat an insult as could be given.

By the thickness of the queue, and the silk used in braiding it, a man was marked for what he was. The Chinese would shave their heads in front—then allow the hair to grow long. Three strands were braided into one, with black silk intertwining. The average length was about two feet, although some aristocrats prided themselves on a three-foot queue. The wealthy men all had large tassels at the end, and used the finest of black silk.

It was because of this silk that teamsters in the pioneer days in California started cutting queues from unprotected and unsuspecting Chinese. That quality of silk couldn't be bought in stores. For the whip-poppers on the end of the ten-foot blacksnake whip, this Chinese silk was perfect.

Whenever a teamster met a solitary Chinese on the road, he caught him and cut his queue to get the silk. The Chinese, so caught, would plead for his life. If he protested too much, or fought back too strongly, he might have been killed. He really didn't have a "Chinaman's chance" on a lonely road. Perhaps this is where the phrase originated. No wonder the Chinese in America hated the queue.

One morning Homer Lea took Liang Chi-chao to Chinatown. He had no idea what he was going to see this day. It was not a Chinese holiday, yet all the shops and restaurants were closed. The streets were crowded with Chinese standing about, laughing, joking, and smiling in anticipation of what was about to happen. The waiters in the restaurants had never been on the street before so early in the morning. But there they were, in full force. The merchants had their hands hidden in the long sleeves of their Chinese gowns as if they were concealing something. And they were. Even O'Banion was holding behind his back something he didn't want the rest to see.

Weeks in advance every detail had been planned and arranged for by Homer Lea. He didn't intend that anything should go wrong on this occasion. And he knew exactly what he was going to say to Liang Chi-chao, for whom this moment had been especially prepared. The cab, in which they had ridden to Chinatown, was parked in front of the Hay and Feed Market on Alameda Street. They had arrived shortly before ten o'clock and stood there chatting with O'Banion.

Exactly as the clock was striking ten, Tommy Gun lifted his bugle. He blew the call to attention—and the crowd became silent. Then Tommy lifted his bugle and gave another call. It was one which had been decided upon previously as the most appropriate call for this particular time. Taps!

As the last notes died away, Soo Hu-hem and his cousin, Soo Hu-king, the two highest noncommissioned officers in the troop, seized a certain Chinese merchant, a man about forty years old. He was a little fellow—and they were big men. It didn't seem quite right that two such stalwarts should pick on this well-behaved elder who was only minding his own business and not offending anyone. But they grabbed him and literally between them carried him to O'Banion. The merchant protested and struggled, but it didn't do him any good. Frightened and not knowing what was going to happen to him, he kept saying over and over, "I am innocent! I am innocent!" He didn't know what he was accused of—but whatever it was, he wanted his friends to know he wasn't guilty. Nobody offered a hand to rescue him—not even his own sons. No wonder he was frightened. It appeared that all Chinatown was against him.

"But I am innocent!" he kept protesting.

"No, you're not!" said Soo Hu-hem. Holding him firmly, and not allowing him to escape, Soo Hu-hem said to O'Banion, "Captain, this is the man! For weeks now we have searched Chinatown carefully. Armed with a measuring stick we have gone from shop to shop, restaurant to restaurant—until finally we discovered this honorable merchant. Captain, this worthy elder has—and we can prove it—the longest queue in Chinatown!"

"I have, indeed!" cried the merchant, proudly.

"Then shall he be the first?" asked O'Banion.

"Yes, yes!" exclaimed both Soo Hu-hem and Soo Hu-king, nodding in approval.

Soo Hu-hem lifted up the merchant's queue for all to see. From behind his back O'Banion brought forth the largest pair of shears he possessed. It was the one he used to trim the horses' manes. Again Tommy Gun started to blow Taps. With one swift clip of the shears O'Banion cut the merchant's queue.

Liang Chi-chao gasped. Everyone else laughed. Soo Hu-hem released the merchant and, bowing respectfully, said gently, "Honorable elder, I trust I have not hurt you. I hope I was not too rough. Are you quite all right?"

"Oh, quite, quite, thank you," replied the merchant, beaming with pleasure. "I am highly honored. See, I am no longer even frightened! It is now the Manchus who will tremble in terror!"

And he shook his clenched fist with his thumb up.

Then it started. From the sleeves of their gowns the merchants brought forth the scissors they had been concealing. And off came the queues!

As fast as they were cut, the discarded queues were thrown to the sidewalk or into the ash cans. Then the Chinese hurried to the barbershops to get their hair trimmed American style. For three days the barbers did a thriving business.

"This is happening today all over the United States," Homer Lea said to Liang Chi-chao. "Every member of the Po Wong Wui in this country—and Canada and Mexico as well—is forswearing his allegiance to the Manchus. Long live the revolution!"

"Daring! Very daring!" murmured Liang Chi-chao. "I hope not premature! Now everyone—and the Empress Dowager—will know!"

"It's our American way of doing things," replied Homer Lea. "The time may not yet be ripe in China, but here in America we have the habit of declaring our independence. The Liberty Bell in 1776 rang to signify to the world that we in America were in our own right free men. Today, in the Chinatowns all over the United States, the Chinese are cutting their queues to declare their independence against the tyranny in China!"

"Excellent!" Then, with tears in his eyes, Liang Chi-chao added, "I am with you. Please cut my queue, too."

Soo Hu-hem was given the honor.

When his queue was cut, Liang Chi-chao said, "If the revolution doesn't succeed now, I shall be forced to live the rest of my life in Japan!"

That night there was another banquet, and General Lea in his address assured him that the revolution would succeed—even though it might take years to perfect their plans, there was no turning back.

Liang Chi-chao replied by saying that he had much to report to Kang Yu-wei—but from this day forth there was hope in his heart, and no longer doubt and despair. For against the combined strength of free men, who are brave enough to declare their rebellion openly, tyranny cannot avail forever. "Liberate the Boy Emperor!" he told them— and promised to do what he could in his own way.

A few days later he went back to Japan. He was in this country only three weeks, and never came again.

When word of his defiance reached the ears of the Empress Dowager, she was furious. Forever after she declared him an archrebel, and never forgave him. His behavior in this country was not according to the rules of proper conduct. He was, even though in disfavor at the time, a citizen of China. The regime of the Empress Dowager was the officially recognized government of China, according to the State Department in Washington. And any act against that government in this country could be—and was—classed as unfriendly.

Diplomatic notes were exchanged. And the U. S. Secret Service was requested to investigate and to find out just exactly what was going on in the Chinatowns all over America!

CHAPTER TEN

The U. S. Secret Service Investigates

ONE morning in St. Louis, where Captain Francis Drischler was drilling the troops, a member of his company came to see him. The soldier was excited and somewhat scared. He told Drischler that a stranger had been hanging around, had cornered him and begun to ask a lot of questions.

"What's going on down here in Chinatown? Aren't some of you Chinese boys doing some drilling nights? What's it all for? Fun? I can't quite believe that. What's the idea back of it?"

The soldier replied that he didn't know, and hoped he gave the stranger the impression he was a stupid Chinese who didn't speak much English.

But, as he said to Captain Drischler, "He will come back and ask more questions. What shall I do?"

Immediately Drischler wrote to General Lea, told him the story, and asked that he be advised how to proceed. Homer Lea said to proceed as usual, that there was to be no change in policy whatever. He also told Drischler to instruct the Chinese not to talk, to pretend to know nothing, and that a reputation for honest stupidity was more to be honored than scorned.

To General Lea and O'Banion this was a matter of grave concern. Why were these questions being asked? And what was behind it all?

There was that man Dingle, for instance, who had been

asking questions, too. This Dingle was often in Chinatown and seemed to like to stroll around with O'Banion.

One morning Dingle said to him, "You know, you fellows are skating on pretty thin ice."

"Meaning?" asked O'Banion, bluntly.

"This drilling down here. Might get you into a jam. If I were you I'd watch my step."

"Why?" answered O'Banion, assuming an air of innocence.

"You must be spending a lot of money on this military academy. Uniforms cost something, and so do guns. That was quite a showing you made in the parade for Prince Liang Chi-chao."

"Thanks," replied O'Banion, as modestly as the politest Chinese.

"You must be making a little something out of this yourself," continued Dingle.

"I'm paid a small salary."

"There might be some trouble in store for you if you aren't careful. A little sugar money in the right spot might help."

"Think so?" replied O'Banion, evasively.

"Yeah. And I'm in a position to help. I know just where to put that money."

"Thanks a lot," said O'Banion, and let it go at that.

He didn't say "Yes" or "No." He just let Dingle go on talking, but the more Dingle talked the more O'Banion began to wonder. And he had more cause for concern when sometime later Dingle was appointed a deputy United States marshal.

But, as he said to Homer Lea, the only thing to do was to be evasive and keep on stalling. The moment they paid anyone money to keep their mouths shut, they were sunk. It would be known then, for a certainty, that something was in the wind, and the Western Military Academy was not so innocent as it appeared on the surface.

And then one morning the matter came to a head. Homer Lea sent for O'Banion and showed him a newspaper clipping he had received. It was from a paper in Wisconsin and following the headline, "Chinese Are After Soldiers," said briefly:

A La Crosse, Wisconsin, militiaman was approached by recruiting officers working secretly for the Chinese government and offered a rank of considerable importance, transportation to China and a salary larger than is given officers of the same rank here. It is said that none but Philippine veterans will be approached. Strict secrecy is being maintained. This Chinese military company is a queer proposition. The real head of it is Homer Lea, the Los Angeles boy who is or claims to be a Lieutenant General in the Chinese Reform Army. There must be some strong inducement for these hard-working vegetable peddlers and laundrymen to be out night after night and week after week to drill, drill, drill. No one knows what it is for.

After reading the story, O'Banion shrugged. "I never approached anyone in Wisconsin to drill the troops," he said.

"I know that," replied Homer Lea. "Puzzling, isn't it? I don't quite know what to make of it. However, here is a horse of another color."

He handed O'Banion a clipping from the *Philadelphia Inquirer*. After blaring headlines, the story started by saying:

United States Secret Service operatives, acting under the personal direction of Chief Wilkie, have discovered evidences that a large proportion of Chinamen in this country are involved in a world-wide conspiracy to overthrow the present Chinese dynasty. . . . In Philadelphia the revolutionary party has headquarters in the heart of Chinatown. In a house on Race Street, near Ninth, which is being watched night and day by the Secret Service men, a body of Chinamen is being drilled daily.

The story then went on to say that these soldiers, it was believed, were being prepared for a general uprising against the Empress Dowager Tsu Hsi, the real ruler of the Chinese Empire. At first Chief Wilkie's men were inclined to doubt the existence of so widespread a plot. But after a week's investigation they discovered they had "been correctly informed."

Then the story said:

As soon as this had been determined Chief Wilkie set the vast and intricate secret service machinery in motion and for weeks hundreds of operatives, many of them with long experience in dealing with the Chinese, have been unraveling clues and ferreting out additional information by which it is hoped that this country will be enabled to lay bare the details of the whole plot before the eyes of the world.

The clipping further said that companies of soldiers were being trained in the various Chinatowns of this country and made the puzzling statement that officers in the National

Guard of Oregon, Washington, and Philadelphia had been approached in the name of the Peking government to train these men. "But all declined," so the paper said, "after the true status of affairs had been explained to them by the Secret Service men."

As Homer Lea pointed out to O'Banion, this newspaper story told him two things: one they already suspected, that they were being investigated by the Secret Service; the other had implications equally disturbing.

Who had really approached these officers of the National Guard? Were they agents of the Empress Dowager? Was she planning to train troops of her own in this country? What a complication that would be!

Suppose a royalist army of Manchus and the Reform Army under General Lea started fighting it out in the streets of Chinatown? That would be something!

"Yet such a movement as hinted at in this paper may be on foot," said Homer Lea. "If it is, we'll be hearing from it."

And they did, later.

However, the immediate problem was the investigation being made by the Secret Service. The best way to handle this at the moment, so thought Homer Lea, was to be so damned brazen about the whole thing that no one would take them seriously. From now on he intended to wear on all occasions his uniform as a lieutenant general in the Chinese Army. He'd tell everybody which army it was—that he was its only general was nobody's business but his own.

Also, while he wouldn't deliberately seek publicity, he wouldn't avoid it. He would give the newspapers stories— weird, fantastic yarns of his adventures in China, and what he was doing here in America. It might make him at times slightly ridiculous, but that didn't matter. His friends knew him for what he was, and who cared what others thought? He would draw several nice, fat red herrings across the trail. His technique would be the well-known "Tell them every-thing—but tell them nothing!"

That very day he telephoned the *Los Angeles Record* and informed them that, if they sent a reporter to Chinatown, they might get a good story about the soldiers supposed to be drilling there. A reporter came and had a long chat with O'Banion. And when his story appeared, the headlines read:

"Chinamen Will Play American Football"

The story said it was all nonsense to believe that the men drilling at the Western Military Academy were planning to become officers in the Chinese Army. True, they had cut off their queues, but they were only wanting to become Americanized. The drilling was just for their own amuse-ment. They paid tuition and expected nothing in return but a good time. They were already organizing a football team and perhaps a baseball nine. In their drill room they were going to install as much of the paraphernalia of a gymnasium as they could afford. They were even planning games for the football team—and hoped someone would challenge them.

When Soo Hu-hem saw the newspaper story he laughed and said, "I know what we should have to kick around for a football—the head of an empress!"

Then Homer Lea had another idea.

"In Pasadena on Jan. 1 there is the Tournament of Roses Parade," he said to O'Banion. "The Secret Service are cu-rious about us, we know that. Why not go the whole hog and let them see that perhaps there is something here to investigate? If we march the troop publicly in this parade, they'll be around. I'll guarantee that!"

But making arrangements for the Chinese soldiers to appear in the parade had not been too easy. One brief clipping in a newspaper said:

John M. York of Los Angeles is to be credited with securing this interesting feature for the pageant.

Judge York, now Presiding Judge of the Appellate Court in Los Angeles, was a young practicing attorney at that time. When the Tournament of Roses Committee asked him to sponsor the Chinese troop, he readily assented. There was some dissension from the district attorney, a retired army officer. He tried to have the United States Army prevent the Chinese soldiers from marching. However, since Mr. York had obtained permission and an order from the Governor of California, nothing came of this.

But, in accordance with the old adage that an ounce of prevention is worth a pound of cure, all the firing pins from the guns the soldiers carried were removed. They were locked up, of all places, in a safe-deposit box in a bank. And there they stayed until the parade was over.

Among the interested spectators in the reviewing stand of the Tournament of Roses Parade in 1905 was an illustrious Chinese, Envoy Wong. He was a representative of the Manchu government and had been sent to this country to be the Imperial Commissioner to the St. Louis World's Fair.

The newspapers said he was visiting Los Angeles, and "his mission has something to do with the Chinese military academy established in the local Chinatown by Lieutenant General Homer Lea. In fact his visit is clearing up some of the mystery that has surrounded that organization. It appears that this company is a sort of West Point, to train officers for the army of the Reform party in China. Wong's visit is said to be the equivalent of casting the Imperial eye over this school. . . . He beamed with geniality upon the garlands of the Tournament; he watched the Chinese soldiers like a cat."

There's quite a bit of double-talk in this story. Anyway, the Chinese soldiers marched, and an official representative of the Manchu government watched them go by.

Some spectators mistook them for Japanese, since they didn't have queues, and cried, "Banzai! Banzai!" Of course this made the Chinese angry, but not once did they respond to the insult. They marched with heads erect and "eyes front," and no word passed their lips.

There had even been hints in the papers now and then that the Orientals drilling in Chinatown were in reality Japanese. And there was another story to that effect on the evening of the parade.

That morning, as O'Banion was marching his troop to the Pacific Electric station where they would take the streetcars to Pasadena, a newspaper reporter by the name of Jack London on the old *Los Angeles Examiner* came running up. O'Banion had met him before. He had been to many of the banquets given for Liang Chi-chao. Homer Lea had told O'Banion that London had written some books and a number of excellent stories and was rather upset at the moment over what he called the Yellow Peril. Always tousled and bedraggled looking, his hair mussed, and a wild gleam in his eye, he took delight in making his newspaper stories as sensational as possible.

So O'Banion was fully prepared when London, pad in

hand, walked beside him as he was leading the troop down Spring Street.

"What are they—Japs or Chinese?" asked London.

"How should I know?" replied O'Banion.

"Well, if you don't know, I wouldn't either," grinned London.

That evening his paper had a story which read:

Jap Soldiers in Los Angeles

The greatest interest was manifested Monday morning in the march of a company of Japanese military cadets from the Western Military Academy through Los Angeles on their way to the Tournament of Roses in Pasadena. "They look natural," remarked Jack London, when he saw them march by. The company was in command of Lieutenant A. E. O'Banion and their marching would have been a revelation to the ordinary volunteer. A ruler would have marked exactly the alignment of their march. They were a steady set of young men and made a fine showing in their bright uniforms and in their light marching order with their Krags and dagger bayonets.

But having the recruits at the Western Military Academy labeled Japanese worried some of the board of directors. One of them hurried to Chinatown. He went with O'Banion to the Armory and saw the guns there.

"Very necessary, I suppose," he said, dubiously. "You can't drill soldiers without guns. But we should do something to make this place look more like a classroom. We need books around. There's too much drilling and not enough higher education. I'll see to it."

A few days later a wagonload of secondhand books arrived at the Armory. Love stories, travel books, and textbooks, battered and thumbed, but they made a nice display in the bookcases some of the soldiers built for that purpose. They came in handy, too, one evening.

The little Wong girl was on an errand for her mother in a near-by store when she overheard a stranger asking questions of the merchant. He was inquiring about the Western Military Academy. Did the merchant know exactly what was going on there? And what *was* going on? Were soldiers being drilled? And if they were, for what purpose? Did they ever have classes in educational subjects?

The merchant was hedging as best he could. When he saw the little Wong girl, he smiled and told her in Chinese to hurry to the Armory and tell Captain O'Banion that there was a stranger asking questions, and he would keep him as long as possible.

Soon the Wong girl returned. She smiled at the merchant and told him in Chinese to tell the stranger to go and take a look at the school for himself.

When he arrived at the Armory, after the merchant gave him directions as to how to get there, the front door stood wide open. Seated on benches were the Chinese students, each with a book in his hand. And standing at the head of his class was O'Banion reading to them from a Bible.

"Come in, come in," said O'Banion to the stranger. "My students are having their class in English tonight."

"So I see," said the inquisitive stranger.

There was nothing he could do about it, so he went his way. The little Wong girl trailed him until he left Chinatown. And once he was out of sight, she came back to the Armory. The English lesson was still in progress.

"He's gone," said the Wong girl to O'Banion.

"At ease," said O'Banion to his students. The books were put away. The doors locked. The guns taken down from the racks—and the evening's drill continued.

Then one day in the midsummer of 1905, on the corner of Alameda and Marchessault streets, a man came up to O'Banion. He had, to all appearances, been waiting for him. The man was standing in front of Suey Yuen's restaurant on Alameda Street, and when he saw O'Banion coming along, he crossed the street and walked up to him.

"Good evening, officer," he said, seeing O'Banion was wearing his police badge.

"Good evening," replied O'Banion, looking him over.

He was a smiling, pleasant, friendly sort of chap, wearing corduroy trousers, puttee leggings, and a cowboy hat.

"I'm Chief Wilkie of the United States Secret Service," he said, introducing himself.

"Glad to know you. I'm Ansel O'Banion."

"Yes," smiled back Wilkie. "So I've been told. I'm visiting here in Los Angeles and thought I'd come down and see Chinatown."

"Could I show you around?" asked O'Banion.

"I wouldn't want to trouble you."

"No trouble at all."

O'Banion was on his way to the Armory for the regular evening drill. But he led Chief Wilkie in the opposite direction. As he passed some Chinese he knew, he spoke to them in Chinese and told them to hurry to the Armory and start their daily English lesson. Then he took his time showing Chief Wilkie about.

After a while, the little Wong girl strolled by.

"Ho la ma," she said in Chinese to O'Banion, meaning,

"How do you do?" Then she added, also in Chinese, "All study hard!"

"Ho, ho," replied the Captain, the equivalent of saying, "Good—good."

So now he could walk Chief Wilkie past the Armory with perfect safety. The doors stood wide open and they glanced in. The boys were all bent over their books, and Soo Hu-hem, at the head of the class, was instructing them in their English lesson.

"They're learning to speak English," said O'Banion.

"So I see," said Chief Wilkie.

And they strolled on their way. But to O'Banion's embarrassment some of the merchants they passed saluted him as usual. He never had been able to get them over that habit. Chief Wilkie noticed this.

"These people down here all seem to know you pretty well," he said. "Should make your work here easy—they all seem so friendly."

"I get along with them okay," replied O'Banion.

But Chief Wilkie was too smart a man to ask O'Banion any personal questions. Their conversation was more or less of the casual nature of two men meeting for the first time and rambling about the streets together, seeing the sights.

But he did say, "I may come down and talk with you again."

"Fine," said O'Banion.

He had no idea from anything Chief Wilkie said just how much he did or did not know. However, Chief Wilkie hinted that perhaps O'Banion could be of some help to him.

"Now and then," he said, "men we are looking for often come to Chinatown. This Chinatown is laid out in such a manner that it would be difficult for anyone to frequent this part of town and not be seen by you."

"Yes," replied O'Banion. "That's the way the streets are laid out down here."

And he took Chief Wilkie for a complete tour of Chinatown. He practically walked his legs off. But he enjoyed talking with him, although Wilkie did most of the talking.

After a couple of hours, he thanked O'Banion for the attention he had given him, shook hands, and went on back to his hotel. O'Banion hurried over to the Armory. They would have to work a little longer tonight to make up for the time lost.

When Homer Lea learned what had happened, he urged O'Banion not to worry.

"It isn't likely we'll get into trouble," he said. "It's possible, of course, but my hunch is that if we mind our own business, the Secret Service will mind theirs. You haven't seen the last of Chief Wilkie, either."

And O'Banion hadn't. Three times in the next six weeks Wilkie came to Chinatown. He was an interesting person, and O'Banion found it a genuine pleasure to show him around Chinatown. He chatted about everything under the sun, and never once mentioned the Western Military Academy. He didn't have to. He knew all about it.

After he had gone, Homer Lea told O'Banion something he had long suspected.

"I think," said Homer Lea, smiling, "we have friends in Washington—and some of them in high places. Obviously, since our government and the government of China are on friendly terms, we cannot have official permission for what we are doing. And since those stories have appeared in the newspapers about us, Chief Wilkie had to come here and look around. But we've treated him very nicely, and when he goes back to Washington, he'll make his report to the State Department. So let's keep right on drilling as if nothing has happened.

"And here's our next step. It may be a very wise move— in the face of all this—to bring Kang Yu-wei openly to this country, make a big fuss over him. And then, what would you think of taking him to Washington to call upon President Theodore Roosevelt?"

CHAPTER ELEVEN

An Interview at the White House

ON FEB. 6, 1905, Prime Minister Kang Yu-wei arrived in Los Angeles accompanied by his three secretaries: Chew Hok-kean, Chu Wu, and an Austrian named Rupert. He was greeted at the railway station with even more fanfare than the reception for Liang Chi-chao. After a parade through the streets and speeches in Chinatown, he was taken to a house on West Seventh Street facing Westlake Park, which had been leased and furnished in true Chinese style for the occupancy of the prime minister during his stay in this country. It was an eight-room cottage, and the furniture had all been borrowed from Chinese merchants. There were heavy, carved teakwood tables and chairs, beautiful draperies, and fine old Chinese paintings.

Even the banquet that evening in Chinatown was the most elaborate ever held. It cost $10 a plate, a lot of money in those days. Live turtles had been brought in from China for the turtle soup. They came in specially made tubs. Other delicacies had been imported just for this occasion. In all there were twenty-two courses. The guests started eating at nine o'clock. It was two in the morning when the last dish was placed before them.

Among the guests present were Governor LaGrange of the Soldiers' Home, Harrison Gray Otis, owner of the *Los Angeles Times,* G. G. Johnson, president of the Chamber of Commerce, and a large number of high city officials, bankers, lawyers, and of course important newspapermen including Jack London, Harry Carr, and Charlie Van Loan.

In the speeches that were made during the course of the banquet, Kang Yu-wei was introduced as the prime minister from the court of the Boy Emperor Kuang Hsu. The point was not stressed that, at the moment, he was at outs with the Empress Dowager, nor was the fact mentioned that the Boy Emperor was a prisoner in the Purple Palace. It was said that Kang Yu-wei was an official representative of the Chinese government. Perfectly truthful—for when the Boy Emperor would be freed and placed back upon the throne again, Kang Yu-wei would be his prime minister. In the meantime, his "official" position no doubt fooled some of the guests.

But that was Homer Lea's idea, and if any of the guests did guess that things were not quite according to the Hoyle of proper diplomatic procedure, they made no comment. They probably wanted to be fooled. After all, someday there might be important banking concessions in China; so the thing to do was to bow politely to Kang Yu-wei and hope he would remember when the time came.

He made a great impression. A large man, weighing over two hundred pounds, thick-chested and dignified, he looked every inch the leader. And when he spoke, in a deep, booming voice, the members of the Po Wong Wui were delighted to accept him without quibbling as their vice-president, secretary, and treasurer. All the bankers and officials present felt it a tremendous privilege to be invited to meet Prime Minister Kang Yu-wei. But he didn't make quite the same impression upon the troops.

The next day he came to the Armory for a tour of inspection. The soldiers were all lined up at attention as Kang

Yu-wei strode down the line. Now, the correct procedure during such inspections is for each soldier, at the command "Port Arms!" to hold his gun in front of him. The inspecting officer takes the gun. The bolt is then opened by the soldier. The officer looks through the barrel to see if the gun is cleaned and oiled. Then he hands it back to the soldier, who closes the bolt and comes to "Order Arms," holding the gun at his right side. And never once does the officer speak.

Proudly the soldiers waited for Kang Yu-wei, their Number One leader, to inspect them. He walked slowly down the line, bowing and smiling. The soldiers stood at attention, as they had been instructed, and not a word was said, not even a flicker of the eyelash responded to Kang Yu-wei's smile of approval.

He stopped in front of one of the soldiers. "Let me see your gun," he said.

The soldier handed it to him. Kang, holding it level, like a baby, looked it over, then handed it back, and said politely, "Thank you." The soldier had to reach for it, and even step out of line to take it. Most unmilitary.

No one cracked a smile while this performance was going on. But after he had gone, they laughed uproariously. Some of them slyly made the comment that he might have asked the proper military procedure.

Even Soo Hu-hem said to O'Banion, "I suppose it's all right. Maybe he didn't really know any better. However, I've heard some vague rumors . . . I don't know. I don't know . . ."

"Don't know what?" asked O'Banion.

"Just don't know yet," answered Soo Hu-hem, cryptically.

In the meantime Kang Yu-wei received the press and other visitors at his official residence. And, since he was the treasurer for the Po Wong Wui, he requested that the money be brought to him.

Funds had been piling up at a great rate. The subtreasuries all over the country were getting huge sums, not only in dues but, now that the Chinese saw the troops being trained and rapid progress made, many wealthy Chinese were making donations. The money was never banked. This, so Homer Lea felt, might arouse suspicion and bring unnecessary questions. And as long as it wasn't banked, there would be no record.

The various subtreasurers, however, he knew to be honest, and since they made reports from time to time on the amounts they had in their possession and the expenditures made, the "books" as such were all in order.

Homer Lea was glad that Kang Yu-wei as treasurer of the Po Wong Wui was here in this country to collect the money. Considering the plans they had in mind, and since Los Angeles was the headquarters, it had been decided that it would be best if the money were all kept here. So word was sent out to the various branches of the society throughout the country to deliver the money to Kang Yu-wei.

And it came rolling in—mostly in bills—several trunks stuffed to the brim. Since Kang Yu-wei was the official and acknowledged head of the Po Wong Wui, he was entrusted with the funds. Ready cash was needed, of course, to carry on the work. But since the sum total of money received— all raised by dues and donations—ran into the hundreds of thousands of dollars, Kang Yu-wei, after discussing the matter with Homer Lea, came to the conclusion that a part of it, at least, should be invested. But it couldn't be done in this country, obviously. So they planned that, when his visit to the United States was over, he would go to South America and invest the money there.

This he later did, taking with him some $400,000. It was invested in rubber plantations. And there the money stayed. No part of it was ever used for the promotion and benefit of the Po Wong Wui in this country.

But the funds left behind, and the money received after that, were entrusted by Homer Lea to O'Banion. It was placed completely in his care. What to do with such a large sum at first bothered O'Banion. Then he decided that—since the money was in loose bills in a trunk—the safest place to keep it would be somewhere in Chinatown.

From previous experience, O'Banion knew that Lum Sum was a man to be trusted. He was about fifty years old and had a stable at the very foot of Marchessault Street. Here he stabled a number of the horses for the hucksters. His living quarters were above the stables—and it was there that O'Banion decided to hide the money. Lum Sum didn't mind a bit what O'Banion did to his home, so one day the two of them ripped up part of the floor and made a trap door. It didn't look the least like a trap door, for various sizes of boards were used. The nails were only dropped into the holes, and not fastened. All that had to be done was to pick out the nails, lift up the boards, and there was a perfect hiding place. There was a grass rug on the floor, and nobody ever suspected that beneath this rug was a trap door and in the floor a small trunk containing thousands of dollars of the Po Wong Wui money.

Only O'Banion and Lum Sum knew where the money was kept. Homer Lea had asked particularly of O'Banion that he not be told.

"It's better that way," he said. "And since I shall never use a penny for myself, why should I even know where it is hidden?"

Always after that, whenever money was needed, a receipt for the sum taken was left with Homer Lea by O'Banion. And all O'Banion had to do was to drop around for a chat with his friend, Lum Sum, and walk out with the money in his pocket.

One evening, before Kang Yu-wei and Homer Lea left for Washington, another banquet was held in Chinatown. The soldiers O'Banion had been training were all on hand, as well as prominent merchants and the leaders of the Po Wong Wui.

Before the banquet started, Kang Yu-wei rose and made a speech. His secretary, Chew Hok-kean, translated for him. To O'Banion's surprise and bewilderment, he learned that Kang Yu-wei was mentioning his name over and over again. He spoke of the splendid training the soldiers were receiving and how gratified he was.

In conclusion he said, "I have been sent here to present this medal to you in the name of the Boy Emperor, Kuang Hsu Wong, for meritorious military service."

Then he pinned on O'Banion's coat a decoration, of which only five were ever given by the Boy Emperor. The medal was of silver. Homer Lea had previously been decorated with a similar medal of gold. It was called the Emperor's Star. On one side was the embossed picture of the Boy Emperor. On the other were two crossed flags; one with the Imperial Dragon on it, and the other the flag of the Po Wong Wui. Around the flags were Chinese characters, which read, "Presented in the name of the Emperor Kuang Hsu Wong in the thirtieth year of his reign."

Shortly after this Kang Yu-wei and Homer Lea left for a trip around the country, visiting the various cities where soldiers were being trained, and eventually arrived in Washington. When O'Banion joined them later in New York he learned from Homer Lea all the details of what had happened. They were staying in New York at the old Waldorf-Astoria Hotel on Fifth Avenue and 34th Street. Here Kang Yu-wei had a suite of rooms and received Chinese from all over the East in fine style.

Homer Lea told O'Banion, "In Washington we first called at the Chinese Embassy and had a long chat with Envoy Wong. You remember him? He was at the Tournament of Roses Parade in Pasadena, an official representative of the Manchu government. Envoy Wong made arrangements through the State Department for us to see President Theodore Roosevelt."

"A Manchu did that?" exclaimed O'Banion, surprised and puzzled.

"Why not?" replied Homer Lea, smiling. "You see, Envoy Wong is secretly on our side."

"Are you certain?" asked O'Banion, dubiously.

"Reasonably so," replied Homer Lea. "I'm not actually certain of anybody. But I think we can trust Wong. At least he helped us accomplish our purpose in seeing the President."

When O'Banion inquired what happened at this interview, Homer Lea handed him a newspaper clipping from *The New York Times* of June 27. It said, in part:

Kang Yu-wei, the head of the Chinese Reform Association, who is traveling through Asia, Europe and America in the interest of that organization, arrived in this city from Washington. In an interview he said, "I had a very fine interview last Sunday with President Roosevelt. He was very cordial. He told me all about the Chinese Exclusion Act, and said he would do all in his power to further the better treatment of the Chinese, and would instruct all American consuls in China to make better arrangements. In view of his remarks, I told him that we had military schools, and were trying to teach the young men English, and all he said was, 'Good.' The President is the best and most strenuous ruler I ever saw. The Reform Association is growing throughout the world. We have several million members. I am quite certain that a great change is coming in China. The Empress Dowager alone stands in our way."

"So you told President Roosevelt about the troops we are training?" asked O'Banion, in surprise.

"Certainly! Certainly!" answered Homer Lea.

"And he said, 'Good!' It's amazing!"

"He didn't really say, 'Good,'" explained Homer Lea. "What he said wasn't translatable into Chinese to Kang Yu-wei. It was a word having to do with an animal, and Kang Yu-wei wouldn't have understood. So I said it was 'Good.' What the President really said was 'Bully.' . . . And now I fully expect to hear repercussions from our interview."

They weren't long in coming. Politics being what they are, no President can make a statement without having his opponents jump down his throat—especially anything dealing with international relations.

A story, among others, appeared in a Los Angeles paper.

It told of the soldiers being trained in America and added, "No federal official seems to have considered that the existence of these corps is illegal, in that the law provides that no body of aliens shall be permitted to bear arms as a military organization in the United States." The story said that Governor Higgins of New York had discovered that military companies existed in his state and Commissioner McAdoo was going to take measures to suppress them.

The story also told the purpose back of this soldier training—to depose the Empress Dowager. Then, boldly facing the facts in the matter, it said,

The Empress likes guns only when they are in the hands of her own men. She cannot well chop off Kang Yu-wei's head, or put a kangue about General Lea's neck, but diplomacy can do often abroad what the headsman does in Pekin. So notes have been passing between Washington and Pekin, Ministers have conferred, and the two State Departments have been agitated about Homer Lea's yellow men in blue and yellow uniforms bearing the buttons of the Reform Association, and the claim made that the existence of these military companies is "an unfriendly act" which the government has been asked to stop.

It was time for someone in authority to make a statement. It came from United States District Attorney H. Valentine. He claimed he had not received any instructions from the Department of Justice, and then said, "There is a statute which forbids aliens from forming any military organizations, but I could not proceed to enforce that provision without instructions from the Department of Justice. In such matters it is the Department of State that takes the first action; if there appears to be sufficient cause to warrant proceedings the Secretary of State communicates with the Department of Justice asking that proper steps be taken, and in turn the officials in the locality concerned are notified what to do. Such matters are in the nature of international questions, and for minor officials to act on their own responsibility might involve the country in serious difficulties."

As Homer Lea pointed out to O'Banion, the United States District Attorney said a great deal—yet on the surface he seemed to say nothing. But what he did say, and said very well, was, for an official statement, a masterpiece of polite hedging.

Then Homer Lea added, "We need not worry. Continue the drilling, and let the boys in Washington make the statements and write the diplomatic notes!"

But this was the least of their troubles. Other forces were secretly at work against them. And one day, to his dismay and surprise, General Lea learned that there was a plot on foot to oust him, and he was no longer considered commander in chief of the Chinese Imperial Reform Army. The authority for this came from no less a person than his supposed friend and ally, Liang Chi-chao.

CHAPTER TWELVE

General Falkenberg Takes Command

THERE is a veil of mystery surrounding the Great Seal of China, called the Seal of Legally Transmitted Authority. Where it is today nobody seems to know for certain; or, if anyone does know, he remains silent.

It may be in Shanghai, or Peiping in the territory occupied by the Japanese, or perhaps it is somewhere in free and fighting China. It might be in Japan—or even in England. That's possible. Or perhaps it has been restored to the Manchus, from whom it was stolen, and is now in possession of Henry Pu Yi, the present puppet Emperor of Manchuria.

But wherever it is today, this is the official seal of the Manchu Dynasty and, according to the old laws, no official document became a decree until stamped with the Seal of Legally Transmitted Authority.

Now, a Chinese never signs his name as we do. Instead, all scholars, diplomats, bankers, and gentlemen use a seal. This consists of his name carved on wood, ivory, jade, or gold, and the imprint of this seal on paper serves as his signature.

The Great Seal disappeared during the Boxer Rebellion in 1900 when the Empress Dowager fled from Peking and her palace was looted by the British soldiers. And she never got the Great Seal back.

But in 1905 it was in the United States and, as the saying goes, thereby hangs a tale.

There appeared one day in San Francisco, General R. A. Falkenberg. He was by no means an amateur soldier but had every right to be considered a militarist of some renown. He had been in the British Army at one time and had even, so it was said, commanded troops in Canada during the Riel Rebellion in 1884. Riel was an agitator who tried to seize the government of Canada. He was ultimately caught, given a fair trial, and hanged for treason. General Falkenberg, even at that time, had the interest of the British Empire at heart. It was also said of him that he had served in the American Army, but just where and in what capacity nobody seemed to know for certain.

In San Francisco he knew exactly where to go to find the troops drilling. Being admitted, he introduced himself. His errand was simple. He announced himself as commander in chief of the Chinese Imperial Reform Army. And as proof, he handed them his commission as general, duly signed on Oct. 5, 1903, by Liang Chi-chao, and stamped with the Great Seal of China.

The soldiers immediately called in the leaders of the Po Wong Wui. They looked at the commission. They examined carefully the stamp of the Great Seal—and pronounced it genuine!

All night long they discussed the matter and asked General Falkenberg many questions. He was given his commission in 1903. This was 1905. Why had he waited two years before presenting it?

"I have been biding my time," replied the general.

"Where did you get this commission?"

"It was given me by Liang Chi-chao."

It was compared with other papers which the Prince had signed while he was in this country. It did not appear to be a forgery. So, in typical Chinese manner, they all listened to what General Falkenberg had to say. But they couldn't understand how the commission had been stamped with the Seal of Legally Transmitted Authority.

There seemed to be no point in doubting the truth of Falkenberg's statements until the matter had been thoroughly aired and investigated. Also, Chinese politeness being what it is, General Falkenberg was accepted then and there as the new commander in chief of the Chinese Imperial Reform Army. They asked for his picture—and it was hung in a prominent spot in the drill hall, where everyone could see.

"And now that you are in command," they inquired, "what are you going to do first?"

"I shall next visit the Sacramento company, show them my credentials as I have you, and then go to Los Angeles to assume complete command."

"But General Lea?" they asked.

General Falkenberg shrugged. "He can, no doubt, find some place where his many talents will be most useful in civil life!"

General Falkenberg then inspected the San Francisco company, in a most military and satisfactory manner, pronounced himself highly pleased with their progress, and congratulated them upon their fine showing. He then said he would return later. In the meantime, they were to carry on exactly as they had been doing. Then he went to Sacramento—and the same sort of thing took place there.

But, of course, the very next morning the leaders of the Po Wong Wui in San Francisco wrote to General Lea. They politely informed him of General Falkenberg's visit, told him they had seen Falkenberg's commission, and that now

—as they understood it—General Falkenberg was commander in chief. The leaders in Sacramento wrote General Lea, also.

Both letters were shown by Homer Lea to O'Banion. And they awaited the arrival in Los Angeles of General R. A. Falkenberg.

One night, while O'Banion was at the Armory drilling the troops as usual, there was a pounding on the door. He dismissed the company, told them to do a little extracurricular glancing at their books, and went to the door.

Standing on the sidewalk were two men in uniform. O'Banion closed the door behind him and waited for them to speak.

"I am General Falkenberg," said one.

"How do you do, sir?" replied O'Banion.

He looked Falkenberg over. He was a short, slight man— about fifty years old, so O'Banion judged. The only thing he didn't quite like about his looks was the heavy—too heavy —black mustache in the approved style of the gay nineties. Falkenberg's uniform was gorgeous to behold. His saber swung at his side. There was gold braid on his shoulders, the Imperial Dragon on his buttons, and the dragon on his army cap.

He introduced his companion as Lieutenant General F. Parmentier. O'Banion was surprised to see him in uniform. He was a Los Angeles architect and never had had, to O'Banion's knowledge, any army experience. A tall, slim man in his middle thirties, very much of a dandy, he was proud of his neat, trim figure and—so the gossips said—wore corsets!

"I have come to take over," said General Falkenberg.

"Take over what?"

"The troops."

"What troops?" asked O'Banion.

Such a statement seemed to puzzle General Falkenberg, but only for a moment.

"The Chinese troops training in this country," he replied. "There's a wonderful organization in San Francisco— another in Sacramento. I have just got them straightened out. Now I've come to Los Angeles to take charge here."

"That's fine!" said O'Banion.

"I should like to come into the Armory and look around."

"Why?" asked O'Banion.

"You are being impertinent, Captain!" blustered General Falkenberg in his best military manner. "I am your commanding officer!"

"If I have a commanding officer, it is General Homer Lea," replied O'Banion, pleasantly but firmly.

"Homer Lea is an impostor," said General Falkenberg. "Have you ever seen his commission as general in the Chinese Imperial Reform Army, Captain?"

As a matter of fact, O'Banion hadn't. So he made no reply. He didn't even have a written commission himself.

"I have been commissioned by Liang Chi-chao," Falkenberg explained. "From now on I am in command of all Chinese troops training in this country. And you are taking orders from me."

"Until I hear to the contrary from General Lea, I am taking my orders from him," snapped O'Banion.

"Stand aside, and let me into the Armory!" commanded General Falkenberg.

"Sorry," replied O'Banion, effectively blocking the doorway. "But we do not allow visitors."

"That is no way to talk to your commanding officer!" stormed Falkenberg.

O'Banion made no reply.

"You shall hear from me about this," threatened Falkenberg.

"That's fine," answered O'Banion. He turned and quickly closed the door in the general's face. It certainly was no way for a captain to treat his commanding officer. Soldiers have been court-martialed for less.

Nor had he and Homer Lea heard the last of this. They were both startled one morning to read an item in the society column of a Los Angeles paper. It was as follows:

A dinner was given on Monday evening at the home of Mrs. A. B. Hotchkiss of No. 400 South Grand Avenue, in honor of His Excellency Kang Yu-wei, the Prime Minister of Emperor Kuang Hsu of China, and his military chief, General R. A. Falkenberg, the commander-in-chief of the reorganized Chinese Imperial Army, who has expressly come down from San Francisco to meet his eminent chief. Gen. Falkenberg was commissioned some years ago by Hon. Liang Chi-chao, adviser in His Majesty's Cabinet of Ministers and colleague of His Excellency Kang Yu-wei. In a graceful speech, interpreted by his secretary, Chew Hok-kean, a highly educated young Chinese student, His Excellency Kang Yu-wei conveyed to those present that after years of travel in many European military countries he had decided to strictly uphold his colleague's—Hon. Liang Chi-chao—official appointment of Gen. Falkenberg, as commanding general, expressing the utmost confidence in Hon. Liang Chi-chao's wisdom.

Among the guests, besides the friends of Mrs. Hotchkiss, there were present Dr. Tom She-bin and Chaw Bin-Chong of San Francisco.

Some explanation of the people concerned may help to clarify the picture—or add to the confusion. Colonel A. B. Hotchkiss was a retired army officer. He was an old man and very wealthy and had a big house in Los Angeles, where he entertained a great deal. Mrs. Hotchkiss was one of the society leaders of the city, and, as O'Banion later discovered, there was some sort of family connection between her and Mrs. Falkenberg. He also discovered, after making some discreet inquiries, that the colonel and his wife were what are known today as fellow travelers. They were not, as all evidence showed, in any way connected either openly or secretly with any revolutionary movement. They had merely opened their home to entertain the friends of one of their cousins.

But Dr. Tom She-bin and his interest were something else again. He was a famous herb doctor, both in Los Angeles and in San Francisco, and an out-in-the-open supporter of the Empress Dowager and the Manchu Dynasty. He flatly refused to cut off his queue on that historic day. While later he did cut it, the reason he gave was that he did not wish to appear too conspicuous. But he was strictly opposed to the Po Wong Wui and said so. Certainly he never donated a penny to the cause. Some of the Chinese respected him for his stand. After all, every man has a right to own ideas, and an enemy who declares himself and lets you know his honest political opinions is much more to be admired than a liar who stabs you in the back.

His business, also, was not so much with the Chinese as with other peoples. He was a man about sixty at the time, very wealthy, and had a large family. Following the queue cutting, he was no longer popular with the Chinese and finally decided to move away from Chinatown. He came to see O'Banion and told him he had purchased a home in another part of Los Angeles, and would O'Banion help him move? O'Banion said he would, gladly. It took four wagonloads to get Dr. Tom's household goods safely out of Chinatown.

There is a possibility that his new home became the meeting place for the Royalists in this country. In any event, the headquarters of the two factions engaged in the struggle for the freedom of China were located in Los Angeles.

Immediately upon reading the newspaper story, Homer Lea picked up the telephone and got in touch with one of his reporter friends. The reporter went to see Kang Yu-wei. He had several questions to ask him. Among them were, "Why is Los Angeles so overstocked with reputed commanders in chief of the Chinese Imperial Army? . . . If General Falkenberg is commander in chief, what is General Homer Lea? . . . As one of these two generals is a fake, which one is it? . . . Is there a Chinese Imperial Army, anyway?"

The reporter said afterward that when he arrived and asked for a statement from Kang Yu-wei, the secretary, Chew Hok-kean, replied that His Excellency was ill and not granting interviews that morning. But the reporter was persistent. He wanted to know if there was any truth in the report that Kang Yu-wei acknowledged General Falkenberg as commander in chief. Chew Hok-kean looked distressed and said he didn't know.

"But you were at the dinner yourself that night and must have heard what was said and the toasts given," insisted the reporter.

"A great many people said a great many things," was Chew Hok-kean's evasive answer.

"But does Kang Yu-wei confirm General Falkenberg's appointment?"

Chew Hok-kean only looked unhappy and shrugged his shoulders.

Then the reporter asked the important question, as he had been instructed to do by Homer Lea: "I understand that General Falkenberg's commission is stamped with the official Great Seal of China."

"Quite correct," responded Chew Hok-kean.

"Then perhaps you can tell me, how did Liang Chi-chao obtain possession of it?"

"That I do not know," answered Chew Hok-kean.

"Where is this Great Seal now?"

Chew Hok-kean brightened. "The answer to that is simple," he said smilingly. "It is here in America—in the possession of His Excellency Kang Yu-wei!"

CHAPTER THIRTEEN

The Prime Minister Explains

NO SOONER had the reporter left that morning than Kang Yu-wei quickly recovered from his illness. A hurried telephone call from Chew Hok-kean asked Homer Lea and O'Banion to come immediately and confer with the prime minister.

When they arrived they found Kang Yu-wei visibly disturbed.

"There has been a newspaper reporter here to see me," he exclaimed. "He was asking me what I knew about General Falkenberg."

Homer Lea seemed surprised to hear this.

"The whole affair is unfortunate," continued Kang Yu-wei. "In the first place, I was tricked into going to the dinner at Colonel Hotchkiss's home. I did not know what it was all about. I have been placed in a most embarrassing position!"

O'Banion thought to himself, He is either the world's most consummate liar, or entirely too stupid to be a prime minister. What Homer Lea was thinking, he didn't know. Homer Lea gave no indication. He merely listened.

"I have been misquoted!" exclaimed Kang Yu-wei.

"You most certainly have!" replied Homer Lea, cheerfully.

"Isn't there something we can do about this?" asked Kang Yu-wei.

"Don't let it worry you," said Homer Lea. "As long as you and I are in agreement—and we are, aren't we?"

"Oh, yes. Yes, of course!"

"Then what does it matter what General Falkenberg says and does?"

"But I don't like this!" exclaimed Kang Yu-wei, beating his chest, which was a habit he had when excited.

"Don't let it bother you, please," said Homer Lea, gently and sympathetically. "Captain O'Banion will continue to train the soldiers, and you and I will work along together exactly as we have been doing in the past. In time, I hope, the whole matter will adjust itself to our satisfaction."

"Thank you—thank you!" Kang Yu-wei smiled politely.

After they left, Homer Lea told O'Banion he didn't believe a word the prime minister had said. He wondered what was at the back of his mind and the reasons for his sudden about-face. He suggested that O'Banion have a talk with Rupert, the Austrian secretary to Kang Yu-wei, and see what he could find out.

Rupert was a blond youngster about twenty-two years old. Slight of build, weighing not more than 125 pounds, he was mild-mannered and soft-spoken. He had been working as a translator in government offices in Japan when Kang Yu-wei met him. An expert linguist he was just the man, so Kang Yu-wei felt, to be of assistance to him in his travels about the world. Of Rupert's background little was known. O'Banion sometimes wondered if he could have been a secret agent in the employ of Japan—or even of Germany. But, of course, that was mere conjecture on his part and he had no way of knowing for certain.

Yet O'Banion liked the youth and enjoyed talking with him. Since he never attended any of the banquets held in the prime minister's honor, but remained at home guarding the money of the Po Wong Wui, it was an easy matter for O'Banion to select a time for a chat with Rupert when Kang Yu-wei was out. When he asked the young man what he knew about the Great Seal, Rupert promptly brought it forth from its hiding place and showed it to O'Banion.

"Genuine?" inquired O'Banion.

Rupert grinned and replied that as far as he knew it was. He didn't know, however, how Kang Yu-wei had obtained possession of it—but here it was and one of Rupert's duties was to guard the Great Seal along with the money. Then he confessed that he didn't particularly like Kang Yu-wei.

"Why not?" inquired O'Banion.

In reply Rupert only shrugged his shoulders.

"You've been around the Chinese so long now," said O'Banion, "that you're getting just as secretive and mysterious as they are. Come on now, what's on your mind?"

"It isn't what's on my mind—but what's on his!" answered Rupert. "And just what he's thinking, how do I know?" Then he added, "I think you and General Lea are doing wrong in letting Kang Yu-wei take this money with him to South America."

"Why?" asked O'Banion.

"In my opinion it could be used to better advantage here in this country than invested somewhere else."

"Kang Yu-wei is the head of the Po Wong Wui. He's the one to make final decisions," said O'Banion.

"Yes, of course," smiled Rupert. "I know that's the Chinese way of looking at things. Number One Boss can do no wrong. What he says goes. All that sort of thing. I only hope one of these days you fellows won't be left holding the bag."

All this interested O'Banion very much. It didn't quite

make sense. Was Kang Yu-wei putting Rupert up to this for some reason of his own? Or was Rupert's dislike of the prime minister genuine?

"Just what would you suggest our doing about it?" O'Banion asked.

"The money is here," said Rupert. "Take it and put it with the rest."

"But wouldn't that be equal to stealing it?"

"I don't see why; you'd not be using it for yourselves. It isn't your money—nothing personal about it."

"But it's in your care," suggested O'Banion. "Then—presto!—it vanishes. How would you explain?"

"I'd just say I didn't know what happened," smiled Rupert. "Kang Yu-wei would probably fire me on the spot."

"And then what would you do?"

"I think you could find some use for me somewhere or other," said Rupert softly.

"You'd like to live in America?" asked O'Banion.

"Yes. It was dull in Japan—not interesting. I like the climate in Southern California, and what you and General Lea are doing is exciting."

It was now O'Banion's turn to shrug his shoulders. Just how far could Rupert be trusted? If his suspicions were correct, it would be a pretty kettle of fish having a spy on their own doorsteps reporting every move they made to—who knows?

"I'll talk this over with General Lea," replied O'Banion, noncommittally. "But in time you might find things here as dull as in Japan."

"I doubt it," said Rupert.

"Tell me," suddenly asked O'Banion, "what do you know about General Falkenberg?"

"Not one damn more thing than you do," answered Rupert.

Which may, or may not, have been true—O'Banion didn't know. But Rupert's idea about the money didn't appeal to him. He reported the whole conversation to Homer Lea and made no comment on his own feelings in the matter.

Homer Lea's reply was typical. With a smile he said, simply, "Don't do it. If Kang Yu-wei has something up his sleeve, let him keep it there. Perhaps Rupert is right. I don't know. I don't really much care. Let Kang Yu-wei take the money with him to South America. It will be wisely invested."

"But suppose we are left holding the bag, as Rupert hinted?"

"We'll just raise the money all over again. That's all!"

"But what about Rupert?" asked O'Banion.

"He's Kang Yu-wei's secretary, not ours. Let him remain so," replied Homer Lea. "For my part, I'd rather have him as a friend than as an enemy. So let's treat him gently, hear all he has to say, but in return tell him nothing!"

If Homer Lea had any real reasons for doubting Kang Yu-wei he did not, at this time, express them too openly. Certainly he did not force any issue. He didn't even ask Kang Yu-wei for any further explanation concerning General Falkenberg. He didn't have to. General Falkenberg himself made a statement.

He gave an interview in a San Francisco newspaper, in which it was said:

The General is a true and trusted friend of all Chinese reformers, and in recognition of his many important services was complimented by Kang Yu-wei, the imperial Privy Councilor of His Majesty, and was presented by Dr. Tom She-bin, for the reformers, a large gold medal.

The newspaper also said that Kang Yu-wei would be in San Francisco within a few days, and then the whole affair would be straightened out. It also hinted that if the general's papers proved to be genuine, there would be an interesting side issue.

But Kang Yu-wei's visit to San Francisco proved an anticlimax. He didn't remain long, and when he left the papers said they regretted his hurried departure, for he had proved himself to be extremely agreeable, was a "tactful guest and an urbane host, as well as a charming diplomat."

And then in conclusion they said, "Besides he added to the net sum of the country's information on military matters by disclosing that General Falkenberg is a commander-in-chief without a command."

When the troops being trained in San Francisco heard this, they promptly turned to the wall the picture of General Falkenberg, his gift to them as their commanding officer. In that undignified position it hung all evening while the drilling continued. The next morning the picture was taken down and thrown into Sacramento Street. What better gesture could they make in response to Kang Yu-wei's denial of the status of General Falkenberg?

What happened next was a story in a San Francisco newspaper, which cleared up a few points, even though the mystery was not fully explained. After reviewing the whole affair, there was this illuminating paragraph:

According to the tales now told, Falkenberg collected a large amount of money from both Chinese and Americans in this city, having gained the confidence of Dr. Tom She-bin, an influential Chinese. One ex-soldier of experience and reputation stated yesterday that he had been offered a high commission by Falkenberg and had accepted it, but that an immediate demand was made on him for a "contribution" of $5 to get a present for His Excellency Kang Yu-wei, besides a suggestion that it would be a pleasant thing to get up a fund for his entertainment. The retired officer stated that, knowing this was not the policy of the organization he thought he was joining, he became suspicious and started an inquiry, which resulted in further exposures, which led the Chinese concerned in the movement to meet on Friday and formally disown Falkenberg.

Later Homer Lea told O'Banion his suppositions in the matter. There was no doubt, he felt, that Kang Yu-wei and Dr. Tom had met in secret and come to some sort of agreement. Then Dr. Tom, under the very nose of Rupert, must have gained possession of the Great Seal. There was no doubt but that the signature of Liang Chi-chao on General Falkenberg's commission was a forgery. To say that he signed it was an easy way out for everybody. If they got caught, somebody had to be blamed; and since Liang Chi-chao was in Japan, it was not possible to ask him the truth in the matter.

There were, however, some unanswered questions. Was the plot an idea thought up by General Falkenberg to further his own personal ambitions? Or was there somebody behind him, and was he merely acting upon orders? It must be remembered he was an English Army officer. When the story broke in the papers, were diplomatic notes exchanged between Washington and London? Who knows?

The plot failed and Kang Yu-wei denied the whole story. It wasn't long afterward that he sailed for South America in the interest of the Po Wong Wui. Rupert went with him, and so did his Chinese secretary, Chew Hok-kean, whom the Chinese in Los Angeles all liked. Even Soo Hu-hem had said he was a man to be trusted.

After his visit to South America, Kang Yu-wei went on to Japan. He came back to the United States twice after that, but his other visits were never publicized as was his first trip to this country.

General Falkenberg faded out of the picture. There was never another murmur from him. He went back to his former so-called civilian occupation of selling oil stocks. Dr. Tom remained silent, too. If they were active in any way, what they did was underground—and nobody knew for certain.

"Lieutenant General" Parmentier remained in Los Angeles, but he ceased wearing his uniform. He always avoided O'Banion whenever he saw him on the street and never spoke to him. He did, however, cause Homer Lea some slight annoyance.

When he failed to receive his commission, he tried to start suit against Homer Lea, claiming he had paid money for a commission that hadn't been forthcoming. Immediately Homer Lea telephoned his attorney, who went to see Parmentier. But Parmentier wasn't able to do anything about it, for, as he confessed, the money for the commission had been paid to Dr. Tom. And since Homer Lea had had no connection in any way with Dr. Tom and General Falkenberg, the suit was dropped without coming into court.

Later, however, Parmentier did achieve his ambition to

become a soldier. He enlisted in the United States Army during the First World War and died on the battlefields of France.

In July of that year, 1905, after Kang Yu-wei had left this country, Homer Lea called O'Banion for a conference. What he had to tell him changed the whole picture of the revolutionary movement.

Things were in a muddle, and something must be done to clarify the situation. At the moment, Kang Yu-wei was the acknowledged head of the Po Wong Wui. And as the head and leader of the revolution, they had no choice but to entrust him with what funds they had on hand. It's a Chinese characteristic always to trust a man, no matter what one's private opinions concerning him may be. No matter what he does to others, no matter what people may say about him, as long as he doesn't do anything to you, give him your confidence. Not your whole confidence, perhaps, but enough. There's always the possibility that what he does to others he may not do to you. So until the time comes when one feels that trust is given too freely—play ball.

"And so far, from all outward appearance, Kang Yu-wei is on our team," continued Homer Lea. "He has a large personal following—and there is no other leader among the Chinese in America at this time. Don't forget or overlook this, however—when the revolution succeeds and the Boy Emperor becomes the head of the government, it is still the Manchu Dynasty in China. Kuang Hsu is a weakling. He'd be merely a puppet in the hands of a clever diplomat like Kang Yu-wei. Have you heard any talk among the soldiers along this line?"

O'Banion said he had, little vague rumors, subtle hints, nothing one could really put a finger on. Some of the soldiers had confessed they didn't like Kang Yu-wei, and after the General Falkenberg affair they wondered if they could really trust him. He'd be the head of the government as prime minister, and, so Soo Hu-hem had grumbled, "Is that what we're fighting for? To keep the Manchus in power?"

When O'Banion told this, Homer Lea replied, "That's the idea in a nutshell. What's really in the back of Kang Yu-wei's mind? Has he any personal ambitions? That I should like to know. It's part of my philosophy to put the cause we are working for above any personal interest. The revolution is greater than any one man, any one individual. Should one person use the revolution for his own selfish ends, it will make matters more difficult for us and take longer to accomplish our purpose. But in the end the revolution will succeed—and not the individual. In the meantime, until we have definite proof to the contrary, we'll continue to trust Kang Yu-wei and play ball with him. However, here is our next step."

He went on to tell O'Banion that when he was in China he had talked with the leader of another secret revolutionary party. This man and Kang Yu-wei did not see eye to eye. They were, in fact, openly in disagreement. And there were, within the revolutionary movement, two opposing factions.

"If this quarrel within a quarrel continues, the revolution may fail, and everything we are doing come to nothing. The two parties must be brought together. I think the time has come to have a talk with this other leader."

"What's his name?" asked O'Banion.

"Dr. Sun Yat-sen!"

"Never heard of him!"

"You will," said Homer Lea, smiling, "for I want him to come to America."

"Good! More parades, more fireworks, more banquets."

"Oh, no. Considering everything, no fireworks, no show of any sort, and no banquets until after we have conferred with him. Dr. Sun has enemies everywhere. He is not even a member of the Po Wong Wui, and certainly not in sympathy with their aims of restoring the Boy Emperor to the throne. He has his own revolutionary party. So there are those who hate him—even here in America. There have been several attempts to assassinate him. That can't happen here. I should like to have him brought into this country quietly and without any fuss whatsoever. In short, I want him smuggled in. Do you think you can arrange it, Captain?"

"It's a tall order," replied O'Banion. "I can only try."

"I have every confidence in you."

"Thanks."

A few days later O'Banion took a trip to San Francisco. The time had come, so he felt, to make use of the man whose life he had once saved—Duke, the highbinder of the tong.

CHAPTER FOURTEEN

A Doctor in a Potato Boat

WHEN O'Banion saw Duke, he asked, "Do you think you could help me smuggle a man into this country?"

Duke's face was expressionless as he answered, "I've heard stories now and then of its having been done. Who's the man?"

"A Chinese doctor—a friend of Homer Lea's—by the name of Sun Yat-sen."

Duke lit a cigarette and took a couple of puffs before speaking. Then, to O'Banion's surprise, he said, "At last the time has come. I've been waiting for this to happen— and wondering when Dr. Sun would visit this country. Liang Chi-chao has been here and so has Kang Yu-wei. But Dr. Sun Yat-sen, the most important man of all, has not even been mentioned."

"Then you know him?"

Duke nodded. "I met Dr. Sun first when he was secretly in this country in 1896. He was on his way to England and stayed only a few days in San Francisco. I was a youngster at the time, and met Dr. Sun through one of my uncles. I heard him talk one evening—there weren't many of us present—but what he said convinced me. I threw in my lot with him. I joined a secret society of which Dr. Sun is the founder and the acknowledged leader. There are not, at the moment, many members of this society in America, and those who do belong have been carefully chosen. The purpose of this secret society is the complete overthrow of the Manchus—and no compromise! Dr. Sun is, in my opinion, the greatest Chinese of this generation!"

Dr. Sun was born in 1866 in Choy Hung, a village in Kwantung, a province of Southern China, of which Canton is the largest city. His family were wealthy and respected for their strict observance of Chinese customs and traditions. When he was thirteen he was sent to Honolulu to school, and there he came in contact with American ideas and ideals. He saw for himself the benefits to be derived from a democratic form of government.

In China he saw the many injustices inflicted upon his people by their oppressors, the Manchus, and when he was only twenty decided to devote his life to their overthrow.

Following his early schooling in Hawaii, he attended the College of Medicine in Hong Kong. He would have studied law, had there been a school of law in China. But the Manchus were not in favor of educating Chinese along those lines. Perhaps being a doctor was much better for his purpose, for it gave him a perfect cover for his political intrigues. As he often said, "Doctors in China are considered politically innocuous."

When he was only twenty-eight years old, he cut his queue, the first Chinese to declare openly his revolt against the Manchus. He was already at that time deeply involved in the revolutionary movement. He had joined, when a student, the powerful secret Triad Society.

But Dr. Sun, while he fully approved of destroying the Manchus, did not accept the restoration of the Ming Dynasty upon the Dragon Throne. The day of monarchs, kings, and emperors was over, he felt. The day of the freedom and the equality of man was at hand. From the very beginning he preached only a republic for China.

His revolutionary activities were discovered by the Manchus and he had to flee the country. In 1895, when he was a fugitive in Japan, he organized his own secret society and made his Declaration of Independence in four words, "Tien Ming Wu Chang," which means "Divine right does not last forever." It was a society of patriots, and when it came more or less into the open in 1899 it was called the Dare-to-Dies.

In the beginning, Dr. Sun tried to persuade other known revolutionists like Kang Yu-wei and Liang Chi-chao to join his movement. But these men had different ideas. What Kang Yu-wei wanted for China was an emperor on the Dragon Throne and a constitutional monarchy not unlike the British form of government. What Dr. Sun wanted was a republic.

He wrote Kang Yu-wei many letters, but the prime minister never answered. Kang Yu-wei felt that the Chinese, bound by tradition and respect for lawful authority, could understand a monarchy. But a republic in China? The very thought was much too revolutionary to be considered seriously.

There were a few who believed as Dr. Sun did. But he was a fugitive from the wrath of the Manchus with a price on his head, a man without a country, and whatever he did he must do alone. So, in disguise, and with the threat of assassination hanging over him, he went about the world preaching his ideas.

On his first visit to America in 1896 he gained a few followers. These men, living in the United States, knew what a democratic form of government meant. They gave

Dr. Sun their support and joined his secret society. Among them were the two Stanford students, Allen Chung and Lou Hoy, and also Soo Hu-hem and Duke. Homer Lea was initiated into this society, too. In fact, it was the first secret society he joined. Therefore, from the very beginning his loyalty was pledged to Dr. Sun Yat-sen and the establishment of a republic in China.

The first revolutionist whom Homer Lea met in China was Dr. Sun Yat-sen. This was secretly in Hong Kong, where Dr. Sun was living at the time in hiding. At this meeting the two men agreed on one thing: each was to go his separate way, but they were to keep in touch. It was also agreed that, for the present, Homer Lea should play ball with Kang Yu-wei and Liang Chi-chao. Their attempts at reform during the one hundred days were well-known, and they were at this time the acknowledged leaders of the revolution. Sun was merely a man with an idea and a few loyal and faithful followers who believed as he did. He told Homer Lea to do what he could in organizing a strong revolutionary party. Perhaps, when the time came, Kang Yu-wei would join forces with Dr. Sun and work for the complete liberation of China.

Everything was progressing according to plan in 1905 when Kang Yu-wei came to America. But would he join forces with Dr. Sun? He would not! You might as well expect the Republicans and the Democrats to drink out of the same loving cup. True, they had one idea in common—the overthrow of the Empress Dowager. But from that point on, they did not agree. What Homer Lea wanted to do was to bring them together and have them unite their efforts in one single cause.

He even brought up the subject when Kang Yu-wei was here.

"I wish," he said one day, "you would cooperate with Dr. Sun Yat-sen, and work toward a democracy for China!"

"That madman!" cried Kang Yu-wei, beating his chest as usual. "A democracy for China? It will not work. China is not yet ready for such a completely revolutionary idea."

"But perhaps if your followers and his joined forces—"

"Impossible. He has no following. Nobody believes in him, not even here in America. I have inquired."

This was only partly true. Homer Lea might have told Kang Yu-wei that Dr. Sun had more followers here than he suspected. But he said nothing. The time for making such a statement had not yet arrived.

"Dismiss Dr. Sun from your mind," continued Kang Yu-wei. "He is a visionary, an impractical idealist. I will have nothing to do with him. Don't let him or his ideas bother you in the least, General Lea. He is in disgrace—even with the Chinese. Nobody listens to him. So put him out of your mind. We are doing very nicely without such a man. The Po Wong Wui is succeeding beyond all my expectations. Should we bring Dr. Sun into the movement, he would only cause confusion. Forget him completely. That is the best thing to do!"

"Yes, sir," replied Homer Lea, meekly. Kang Yu-wei seemed satisfied.

And that was as far as Lea was able to get at that time with the prime minister. It was, any way you look at it, a difficult situation for Homer Lea. Here he was faced with a revolution within a revolution, and a secret party working inside a secret party. And so, when Kang Yu-wei went to South America, there was but one course open, and that was to bring Dr. Sun to America for a conference and see what could be done. But he had to be brought in secretly.

Duke was delighted to be chosen by O'Banion to do this.

"I know whom I can depend upon among the secret followers of Dr. Sun," he said. "But let me warn you—only you and I must know who they are. We must not mention to anyone the names of those who help us!"

"Obviously not!" replied O'Banion. "I understand perfectly."

"It may cost money," said Duke.

"We have it. How much?"

"I'm not certain. I shall let you know. It may take some time to arrange matters. But I promise to work as fast as I can."

O'Banion returned to Los Angeles. A few weeks later he received a letter from Duke. It said briefly:

Dear Captain:

I have a cousin, a very honest fellow, who is badly in need of one thousand dollars. Could I arrange a loan from you for this amount? He promises to return the money with interest within six short weeks. If you could come to San Francisco and bring this money with you and meet my cousin, I am certain you would find him as worthy a person as I am totally unworthy, but still your friend,

Duke.

O'Banion destroyed the letter and immediately paid a visit to Lum Sum in his living quarters over the stable. Later that same day, with the cash in his pocket, he went to San Francisco and there met Duke's cousin.

The man was a steward on a boat plying between San

Francisco and Honolulu, where, so Duke told O'Banion, there was a doctor at the moment whom his cousin wished to see. It was night when they called on the steward at his rooms. He was a fine-looking Chinese, suave and gracious, and exceedingly proud of his position as a steward on a passenger boat.

As Duke told O'Banion, "He can be trusted thoroughly. He is a blood cousin of mine; otherwise I would not pay him in advance. A man can have a lot of fun in Honolulu on a thousand dollars. However, you understand this money is not for himself. There may be palms to be greased along the line, and my cousin feels he must be prepared. Okay?"

"Okay!" replied O'Banion.

But in typical Chinese fashion, when O'Banion met the cousin, not a word was said concerning the reason for his visit. They chatted about the weather, discussed various topics of interest, and when they left, Duke laid an envelope on the table. O'Banion had previously given him the money.

"Have a nice trip," said Duke.

"Good luck!" echoed O'Banion.

"Thank you," said the steward, and put the envelope in his pocket.

As they went down the street, Duke said casually, "My cousin says he likes you very much. And he hopes he'll see you again when he returns from his trip to Honolulu."

"When will that be?" asked O'Banion.

"In about six weeks—say around Sept. 20?"

"I'll probably be in Frisco at that time," said O'Banion.

He had learned to enjoy this Chinese double-talk as much as the Chinese themselves. The Chinese, having a keen sense of humor, love a joke. So do the Irish. So O'Banion and the Chinese got along well together.

"My cousin is a very thoughtful man," continued Duke. "He never forgets a friend. And I think—perhaps, Captain, although I do not want to boast—that when my cousin returns from Honolulu, he may have a present for you. A present for General Lea, too."

"Fine. I know the general will like that."

"Good night, Captain."

"Good night, Duke!"

Six weeks later O'Banion was again in San Francisco. He hadn't sent Duke word that he was coming, but when he appeared at the place where the soldiers were drilling there was a message from Duke: "I'm home. Please drop around."

When O'Banion arrived, after climbing the steep stairs and being looked over by Duke's wife through the peephole, he found Duke alone.

"My cousin's back from Honolulu," he said, happily. "His boat's docked, and all the regular passengers are being let ashore. Just as soon as his duties are finished, he'll join us here."

They didn't have long to wait. The cousin came in smiling, and bursting with good news.

"Did you have a successful trip?" asked Duke.

"Wonderful. Everything worked out very smoothly."

"Between cousins there are no secrets," said Duke. "How did you do it?"

The steward smiled and said, "When in Honolulu, first of all, I contacted the merchant you told me to see. A very intelligent man. I liked him. I was in bad health, as you know. But he kindly suggested the right doctor. I called upon him at once. The doctor told me that, because of my bad health, I should remain quietly in my quarters during my stay in Honolulu—and he would come and see me. And he did twice—carrying his little medicine bag. A most unusual doctor—for, instead of medicine in the bag, he had clean shirts, books, papers, and other personal articles. These—strange to say—he always left with me. Then on the day the boat was to leave, a most unfortunate thing happened. The doctor came aboard with the passengers—but when the boat sailed, he forgot to go ashore. And there he was in my stateroom!"

"A most tragic occurrence," said Duke. "What did you do then?"

"Locked the door and told him to remain there until we docked in San Francisco. I brought him food, took good care of him. Those few ship's officers who got too curious as to what was going on immediately recovered from their curiosity when I gave them a cash present!"

"Very good," said Duke. "Where is the doctor now?"

"Locked up in my stateroom," replied the steward. "And you've got to get him off the boat. He can't walk down the gangplank as did the regular passengers. He has no papers!"

"And you are a very nervous man," teased Duke.

"Very nervous. That's what ailed me in Honolulu. But now it's your turn to be nervous!"

"Not at all! I've made all arrangements," said Duke.

"But will they work out smoothly?"

"They'd better!" answered Duke, grimly. "It's still early in the evening. Let's get going!"

Then he told them his plans.

He had already spoken to Charlie Lung. Lung, a young man in his early twenties, was well-known in San Francisco. Everyone called him the Potato King. He controlled the hauling of potatoes down the Sacramento River from Stockton, which was the heart of the potato country. Lung had a number of boats, all painted red. They were some twenty or more feet long, with a square cabin in the middle. In Stockton the potatoes were loaded onto barges, then the boat, whistling merrily, towed the barges—often as many as three at a time—down the river and across the bay into San Francisco.

They were manned, of course, by a crew of Chinese. Seen so often and frequently as they scooted in and out among the huge steamers and freighters at anchor, nobody paid much attention to them.

"Hi there, little potato!" the sailors on board the sea-going vessels would shout to the Chinese. And the Chinese would grin, wave back, and go about their business. Such innocent-looking little boats, really.

And since by day and night they were always dashing about the bay, it was on one of these boats that Duke had planned to take Dr. Sun off the steamer.

The skipper of this particular boat was a man he could trust. Nor was it the first time the boat had been used for such a purpose. He also knew exactly who Dr. Sun was and realized the importance of bringing him safe ashore. But the crew this evening were not told. To them, the man they were carrying from the steamer was just another Chinese seeking refuge in this country. And once they landed him, he would go about his business, and they'd never see or hear from him again.

All arrangements with this skipper having been made, the next step was to inform him that tonight was the time set. So, first of all, Duke led O'Banion and the steward to a certain address on Washington Street. Here was a Chinese store that, typically, sold everything from suspenders and

underwear to antiques and curios; from dried, imported
Chinese foods to green groceries. During the day the owner,
a man about fifty, always wore American clothes. But when
evening came and he closed the doors, he put on a long
Chinese gown, forgot the business cares of the day, and took
out his books and scrolls to devote his evening to the study
of the classics. Only his most intimate friends were allowed
to interrupt him, and then only on matters of great importance. To these few he had given a secret knock upon his
door. This was the only rap he ever answered.

But this evening he had been expecting Duke and admitted him immediately. He greeted O'Banion and the
steward courteously, keeping his hands folded in the sleeves
of his long black gown. With him was another elderly Chinese, also wearing a Chinese gown, whom O'Banion recognized as one of the important leaders in Chinatown, and
a generous contributor to the Po Wong Wui. He was later
to learn that these two men were the most important Chinese in San Francisco.

"Tonight is the night for our boat ride," said Duke.

"Good!" exclaimed the merchant.

He went to the telephone and had a short conversation
in Chinese.

"The skipper will be here at once," he said. "While we
are waiting, will you do me the honor of having a cup of
tea with me?"

Soon the skipper appeared, a short, stocky man who
wasted no time on formalities.

"My crew is waiting," he said.

"Nothing must go wrong," explained Duke.

"I hope nothing will!" answered the skipper.

Then Duke turned to his cousin, the steward. "You had

better go back to the steamer now," he said. "You have already spoken to the officer in charge tonight?"

"Yes, yes," nodded the steward. "I told him where he could go to buy a very nice present for his wife. I even advanced him sufficient cash to pay for the present. And so tonight he has said—or at least hinted to me—that he will not be curious as to what I may or may not do aboard the steamer."

"I hope he'll keep his word," said Duke.

"I think he will. I've done business with him before!"

"How will I know when everything is ready?" asked the skipper.

"I have long ago," answered the steward, "established a reputation for being eccentric. I do my laundry sometimes at night. I tell them Chinese way—dry better if not too much sun. They laugh and think it strange. So tonight when I get back to steamer I hang laundry on port side. When you see me hanging laundry—and I shall shake carefully three garments three times before hanging them—you will know everything is ready!"

Then the steward excused himself, bowed politely to the two Chinese elders, shook hands with Duke and O'Banion, and left.

"And you have made all arrangements?" Duke asked the skipper.

"All but paying the men who will help me tonight," he answered.

"How much?" asked Duke.

"Two hundred and seventeen dollars!"

"Why not three hundred?"

The skipper looked hurt, as if Duke had doubted his honesty. "Should we be caught," he mumbled, "it would mean prison for us all. And each man values his freedom—considering the risk he is taking—at a different price. One says fifty dollars. Another fifty-seven. One lost last night at fantan. He wants a hundred. Another needs a new pair of shoes and hat. He asks for only ten dollars."

Duke grinned and counted out the money.

"And just how are you going to manage it?" he asked.

"We shall sail around the bay a bit first—as if for pleasure," said the skipper. "We often do at night. No one thinks twice about it. We shall be towing a dory—a small flat-bottomed boat. When we see the signal we shall come close to the steamer, and the dory will be turned loose. There will be a man in the dory. Then our friend will climb down the rope ladder over the side of the boat—step into the dory —and be rowed away. We shall then turn about with our potato boat, pick up the dory and tow it into the wharf where the potatoes are usually unloaded. Very easy. Very simple. We've done it before."

"Good!" said the Duke.

"Good!" echoed the elders.

"Could I go along with you?" asked O'Banion.

Duke thought a moment, and then said politely, "I think it's best not, Captain. If anyone saw you on board the boat, it would seem most unusual, and questions might be asked. Some other time at night we can take a pleasure trip about the bay. But tonight I think it best if you come with me; we shall await the arrival of our guest at my home."

"Okay," said O'Banion, but he was disappointed, for the danger involved appealed to his love of adventure and he wanted to be in the thick of it.

But he couldn't help thinking how different was the arrival in this country of this unknown doctor from the receptions given Liang Chi-chao and Prime Minister Kang Yu-wei. He hoped the good doctor would be worth all the risks involved.

"When we have landed, then what?" asked the skipper.

"Dismiss the crew. Tell them to go home to bed and forget about it all. Then you, coming in another direction, bring the stranger to our shores to my home. We shall be waiting for you there. Good luck, and don't get caught!"

"Good luck!" said the elders, nervously.

Making no reply, the skipper quietly slipped out the door and closed it softly behind him.

Duke turned to the two elders. "It is now almost ten o'clock," he said. "I am going home—and if the Captain is not yet sleepy, perhaps he will come with me?"

"And when did you think I had decided not to see this thing through?" asked O'Banion, angrily.

"Never once!" smiled back Duke.

The two elders began to chatter excitedly in Chinese.

Duke politely let them have their say, then calmed them down by inviting them, too. "I was hoping you would express the wish to come," he said, "for I have arranged a banquet for tonight. It will be sent in from a near-by restaurant. Some feed, too! Twenty-five bucks, Captain. All the Chinese delicacies—some, perhaps, you've never tasted before. I ordered it three weeks ago! And now"—he turned to the elders—"I think it best if we all go our separate ways, and meet again at my humble and unworthy home. But soon—soon!"

It was wisest, so he thought, that they not be seen walking through the streets together. One by one they left the store, Duke going first.

When O'Banion arrived, Duke's wife had already set the

table for eight: wineglasses, dishes for the sauces, teacups, and chop sticks all neatly laid out. Soon the two Chinese elders arrived. There was nothing to do but wait.

Time had a way of dragging that evening. While there had been no specific hour set for the skipper to appear with Dr. Sun, O'Banion couldn't keep his eyes off the clock. Every minute that passed without Dr. Sun's appearing meant, perhaps, that something had gone wrong. It was a terrific strain.

Even the elders and Duke were nervous, although they made every effort to hide their fears beneath a surface calm. But O'Banion wondered what thoughts were going through their minds behind their placid, seemingly indifferent faces.

"Do please join me in a drink, Captain," said Duke.

O'Banion, who had been pacing the floor, readily assented.

The elders nodded their approval. They sat twisting their fingers and now and then adjusting their long Chinese gowns. O'Banion felt that he had never seen two such nervous Chinese. Knowing that others were feeling the strain even more than he, helped calm him. But the elders smoked one cigarette after another and puffed away incessantly, their cigarettes in long, carved-ivory holders. Conversation lagged. Two long hours passed—and still no word.

"Take it easy, Captain!" said Duke. "Look at me, I'm as cool as a cucumber!"

"Like hell you are!" exclaimed O'Banion.

"Like hell I am!" answered Duke.

Shortly after midnight there was a rap on the door. Duke rose quickly. The others fell silent. Pushing back the iron on the peephole, Duke cautiously looked out. The voice of the skipper reassured him, and he quickly unlocked and

DR. SUN YAT-SEN

swung open the door saying, "Loy choy ya," meaning "Come, sit down!"

Into the room, followed by the skipper carrying a single, well-used, black cowhide bag, stepped a short, slender, middle-aged man. He had a small, black mustache, keen, sparkling eyes, and a kindly smile.

"I am Dr. Sun from Honolulu. Good evening!" he said, calmly.

The elders jumped to their feet and bowed. Then Duke introduced himself and in turn introduced the doctor to everyone present.

As he shook hands with O'Banion he said, "I have heard a great deal about you from Homer Lea."

"What kind of trip did you have?" asked Duke.

"Very pleasant, thank you," answered Dr. Sun. "I was well taken care of. You gentlemen managed everything beautifully. You must have a fine organization in this country!"

He spoke English with an accent, and slowly, as if selecting every word with great care. Kindly, simple, and modest, his manner put everyone whom he met immediately at ease, and his obvious honesty and sincerity impressed friend and foe alike. Such was his personality that he could talk himself out of any difficult situation.

"What kept you so long?" asked Duke of the skipper.

"Why hurry?" answered the skipper, shrugging his shoulders. "Have you been nervous?"

"Yes," said Duke, truthfully. "We were afraid something had gone wrong."

"We merely took our time," said the skipper. "Had we seemed to be in a rush, someone might have grown suspicious."

"So nothing happened?" insisted Duke.

"Oh, yes."

"What?" asked Duke, impatiently.

"The steward, in signaling to us, dropped a shirt overboard."

"The delay was my fault," said Dr. Sun. "We lost some time while I fished it out of the water. Could it be laundered tomorrow and returned to him? It was most unfortunate."

Duke and O'Banion laughed. "I'm glad that was all!" said Duke.

"And now, may I ask, what are your next plans?" asked Dr. Sun.

"First, shall we have something to eat," suggested Duke. "And then, Dr. Sun, we are driving you immediately to Los Angeles—where General Lea is waiting. Captain O'Banion has an automobile."

Duke's wife, who had slipped quietly out when Dr. Sun had arrived, came back bringing with her the dinner from the restaurant. She didn't join them at the table, but sat in the room at the back.

It was two o'clock in the morning when they finished eating. Duke asked Dr. Sun what his wish was in the matter—whether to remain overnight in San Francisco or start immediately for Los Angeles. He decided to go on.

"But it's a long ride—and tiring," said Duke.

"I have traveled many miles," smiled Dr. Sun, "and have many more yet to go. However, before we start, every man has his little vanity. Mine—you see—my mustache!"

O'Banion had previously noticed that it did look completely wilted. So they sent the skipper out for some wax for the doctor's mustache.

The merchant whispered to Duke that Dr. Sun should

have a new hat. He had lost his own hat, and the one he was wearing had been given him by the steward. It simply didn't fit. Much too small. Then, too, Chinese leaders in those days always wore plug hats especially when they attended banquets and public functions. So Duke hurried out to borrow the proper hat.

He came back with two: a high silk plug hat and a caddy. O'Banion decided that the caddy was the better of the two for Dr. Sun. But they took the silk hat along for use at some future time.

By the time Dr. Sun had neatly waxed his mustache, they were ready to start. O'Banion had got the automobile and parked it a block away from Duke's home. Dr. Sun made the proper adieus, profusely thanking the skipper and the two elders for all they had done for him. Then off they started.

"I hope luck is with us," said Duke.

And it was until they reached the outskirts of San Francisco—then pop!—a tire had blown. Duke immediately got out and looked around.

"I knew it!" he said. "I knew it would happen about here!"

"Why right here?" asked O'Banion.

"Have you a dollar on you, Captain? I've nothing but a handful of change. Please let me have a dollar for these two halves."

Wondering what it was all about, O'Banion handed him a silver dollar. Duke, to O'Banion's surprise, took the dollar and threw it as far as he could.

"Now I've got rid of my bad luck," he said. "Let's fix the tire."

When it was done and they were on their way again,

O'Banion asked Duke the meaning of this strange performance.

"Confession is good for the soul," said Duke, "and I'll confess. Some years ago I spent the evening with a very charming Japanese lady in a house across the street from where the tire blew out. In the morning she wanted a dollar more for her favors than the price agreed upon early in the evening. I refused to pay it. A bargain is a bargain! But I did wrong. For until I paid her the dollar, bad luck would always haunt me at that spot. I am not superstitious, Captain, but you know how it is!"

The roads were terrible—this being in the days before paved highways. But never once did Dr. Sun complain of the jolting. Now and then during the day they stopped to get coffee and sandwiches and once in a while pulled the car over to the side of the road and took a short nap. Nor was Dr. Sun averse to washing his hands and face as Duke and O'Banion did in the ditches at the side of the road.

Preparing for this secret meeting with Dr. Sun, Homer Lea had gone to North Long Beach and rented a house. He had informed his family he would be away for a few days. But he had not told them, or anyone else, whom he was meeting, and just why he was taking this small house in North Long Beach. So it was here, quietly and without any fuss, that O'Banion and Duke brought Dr. Sun to meet with Homer Lea.

It was around nine o'clock at night, after a long and tiring journey, when they arrived. Homer Lea was waiting. Dr. Sun was worn out, and after a hot supper, which Homer Lea prepared, he retired.

The next day began a secret conference between Dr. Sun and General Lea. The daily routine was simple. Duke went to Los Angeles and did the marketing. O'Banion got up early in the morning and started the coffee boiling. Then, after breakfast, Homer Lea and Dr. Sun would talk all day— and often far into the night.

If there had ever been any doubts in the mind of either of these two men as to whether or not they could work harmoniously together, this conference swept them away. Dr. Sun had, even at his first meeting, convinced Homer Lea of his sincerity, but now he was certain that it was Sun, and not Kang Yu-wei, who was the right leader for the revolution. From this time on Homer Lea was one hundred per cent for Dr. Sun and his ideas for a republic for China. What these two men decided upon—a humble doctor in exile with a price on his head, and a boyish American general in a Chinese revolutionary army—and the plans they made at this meeting formed the course that was followed.

Finally, when the conference was completed, it was decided to take Dr. Sun into Los Angeles and have him meet the members of the Po Wong Wui. Each man took upon himself a specific task. General Lea was to continue to prepare and lead the army for the day of liberation. Dr. Sun assumed the responsibility of swinging over to his view of the revolution all the members of the Po Wong Wui. A gigantic undertaking! But their plans were carefully thought out.

The unforeseen was that, while in Los Angeles, an attempt would be made upon the life of Dr. Sun.

CHAPTER FIFTEEN

Two Men with Queues

IT WAS Dr. Sun's wish that he meet openly and publicly the members of the Po Wong Wui. At first Homer Lea was doubtful of the wisdom of this.

"You have many enemies," he said, "and there have been attempts made upon your life. That might be again."

"Yes, yes, I know," replied Dr. Sun, smiling and shrugging his shoulders. "But I cannot forever work in silence and in secret. I must, sooner or later, come out and declare myself. There is no time like the present. The longer I delay, the longer the sufferings and injustices to my countrymen continue in China. What is one man's life when a revolution is at stake?"

"But at this time—you are too valuable a man!"

"There will be others to take my place!" said Dr. Sun.

So, following the Chinese custom of always combining the pleasures of dining with important business, invitations to a banquet on Sept. 30 were issued by Homer Lea.

Dr. Sun had been in Chinatown on two previous occasions. He had appeared at the Armory one evening with Homer Lea. It was an inspection of the troops, but the soldiers were not aware of it. Dr. Sun merely sat at one side and watched the soldiers drill. He wasn't introduced; or did he make a comment of any sort. No questions were asked and nothing was said.

However, O'Banion noticed that Soo Hu-hem, Lou Hoy,

and Allen Chung watched carefully to see if there was among any of the soldiers a flicker of recognition. If there was, O'Banion didn't see it. Impassive as ever, and attending strictly to business, the soldiers went through their paces. To them, seemingly, the man with Homer Lea that evening was just another of his friends.

Then, too, Homer Lea had driven Dr. Sun about Chinatown. But the Chinese paid no attention to him. In fact, he didn't look too much like a Chinese. With his waxed mustache, and the derby hat he wore, spick and span in his neatly fitting clothes, he could easily have passed as a visiting Frenchman. And since he never said a word when there were any Chinese talking to Homer Lea, nobody bothered about him.

However, on the night of the banquet, it was another story. In all some 600 men were present that evening. Homer Lea had invited all the troops and the leading merchants of Chinatown, as well as some twelve American friends; among them being John Alton of the Farmer's and Merchant's Bank, two young attorneys of Los Angeles, John York and Marshall Stimson, and a few newspapermen.

The banquet hall was in a Chinese restaurant on the corner of Marchessault and Alameda streets. It was on the second floor, up a flight of stairs, at the head of which was a sort of alcove, covered with long, heavy draperies.

The hour was set for eight o'clock. O'Banion drove Dr. Sun and Homer Lea in from Long Beach. When they arrived at the banquet hall, the guests were waiting outside on the street. At the door stood two armed guards. The soldiers were already upstairs in the banquet hall, seated along the walls, wearing their uniforms and fully armed.

O'Banion, since he was responsible for Dr. Sun's safety,

went first. Behind him were John York and Marshall Stimson, with Homer Lea and Dr. Sun next. And then the guests, since the stairs were steep and narrow, followed behind in single file.

When O'Banion got to within three steps of the head of the stairs, he suddenly saw a movement behind the draperies. Inside the door were seated Soo Hu-hem and Duke, calmly waiting. The movement behind the draperies aroused O'Banion's suspicions. With a quick gesture he pushed them aside. Standing there were two strange Chinese, with long knives in their hands.

O'Banion grabbed them by the scruff of their necks and, as he later said, "smeared them." That was his way of saying that he cracked their heads together. And then, for good measure, he rapped them over the head with the butt of his revolver. Their knives fell to the floor. Immediately Duke and Soo Hu-hem were on their feet. In a flash they picked up the knives, grabbed the startled men, and hustled them out through the kitchen. As they left, O'Banion noticed that one of the men, whose cap had fallen off, wore a queue!

It was over quickly. The only persons who saw the affair, save the soldiers in the banquet hall, were John York and Marshall Stimson.

"What's doing?" asked John York.

"Nothing, nothing at all!" replied O'Banion, and then quickly, to stop further comment, he shouted his command to the soldiers:

"Attention!"

They snapped to their feet, and the look of surprise and astonishment on their faces faded. In a twinkling they were calm and impassive, well-trained soldiers, with eyes straight ahead.

O'Banion stepped from the door and signaled to General Lea to enter the hall. Quite unaware of what had happened, he came in smiling with Dr. Sun and led him between the rows of soldiers to the speaker's table at the end.

Even when the banquet started, the soldiers made no comment among themselves about what they had seen. It was their Chinese way. While the first few courses were being served, Duke and Soo Hu-hem were not present. The banquet had been in progress for about an hour when they entered quietly and sat down at a table near the door. They were calm and self-possessed and acted as if nothing had happened.

O'Banion looked at Duke and raised a questioning eyebrow. Duke, without smiling, slyly closed one eye in a slow wink. Everything must be all right, thought O'Banion. Tomorrow, possibly, he would find out what happened to the two men.

Dr. Sun spoke, of course. He was introduced by Ho Lee, but his name was not mentioned.

"Who is he?" Harry Carr, the newspaper reporter, asked the Chinese seated next to him.

"No savvy!" was the reply, in such a tone as to discourage further questions. So the reporters present that evening didn't know they were listening to the real leader of the revolution, Dr. Sun Yat-sen. Had they known, his name at that time would have meant nothing to them.

Sun's speech was a model of tact and diplomacy. He congratulated the soldiers on the splendid showing they were making. He told them how proud they should be to be a part of the coming revolution. He spoke of what it meant to free China. He told them he, too, was working for the same cause, and urged them, "Carry on!"

The Chinese were impressed with him. They saw that he was a frank, honest, sincere man and were glad to know that this friend from Honolulu was on their side. But just what part he was ultimately to play, they didn't know for certain. That they were to learn later. To them, this evening, he was but another revolutionist and a friend of General Homer Lea. That was enough. He was now their friend, too.

The banquet didn't last too long. Nor was it nearly so elaborate as the banquets given Liang Chi-chao and Kang Yu-wei. But it was sufficient and served its purpose. When it was over, O'Banion drove General Lea and Dr. Sun back to Long Beach.

He told Homer Lea of the attempted assassination on Dr. Sun.

"Did anybody see it?" asked Homer Lea.

"All the troops," replied O'Banion. "And also York and Stimson."

"Who took care of the men?"

"Soo Hu-hem and his cousin from San Francisco."

With a big smile Homer Lea replied, "That's good. Let's not mention it to Dr. Sun."

"Why mention it at all?" said O'Banion, bluntly. "Certainly the soldiers won't talk, and I'll phone York and Stimson in the morning to keep still."

"That's the way to handle it," said Homer Lea. And then, after a moment, added, "Unfortunate, of course, that anything like this should occur. And yet I am glad it happened. It definitely proves what I have long suspected—there is great opposition in this country, at the moment, to Dr. Sun."

The next morning O'Banion dropped around to see Soo Hu-hem. They spoke of the banquet the night before, the speech made by Dr. Sun, the weather, and other topics. O'Banion knew better than to ask questions. It was one thing in dealings with the Chinese that simply wasn't done. If Soo Hu-hem wanted to tell him anything, he would of his own accord; but for O'Banion to inquire and display too much curiosity would have been bad manners. And if Soo Hu-hem did tell him anything, he was certain it would be in double-talk.

Finally Soo Hu-hem, without a word, brought out two knives and laid them on the table. They were American-made, vicious-looking knives, each about ten inches long, with a brown wooden handle and a razor-sharp edge.

O'Banion picked up one of them.

"Plenty wicked," he said. "Sharpened to a fine point—I could shave with this knife."

"Yes," grinned back Soo Hu-hem, "or even cut off a queue or two."

That was all that was said. What had happened to the two men, he never knew. Of one thing he was certain, it wasn't the first time men had disappeared and had never been heard from again. He also felt that, in the future, he could always trust both Duke and Soo Hu-hem.

But, of course, he wondered who the two men were. He also wondered who had hired them. Had it been the Empress Dowager, whose secret agents followed Dr. Sun wherever he went? Or had it been someone else? It would be useless to try to find out. The Chinese, even if they knew, wouldn't talk.

He also wondered how they had managed to hide behind the draperies. Certainly they never could have got there on their own. Someone whom he knew—and possibly trusted—had placed them there, probably earlier in the evening. It might have been one of the cooks in the kitchen. It might have been almost anybody on the inside. In any event, he reasoned, they had been standing there a long time. Tired of standing, they had moved and betrayed themselves. Who were they? And why?

He never learned the answers. In time it didn't matter, but during the remainder of Dr. Sun's stay in this country he was doubly careful.

It was during this visit that the final plans for the coming revolution were outlined with Homer Lea. And step by step those plans were put into operation.

The drilling of the soldiers had been going on now for two years. Their training was practically completed. And the plan, from the very first, was to send them ultimately to China to become leaders in the secret revolutionary army.

So they proceeded cautiously, one thing at a time. The first step was discussed one morning. After breakfast Homer Lea called O'Banion into the conference between him and Dr. Sun. He quickly came to the point.

"Dr. Sun wants secret agents planted in China. Do you know of anyone who can do this?" he asked.

"What will you do with them after we plant them there?" O'Banion inquired.

"Use them as contact men and establish hideouts for any one of us who may wish to go to China."

O'Banion thought a moment, then said, "It will cost a lot of money!"

"We don't care about that. The funds of the Po Wong Wui are at our disposal."

"If more is needed, I shall do what I can," said Dr. Sun, softly. "The money will be raised somehow or other."

"Well?" said Homer Lea, looking at O'Banion for his answer.

Unhesitatingly O'Banion replied, "Tell me exactly what you want done—and then forget about it."

Homer Lea, a twinkle of satisfaction in his eye, nodded gravely. "We have the plans here of where these men are to go, and whom they are to see first. Look them over, Captain."

On a single sheet of paper were the names of three men and three cities in China. That was all. Carefully O'Banion read it over—not once, but several times. Then he handed the paper back to Homer Lea.

"I've got it," he said, and tapped his forehead.

Striking a match, Homer Lea burned the paper. Then he turned to Dr. Sun and said, "We need worry no more on this score!"

"Fine!" said Dr. Sun. "When can you get started on this, Captain?"

"P.D.Q.—in other words, today!"

An hour later O'Banion telephoned Duke, who was still in Los Angeles. That evening he had a long talk with him. The next day Duke left for San Francisco.

Shortly after this Dr. Sun started on his return to Honolulu. Or did he? Arrangements for his trip home were the same as those which had brought him into this country. Only this time, it was a different boat and another steward. On the day of the sailing O'Banion went on board the boat with Dr. Sun. They walked on in broad daylight, like visitors coming aboard to wish bon voyage to friends.

But O'Banion and Dr. Sun wasted no time in formal fare-wells. In fact, they didn't even say good-by to each other. For somewhere in the crowds on the decks, they were sepa-rated. And O'Banion, after rambling about awhile, walked down the gangplank alone and out onto the streets. He didn't wait for the boat to sail.

That evening he went around to see Duke. They had planned to meet and discuss the final plans for sending the secret agents to China. When he arrived at Duke's home he was due for a surprise. In a corner he saw a black, well-used cowhide bag.

"Isn't that Dr. Sun's bag?" he asked.

"Yes," nodded Duke.

"What a hell of a note—his forgetting it!"

"He didn't forget," replied Duke.

The expression on O'Banion's face, bewilderment min-gled with curiosity, amused Duke. But O'Banion asked no questions. He scratched his chin and waited for Duke to explain—if he would.

Duke also scratched his chin and smiled.

Then he said, "Don't worry about Dr. Sun, Captain. He's been in this country before. He can find his way around. He likes America very much. He's a great traveler. Likes to go places and do things."

"But what shall I tell General Lea?"

"Report that, like a good soldier, you've carried out his orders—and saw Dr. Sun safely aboard the boat!"

"I sure did," said O'Banion.

"Yes," echoed Duke. "That's the way it was."

Then he smiled and shrugged his shoulders. "Your

responsibility is over," said Duke, politely. "Now mine begins."

"Good luck!" said O'Banion.

"Thanks, I'll be needing it," exclaimed Duke. "Arrangements for sending the men to China have all been completed. And now, Captain, I've another surprise for you. Among the men who are going is someone you know very well."

"Who?" inquired O'Banion.

"Myself," answered Duke, simply.

"But why?"

"It's a very dangerous mission. I couldn't ask others to do it unless I went along, too. It's like the Golden Rule. 'Do not ask others to do what you would not do yourself.' So I am going. But I won't be long. A few months, possibly a year. I shall write you from time to time."

"Would that be safe?" asked O'Banion.

"Perfectly. I have thought up a very nice code we can use. I shall tell you about it, so that you will know exactly how I am progressing."

"Okay," said O'Banion. "All your plans made?"

"Down to the last detail. I am taking two men with me. Everything has been arranged. I didn't tell you, Captain," continued Duke, soberly and without smiling, "but we are going to China to start a baby factory!"

"A what?" gasped O'Banion.

"A baby factory! Don't be surprised, Captain. It's nothing unusual, really!"

CHAPTER SIXTEEN

Secret Agents in China

ONE of the outstanding members of the company in San Francisco was Sergeant Lum Sing. Quick-witted, an excellent soldier, he knew all the answers. In Fresno there was another exceptional young man, Sergeant Quong Soo. Both men were leaders in their groups and Duke, through long association with them, knew they could be trusted.

As Duke explained to O'Banion, "We are sailing in four days' time for China. Their papers and mine are all in order. We're leaving quite openly, and nobody is asking questions. In fact, many farewell banquets are being given us. And all our cousins are saving their money to buy wedding presents. You see, Lum Sing and Quong Soo are going to China to be married. They have brides waiting for them there—and so that's how it is!"

"But what about yourself?" asked O'Banion. "What excuse are you giving?"

"The same! I'm going to be married, too!"

"But you already are married!" exclaimed O'Banion.

A look of surprise and dismay swept over Duke's face. "But, Captain, have you never heard of the Chinese custom of having more than one wife? It has all been arranged. My Wife Number One is doing the usual polite protesting. But, custom being what it is, what can she do? My friends are all congratulating me. To be able to afford two wives— one here and one in China—is sufficient proof that I am a very good man!" laughed Duke. "But my wife will be quite reconciled to her fate when I return from China alone."

Four days later, Duke and Lum Sing and Quong Soo walked up the gangplank and boarded the ship sailing for China. A number of their friends went to see them off.

"Come back soon—with your wives!" they cried.

But Lum Sing and Quong Soo never returned to the United States. They remained in China and were active in their secret work until the revolution was over, and then O'Banion lost track of them.

They settled near Amoy, a seaport town, not far from Canton. This was quite according to the plan made by Dr. Sun. Lum Sing and Quong Soo bought farms. The money came from the Po Wong Wui funds, of course—some ten thousand dollars. This had to be smuggled in. But Duke did it quite nicely. O'Banion fixed up the money for him, a neat package of bills—and handed it to the steward on the boat the day before the sailing. So, when Duke and the two sergeants went aboard, there was nothing in their luggage to arouse suspicion.

Lum Sing and Quong Soo really did get married. On a farm, up the river, not far from Amoy they raised vegetables —and their families—and to the outside world behaved like two quiet, hard-working farmers. This was the main base in China, through which all the underground work was to be managed.

Other agents were to be placed elsewhere, according to instructions given by Dr. Sun. Therefore, as soon as Lum Sing and Quong Soo were happily married and had started farming, Duke gave them his blessing and went on to Macao.

From there he wrote a letter to O'Banion, saying in part:

"I have been visiting lately in Canton, but am now in Macao. This is a charming city, a delightful spot. It is an art center and many artists, poets and writers live here. It is most picturesque place, and people are constantly coming and going. It is most accessible by water, on the sea, like Long Beach. And do you remember that day at Long Beach when you amused us by cutting off the tops of carrots? I was telling some friends here about it—and how we wished we grew carrots in China—the American variety, of course. I wish I had a couple of carrots with me to show them how it is done. And what good carrots you grow in America. I think I shall soon take a trip to Hankow—and shall write you from there."

An innocent letter and a trifle silly. But O'Banion knew exactly what Duke meant. It was the code agreed upon before Duke left. What he was really saying was this: "I have made contacts here in Macao according to plan—and send over two men to act as secret agents here."

These men had previously been selected by Duke: two sergeants from the Los Angeles company, Lee Dack and Sui Lung, among the smartest of the cadets. The plan was to smuggle them out of the country, and all arrangements for this had been made by Duke before he left for China. So, when Duke's letter arrived, O'Banion went to San Francisco to see Charlie Lung, the Potato King who had been such a help in getting Dr. Sun off the boat.

Charlie Lung knew all the seamen along the water front in San Francisco Bay. He knew the honest, hard-working sailors as well as the derelicts, the drifters, and the rowdies. He also numbered among his acquaintances a few professional smugglers. Having given the matter much thought, he felt that one smuggler whom he could trust—for a price—was a Hollander, by name of Herman Osterhaus.

In the underworld, Herman Osterhaus was famous. He had been a smuggler all his life. His home was in San Diego, but he came to San Francisco on this occasion to meet O'Banion. He was a stocky, heavy-set man about fifty-seven years old. Uncouth, a hard drinker and a tough fighter, he was, however, tight-lipped. Even though he made his living outside the law, he had his own code of honor as a smuggler. As long as he was paid his own price, he never discussed his business with anyone.

His method of working was rather simple. He would often sign on board a boat—both passenger and freighter—as a seaman. And he knew, almost instinctively, just where to pass the "sugar money" to officers and crew alike to accomplish his purpose. In San Diego Bay he had an old sailing vessel which had been dismantled. This was his home, and here he lived when he wasn't at sea.

When Charlie Lung and O'Banion talked with him and asked his price for getting two Chinese secretly into China, Osterhaus replied, "I'll make you a special price on this job, provided we ship these men—not from this country—but from Mexico."

"Why from Mexico?" asked O'Banion.

"Easier, safer, and cheaper!"

O'Banion looked at Charlie Lung, who nodded in agreement.

"What's your price?" asked O'Banion.

"Five hundred dollars each—paid in advance!"

"Okay!" said O'Banion.

A few weeks later he had a letter from Osterhaus, mailed from Mazatlán, Mexico, a seaport on the west coast, saying briefly, "I'm now in this town. If you got any friends here tell them to look me up."

Lee Dack and Sui Lung went immediately to Mazatlán. They were put aboard a boat by Osterhaus and sailed for Canton. In due time O'Banion had a letter from Duke, in which he said that to his great surprise he had met two old friends in Canton and they had had a good time at their reunion. These friends, so Duke informed O'Banion, were merchants living in Macao and, since they were smart young fellows, he knew they would be successful. He also said that Hankow was a good city for business, and he felt that if a couple of young men, as bright and alert as his Macao friends, were located there, the chances for their success were good.

The men chosen to go were Ming Toy and Sam Tick of San Francisco. They, too, took a trip to Mazatlán to visit their friend, Herman Osterhaus, and shortly afterward sailed for China.

The scene was now all set. Six secret agents had been planted in China. It had taken time, of course. But in Amoy were two hard-working farmers; in Macao and Hankow, two honest and law-abiding merchants. Their neighbors respected them. They minded their own business, never engaged in any political arguments or discussions, and did nothing that in any way would arouse suspicion.

They even pretended not to know each other. Certainly, between the merchants at Macao and Hankow there was never any correspondence. Nor did the farmers in Amoy ever go to those cities to visit their friends. There was no occasion for suspicion—for, to all appearances, these men were strangers to each other. That, too, was part of the plan.

The time would come, of course, when they would be in touch.

In the meantime, they were to wait until the day came when they would receive their instructions from headquarters in Los Angeles. So they worked hard to gain the confidence and respect of their neighbors and establish a reputation for honesty and simplicity of living. In a few years, there would be plenty to be done. But for the present, there was no hurry. Once they had established a good "front," anything might happen behind the scenes—and did!

Then one day there came another letter from Duke. In it he said briefly, "I have just returned to Canton from a little trip to Japan. While in Kobe I visited an old friend. He is doing nicely there—and says in a couple of months he'll be on top of the world."

Again a message in code, and one that O'Banion had been waiting for. What it meant to him was simply this: the Japanese agent previously planted in Kobe had made all arrangements. He had been sent to Kobe to see if he could somehow or other obtain possession of the secret war plans of Japan. The answer had come from him—he could.

CHAPTER SEVENTEEN

The War Plans of Japan

BACK in 1903, some three months after O'Banion had started drilling the troops, Homer Lea came around to the Armory one evening. When the night's work was over, he went with O'Banion for a bite to eat. After they had finished, he laid on the table a hastily sketched map of Asia.

"I have drawn this from memory," he said. "It isn't accurate, nor is it complete. I saw the original in the headquarters of the Japanese Naval Office in Tokyo when I was there in 1901. It is part of the secret war plans of Japan."

Then he went on to tell O'Banion that it was his firm conviction that Japan was planning to conquer all Asia and set herself up as the supreme power in the East. The Japanese might even be including in their plot for domination an attack upon the United States. It was not outside the realm of possibility.

The first hint he had had of Japan's warlike intentions came from a reading, in 1899, of Rudyard Kipling's *From Sea to Sea* in which Kipling warned of the growing strength of Japan and said concerning her army, "They are bad little men who know too much."

Homer Lea's suspicions were confirmed when he was in Japan with Kang Yu-wei and Liang Chi-chao. The too cordial reception given them by the Japanese lacked sincerity. There was no reason for their overwhelming display of friendliness to three lonely exiles if they didn't have some purpose of their own concealed up their long sleeves. And then, one day, some Japanese naval officers broke down and told Homer Lea the truth.

They even, in the headquarters of the Japanese Navy, showed him a part of some secret plans they had drawn up. Japan, so they informed him, was progressive. She was adopting modern ways—and unlike Old China, who was far behind the times in this dawn of the twentieth century, Japan was already anticipating the day when she would be the ruling power in the Far East and all Asia. China was weak. Torn by civil war, her internal affairs in a muddle, she needed the strong hand of Japan to set her straight. And that was exactly what Japan intended doing. So why shouldn't Homer Lea join forces with the winning side? They offered him a commission in the Japanese Army. But he declined.

As he told O'Banion, "I was suspicious. I thought at the time—and I still think—that I did not see all the secret plans Japan is making. I'd give my eyeteeth to know in detail what those Japs are up to. But I didn't say 'No' to their offer to make me a general in the Japanese Army. I said I'd think it over. And I'm still thinking. I did tell them, however, that my first loyalty in this matter was to China— and until I knew for certain that we would fail with our plans for the liberation of the Boy Emperor, I couldn't very well accept a commission from Japan while still wearing the uniform of a general in the Chinese Army."

Then he went on to say that already Japan had begun her campaign. She was sending merchants into China and America—an advance guard of seemingly friendly people. In China, the patriots were beginning to resent this. They didn't like Japan's intrusion into their country, nor her meddling in their internal troubles. And the Manchu Dynasty was obviously playing ball with the Japanese imperialists.

"What I should like someday," said Homer Lea, "is to see a copy of the original war plans of Japan."

O'Banion shrugged his shoulders. "I wish I knew some way to get them for you," he said, "but a man can't just walk into Tokyo and pick them up. It's not so easy as all that!"

"Obviously," replied Homer Lea.

But he suggested that O'Banion bear it in mind. It might take a long time—months, even years—but someday they might have an idea how to go about this. And there the matter rested. O'Banion, however, didn't forget.

When he first went to work in Chinatown drilling the troops, there were no Japanese. Then a family moved in at the corner of Marchessault and Alameda streets. They opened a barbershop with—of all things—a Japanese lady barber. Their customers were Chinese. At first no one suspected them. But in the light of later events, it was seen— and too late—that these Japanese were the forerunners, the first spies sent to this country for a definite purpose.

It was as Homer Lea had said—the advance guard of the Japanese Army was here, laying the foundations for the day of conquest. And their first purpose was to take over the truck farming in California and to put the Chinese out of business. They succeeded, too.

What better place than the barbershop for the Chinese farmers and hucksters to talk, and the Japanese to listen? They obtained all the information possible and studied the methods used, not only in farming, but also in selling the produce on the market.

Then a Japanese family opened a small general store on the corner of Ferguson Alley and Alameda Street. This was an elderly couple, dignified and unassuming. They sold Japanese sake, among other things, and were very, very polite. Other Japanese began to arrive, and this store was their headquarters in Los Angeles. It wasn't long until some seventy-five Japanese farmers were living near Chinatown. They were well-behaved, well-mannered, and friendly.

It was popular, in those days, to speak openly of the "sinister Chinee." That was the name given them, and it stuck —right up to Pearl Harbor, as a matter of fact. No one ever thought of speaking of the Japanese as "sinister." They flocked to churches, were converted wholesale, and became the great friends and willing little helpers of our well-meaning home missionaries. They were spoken of affectionately as the "polite Japanese."

But their behavior when they sometimes lost at gambling was all too indicative of their real nature. O'Banion often had a lot of trouble with them. As police officer, it was his duty to keep the peace. And whenever a street fight occurred he invariably discovered it was the Japanese who started it.

Those nights when they'd lose heavily at gambling, they'd turn off the lights, grab what money they could, and start a fight—while the thieves fled to the streets. The Chinese soon got wise to this trickery, and the result was a free-for-all that sometimes had the proportions of a small riot. The police would arrive and break it up. Knowing the Japs were the instigators, they'd go for them.

One big policeman had an effective method. He'd grab one of the Japs by the back of his neck and use him as a club to mow the rest of them down. But whenever a Jap got knocked down, he'd rise, murmur politely, "Thank you!" then scamper off as fast as he could.

This aroused O'Banion's curiosity. It wasn't, he thought, a normal reaction. So one day he asked a Japanese why it was.

The Jap smiled politely and said, "Told in Japan before we came here no matter what happens to us in America, always say, 'Thank you.' "

"Even if you're mad as hell?"

"Even mad," replied the Jap blandly.

That the Japanese had a definite part in slandering the Chinese and were largely responsible for the origin of many of the rumors about them there is no doubt.

It took time for the Japanese to take over the huckster business in Southern California—but it wasn't difficult. As a rule, the Chinese farmers all rented their farms, sometimes on a sharing basis, and sometimes paying in cash. The owners found it most satisfactory, for the Chinese knew how to treat the soil properly and always paid the rent promptly.

But slowly and surely the Japanese began buying up these farms. They had a well-financed organization for just this purpose. Now, most of the Chinese had verbal agreements with the original owners—but when the farm was sold, the Chinese were told politely that their lease was terminated. The Japanese took over. And, before anybody was really aware of what was happening, the Japanese owned the former Chinese truck farms.

They also stepped in and soon controlled the huckster business. When O'Banion first went to Chinatown there were some four hundred horse-drawn vegetable wagons supplying the markets and the housewives. Each Chinese had his own route. One of the wily Japs would ingratiate himself into the friendship of the Chinese driver. He'd want to go along on the route "to help," so he said. In this way he learned all the tricks of the trade.

Then, when the Japanese farmers began farming, they were loath to sell their produce to the Chinese hucksters. And the Chinese ultimately didn't have a chance. They began selling their horses and wagons to the Japanese. In a few years the Japanese had gained complete control of the produce markets in Southern California. And from that day until the present war—when the Japanese were interned—they had a monopoly. They even refused to do business with O'Banion and his Hay and Feed Market; so in time he, too, was forced out. The Japanese fooled him just as much as they did the Chinese.

To get hold of the Japanese war plans was always in the back of O'Banion's mind. And he felt the best way to obtain them was through a Japanese. Some one of them—if paid well enough—would turn traitor. His problem was to find the right man. And he also knew he must proceed cautiously.

The first thing he did was to contact a Japanese who, he thought, might give him a lead. The Japanese passed his Hay Market constantly on their way into Chinatown to gamble. He had some seventy-five to pick from. There was one who passed by every night. O'Banion liked his looks and got to talking with him. He thought the man might be a possibility, so now and then he gave him $2 or $3.

"Make a bet on this for me," he'd say. "If you win, we'll go fifty-fifty!"

But O'Banion never won. It didn't matter, for he became friends with this Japanese and it wasn't long before he knew all about him—where he came from in Japan, his business there, his family, and so forth. But it was all to no avail.

What O'Banion wanted to find was a man who had been raised on a sampan, with family connections in the army or navy—a seafaring man by profession. This particular chap was a farmer.

Through him O'Banion met other Japanese—also farmers. There wasn't one among them who had a relative of any sort in the army or navy—and O'Banion pumped them all. Eventually he told Duke what he was looking for.

"I've worked over this lousy bunch of Japs—and not a damn one has ever been anyplace but on a farm!"

"I honestly think they've been telling you the truth, too," said Duke. "But cheer up. I believe I know the very man!"

"Where is he?" asked O'Banion.

Duke grinned. "Right at your back door."

Thus, after all his months of trouble, practically on his own doorstep he found just the type of man he was looking for. Back of the Hay Market on Napier Street was a Japanese bathhouse. It was a two-story brick building, with only a four-foot alley between it and O'Banion's place of business.

The bathhouse was run by two sixty-year-old Japanese, a man and his wife. Periodically—every three to five months—the man would go on a rousing old-fashioned drunk. And when drunk his greatest pleasure was to throw his money around. He'd often come into the Hay Market, drunk as a fool, take out a handful of money, let out a whoop and a holler, and throw it into the hay. The next day O'Banion picked the money up and returned it to the man's wife, as usually following these drunken bouts the Jap would sleep for a day.

Now and then, at the wife's request, O'Banion would take the Japanese home and handcuff him to the bed, so he could sober up. He'd fasten the man's right hand and left foot to the bed, and leave him there. It invariably did the trick—and the old Japanese was repentant, until the next time.

He had been in this country only a few months when a helper appeared on the scene—a young chap about eighteen years old. His name was Togo Taymoto. He was a quiet, well-behaved lad, speaking broken English. O'Banion had seen him around but never paid any attention to him. He worked hard, cleaning up the bathrooms, laundering the towels, and doing all the odd jobs about the place. He never gambled, seemed to save his money, and had no bad habits.

As Duke told O'Banion, "He's the man for you. Comes from a family of fishermen at Kobe. He was born on a sampan, raised on a sampan, and has uncles in both the army and the navy—some of them high officials. Now what?"

"Why not drop around one of these days and take a bath there?" suggested O'Banion. "Give him a good-sized tip; perhaps he'll talk freer with you after that."

So Duke did. Taymoto's eyes sparkled as he saw the money Duke handed him.

"America rich country," he said. "Everybody make plenty money here."

"Yeah," replied Duke. "I know how you can make a lot more, too."

"Tell me," said Taymoto.

"Soon as you get a chance, go talk with Captain O'Banion. You can trust him—and he has lots of money."

Shortly after that, Taymoto came into the Hay Market. There was a room at the back where O'Banion knew they could talk without being disturbed. He didn't, of course, at once bring up the subject in mind. He wanted first to know all about Taymoto.

"How long have you been in America?" he asked.

"Just a few months," answered the boy.

"Why did you come?"

The answer was honest and to the point. "To make money. Good place to make money. Japan never make money."

"I suppose when you've made enough, you'll go into some business here?"

But Taymoto shook his head. "No; when I make enough, go back to Japan and get married."

Then Taymoto told O'Banion all about himself and his family. They were poor fishermen, living in the harbor on their sampan, and sometimes making a little extra money by peddling to the boats at anchor. He had a girl he wanted to marry, but he was so poor that marriage was out of the question. That was why he came to America. An ambitious lad, enough American dollars meant freedom from a life of toil in Japan, and also would make him a man of importance.

It was on this score that O'Banion appealed to the boy. With money he could have great face, just like his uncles in the navy.

"Yes," said Taymoto. "Look what they have done. I want to be somebody, too."

One day O'Banion asked point-blank, "How would you like to go to Japan right now and have in your pocket enough money to get married?"

"No get in trouble?" asked Taymoto, cautiously.

"Not a chance of trouble and plenty of money besides."

His curiosity was aroused, and he wanted to know just what was expected of him. By this time O'Banion was convinced that, if anyone could do what he wanted, Taymoto could. But he still proceeded cautiously. In any event, considering the plans being made by Homer Lea, to have an agent of sorts in Kobe might one of these days come in handy. On this point he made a proposition to Taymoto.

Now and then, he knew, the revolutionists would be not only sending men into China, but bringing them out. So what would be better than to have someone in Kobe to help on this? From America to Kobe—and then from Kobe to the coast of China.

Taymoto fell for the idea immediately. O'Banion promised him enough money to buy a house in Kobe, get married, and also be able to put something aside. He would, however, have to pose as a fisherman for a time. That didn't bother Taymoto. He could be patient and bide his time. A boat was bought for him—the best that money could buy. It was made especially at the Crowley shipyards in San Francisco, the total cost being around $2,000—a lot of money for a boat in those days.

Taymoto was now a changed lad. New hopes—new dreams —and O'Banion was his friend. What could he do to show his gratitude for this rich American who had made all this possible?

O'Banion told him exactly what he wanted. There were certain plans the government had. He'd like a copy. When Taymoto asked why, he replied that he wanted to write a book about them. Homer Lea's name was not mentioned.

"If you can obtain a copy of these plans for me from one of your uncles—I'll give you $5,000!"

Taymoto gasped. With $5,000 he would be a rich man for the rest of his life in Japan. He told O'Banion he'd try. He didn't promise, of course. But perhaps when he got to Japan and had a talk with one of his uncles, who knows? His uncles, because of their position, were important men and highly respected. Yet, on the other hand, their pay was very low. Some extra money would come in handy. It might take time—but he thought it could be done.

When O'Banion told Duke how well everything was working out, Duke made a wry face.

"Smiling little traitor, isn't he?" said Duke.

"I wonder if his conscience bothers him?" asked O'Banion.

"I doubt it! However, just a tip, Captain. Don't give him the five thousand until you have seen the plans—and know they are genuine."

The boat for Taymoto was finished and shipped to Japan. O'Banion gave the boy money for a ticket home, enough cash to buy a house, and a little extra as a wedding present. So, in October of 1905, Taymoto sailed for Japan.

It was arranged that messages to O'Banion be sent through the owner of the bathhouse. This elderly Japanese knew nothing about what Taymoto was doing for O'Banion. He had been told as little as possible. But, knowing O'Banion was Taymoto's friend, he relayed news from time to time about how Taymoto was getting along back home.

No sooner had Taymoto landed in Japan than he went to visit one of his uncles. But this uncle was cautious and told Taymoto he would have nothing to do with him. He said he was afraid he wouldn't get his money. Another uncle had no such doubts. There were any number of blueprints of the plans in the army and navy offices, but just how this uncle got hold of one of the copies for O'Banion, Taymoto never told. It was for a price, however. And Taymoto had troubles of his own. When the first uncle got wind of what had happened, Taymoto had to pay him to keep still. His $5,000 didn't stretch as far as he had thought it would!

But he got the plans, and when Duke saw him in Kobe, he was told they would be waiting for O'Banion when he was ready to come and get them.

It was Herman Osterhaus who smuggled him in.

Herman Osterhaus operated chiefly from Mazatlán, Mexico. But it was not difficult, when there was someone to be smuggled out of the country, to reach Herman from the United States.

Between trips across the ocean he lived in San Diego on an old boat. It was drawn up at the back of Neely's store on the water front. Living with Herman was his brother John, an older man with snow-white hair. There was no question how John made his living. He had a high-powered boat of his own, which could be chartered now and then for fishing parties. Anchored in the bay, right near Herman's boathouse, it was innocent enough looking.

Not even old man Neely who ran the store knew exactly the main use of the boat and the real business John Osterhaus was engaged in. He really didn't want to know. He was paid to look the other way and keep his mouth shut.

It was at John Osterhaus's suggestion that, early in the game, O'Banion made Neely's acquaintance. So, now and then, O'Banion drove down to San Diego and stopped in to see him. He was a gentle old man, kind and friendly. They'd sit in the back room, overlooking the bay. When it came time for O'Banion to go, he left some money on the table. Neely paid no attention to this—did not even look at the money or make a comment of any sort. But as soon as O'Banion had gone, he pocketed the money and, no doubt, wished that O'Banion would drop in often. This was the way Neely worked with John Osterhaus, and it was understood between them that he wasn't ever to speak of the people who now and then went through his store and onto the boat at anchor in the bay. From his dealings with John, he knew that one of these days O'Banion would be wanting something—but should anyone ever ask he was to say he had never heard of him.

In time he came to ignore O'Banion completely. He paid no more attention to his comings and goings than if he were a harmless house cat. And always O'Banion left money on the table. The amount varied according to what he was doing—and who would join him on the boat.

That evening when he appeared in Neely's store carrying a small handbag, Neely never even spoke. John Osterhaus was waiting for O'Banion. He went aboard the boat, and they slipped out of the bay toward Mazatlán. Osterhaus had one helper, a young Russian named Paul Beezoff, a short, heavy-set, taciturn chap about twenty-four years old.

It took four days to get to Mazatlán. The boat was loaded with fuel oil, enough to go and return. There were even drums of oil lashed on the deck. Herman was prepared for O'Banion's coming. He was, on this occasion, an officer aboard a freighter bound for Japan. The freighter was waiting, ready to sail.

O'Banion didn't go ashore in Mexico. That night he was transferred from John's boat. Herman Osterhaus put him up in his cabin. And certain of the ship's officers received their cut from the $300 O'Banion gave him. All during the trip no one spoke to O'Banion or paid any attention to him. He didn't, however, parade the decks, since the freighter carried a few passengers. It was a long dull trip to Kobe, but he remained quietly in his cabin.

At Kobe in the harbor the sampans swarmed around like bees. The fishermen were always wanting to sell something to the sailors and passengers: fresh vegetables, eggs, souvenirs, a suit of clothes even; anything a man might want could be bought in this manner. They'd come every day, and since often their prices were less than ashore, it was a good way to make purchases—a good way to get O'Banion off the boat, too, without being seen.

As soon as they had dropped anchor Osterhaus went ashore and, at the address O'Banion had given him, found Taymoto and gave him his instructions. He was to come to the freighter that night in a sampan and was to remain behind when the other sampans left, around ten o'clock. His was to be the last boat to leave, but in the meanwhile he was to behave exactly like the others.

Purchases from the sampans were passed up on long bamboo poles with baskets on the end. So, when O'Banion was ready to go ashore, his luggage first of all was passed to Taymoto in one of those baskets. When night fell and the other sampans had gone, he slid down a rope ladder and into Taymoto's sampan.

Taymoto took him immediately to his new home, a small house, but neat and clean. Taymoto said it had just been built. For three days, while the freighter was being unloaded, O'Banion remained with Taymoto. He never went outside; not even Taymoto's neighbors knew he had a visitor.

The day before O'Banion returned to the boat in the harbor, Taymoto handed him several sheets of paper, each some eight inches wide and two feet long, covered with Japanese characters. There were several maps—and among them O'Banion saw maps of the western coast of the United States. O'Banion wrapped up the plans in a piece of old paper and thrust them into his inside coat pocket.

"Thank you, Taymoto," he said. "You'll be hearing from me. later."

"Yes, yes," smiled Taymoto, politely. "Let my uncle know, please." Meaning, of course, the bathhouse proprietor.

Later that day, O'Banion went aboard the freighter again. No one knew that he was carrying these secret war plans out of Japan. And O'Banion took every precaution. He never thought of putting them into his luggage. That would have been too dangerous. He kept them in his pocket. And since nobody but himself and Taymoto knew he had them, they were perfectly safe.

He didn't even know—not being able to read Japanese— if these were what Homer Lea wanted. But Taymoto had told him they were the real thing, and since he was willing to trust O'Banion for the $5,000 agreed upon, O'Banion believed him.

When he arrived in Los Angeles some weeks later he gave the plans to Homer Lea. Immediately they were translated, and Homer Lea pronounced them genuine. There were even more details than he had seen on his visit to Japan.

"They're worth the five thousand you paid for them," he told O'Banion.

"I haven't yet," answered O'Banion, "but I shall."

He told the Japanese at the bathhouse to write to Taymoto and tell him that everything was okay—and that one of these days he would return all his kindnesses. Taymoto understood. He waited two years for his money. On his next trip to Japan—this time on his way to China—O'Banion paid Taymoto in cash.

The last O'Banion heard of Taymoto was in 1911. He was

the father of several children—rotten rich and living in style. If alive today, he must be almost sixty years old.

It was the information in these secret war plans that furnished Homer Lea with the material for his book *The Valor of Ignorance*. Published in 1909, it pointed out clearly the Japanese plan of attack, not only upon the Philippines, but also upon our western coast. He made the prediction that Manila would fall to the Japanese in "less than three weeks." It actually happened in twenty-six days.

The book was dedicated to the Hon. Elihu Root, Secretary of State, and had introductions by Lieutenant General Adna R. Chaffee, late Chief of Staff, United States Army, then retired, and Major General J. P. Story, also retired, who said that the book should be read by every "intelligent and patriotic citizen of the United States."

When the book appeared the reviewers were of divided opinion. Some said it told "a story which every American would do well to ponder." Others were violent in their denunciation, among them Dr. David Starr Jordan, president of Stanford University. Dr. Jordan was a belligerent pacifist and believed in arbitration. In fact, in Robert Young's *The Impudence of Charlatanism,* in the World Peace Foundation Pamphlet Series, Vol. II (1912), reprinted from *Japan Chronicle,* published first in Kobe (!) Feb. 11, 1912, is a letter in which Dr. Jordan spoke of Homer Lea as an "ambitious romancer" and said that his book *The Valor of Ignorance* was worthless nonsense. The book may be slow reading in spots, but Pearl Harbor proved it wasn't nonsense!

But in 1909 the American public was indifferent to the warning. In time the book was forgotten, and copies could be purchased on the stalls of the secondhand bookstores for ten cents.

Then came Pearl Harbor—and what Homer Lea said would happen did happen. In 1942, Harpers reissued the book and said in the jacket blurb that thirty-three years later Homer Lea's amazing prophecies of Japan's warlike intentions toward the United States were coming true.

CHAPTER EIGHTEEN

Two Farmers at Amoy

ONE day in 1907, O'Banion dropped around to see Lum Sum, in whose living quarters above his stable was kept the money of the Po Wong Wui. The two men pushed aside the grass rug, lifted the trap door, and from the trunk concealed beneath the floor took out $180,000 in cash. This was the exact sum needed for a certain purpose.

"Be back soon, I hope," said O'Banion, bidding good-by to Lum Sum, who quietly nodded and made no comment.

O'Banion hadn't felt it necessary to explain to Lum Sum that he was going to China on a secret mission for Dr. Sun Yat-sen.

It had been during Dr. Sun's conferences with Homer Lea in 1905 that plans for this trip to China were made. In discussing the matter one evening, Dr. Sun drew a map.

On this map a line was drawn from Hankow to Nanking, and another to Shanghai. Inside this triangle is the rich Yangtze Valley. As Dr. Sun said, whoever controls this territory stands a good chance of controlling China. (It is now, as we know, in the possession of Japan—and here was launched her first attack in the present war against China.)

Inside this triangle, as Dr. Sun explained, were stationed the principal garrisons of the army of the Empress Dowager. Outside the triangle, in the hills, were the armies of the brigand chieftains, at constant guerrilla warfare with the Royal Manchu Army.

These brigand chieftains were in command of the loyal Chinese whom Homer Lea had led during the Boxer Rebellion. After their defeat they had fled to the mountains and been told to wait, in the meantime gathering what soldiers they could for their ragged, outlawed armies. The time would come someday—it was hoped—when word from their former commander in chief, General Lea, would reach them.

Seven years later word came. The plan was this: to send someone to China to talk with the brigand chieftains and to buy up certain disgruntled officers in the Royal Manchu Army. A list of possible names was given Homer Lea by Dr. Sun. Also Kang Yu-wei furnished some names. The brigand chieftains, however, were known to only Homer Lea.

As he often said to O'Banion, "I am going to arrange this so that it will be the nearest thing to a bloodless revolution that the world has ever known. In many instances, we may have to buy our way through. But it will be cheaper in the long run, for dollars are less valuable than the lives of men, and money spent is less messy than blood spilled."

The first step in this plan had been taken when Lum Sing and Quong Soo were planted as secret agents in Amoy, and the others in Macao and Hankow. Lum Sing and Quong Soo had been living in Amoy now for almost two years. To their near-by neighbors they were ordinary farmers, and not particularly good ones at that. They appeared to be rather stupid young men, in fact. They did some farming, but they never overworked. Had their neighbors only known the truth—that these two men had more important matters to attend to than the growing of vegetables—tongues would have wagged. And in time the soldiers of the Empress Dowager would have descended upon these humble farms, and there would have been another beheading in the public square.

So Lum Sing and Quong Soo—slow and deliberate, as the Chinese always are—took their time and proceeded cautiously. As innocent-appearing farmers, it was easy for them occasionally to visit the camp of one of the brigand chieftains. At first they merely became acquainted, but, being well-trained soldiers who knew all the tricks, they sized up the camp, knew its strength and the temper of the men.

Finally, after having established friendly relations and learning that the brigand they were talking with was still loyal to the cause of freeing China from the Manchus, they brought up the subject of money.

"I think I know where you can get some cash," Lum Sing would say.

"Fine, fine," the brigand chieftain would reply, and would want to know more.

Then would come another long delay, while the two farmers gave the brigands time to think matters over. And since there were some seventy-five of them, Lum Sing and Quong Soo had plenty of work to do besides farming.

Once quite certain that the brigand chieftains were interested, the two agents would come to the point. They posed as good fellows, not wanting to make money themselves, but perfectly willing to do a favor for a friend.

Lum Sing would say, "There's going to be a rebellion, and soldiers are needed. Just what you are expected to do will be told you later."

"How much money can I get?" would be asked.

"What can I tell about you to the man who has it?"

The brigand chieftain then told of the number of soldiers in his company and all other necessary details. Thereupon, after a certain amount of bargaining, a fixed sum was decided upon.

This information was sent to Homer Lea in the code Duke had arranged during his first visit to China. After his return to the United States, Lum Sing and Quong Soo wrote to him often in Chinese. The letters were simple. For instance, Lum Sing would write that somewhere near Hankow he could purchase three hundred pieces of very good jade for only $1,000. And he would often add, "This is very topside jade!" This meant, of course, that the brigand in this instance was a high-class man. Sometimes Quong Soo would write to Duke and tell him the number of vegetables he had taken to market, and the amount of money paid him for his produce. So, in time, Homer Lea and O'Banion knew exactly how much money was needed in China for this purpose.

The brigands were the first to be approached. The viceroys and the commanders of the Royal Manchu Army were next on the list. The method for getting in contact with the officers was practically the same as with the brigands. However, it was the two agents in Hankow, Ming Toy and Sam Tick, who did this. These agents, also trained army men but professing complete ignorance of military matters, could get into the camps, size up the soldiers, and know as much about the strength of the camp as the officers themselves.

The Manchu officers were not paid too highly by the Empress Dowager. All the agents had to do, therefore, was to offer them more money than they were receiving. They were not told on which side they would someday fight.

"Be prepared. It is for China. We shall let you know," was all that was said.

Many of these men were patriots at heart and already sympathetic to the cause of the coming revolution; so buying them up was not too difficult for the secret agents of Dr. Sun.

Naturally, some were to be paid less than others. The Chinese always love a good bargain; so there was often much dickering before the price was finally decided upon. A few were to receive as low as $500, others $1,000.

Some of the brigands got wind of what was going on and demanded more money. They were entitled to it, for now and again, with part of the money they were to receive, they could buy up the army of another brigand chieftain and combine their two forces. A few really smart men got the price up to as high as $5,000. It began to have the appearance of a racket, but by this time word had reached Homer Lea that just about all the men needed were ready to serve. The time had come for O'Banion to go to China and pay off.

Early in the summer of 1907, O'Banion appeared one day at Neely's store, carrying with him, besides his usual luggage, two packages done up in brown paper. He had previously made arrangements with Herman Osterhaus to be taken secretly once again to Kobe, where, he said, he was planning to remain for two months. But what he didn't tell Osterhaus was that from Japan he was going on to China, for that wasn't any of Osterhaus's business.

Nor did he tell Osterhaus what was in the two packages. "Groceries," O'Banion said in explanation. Had Osterhaus known that the packages contained rolls of money, totaling around $180,000, O'Banion might never have reached his destination. He was fully armed and prepared for any emergency, but the only men he really trusted with the knowledge that he was carrying so much money were Homer Lea and Duke.

The bills were of large denominations. It was easier to make two packages than one, and they were so wrapped— in heavy brown paper and tied with plain stout cord—that they looked as if they contained cheap goods of some sort.

From San Diego, O'Banion was taken by John Osterhaus to Mazatlán, Mexico, and from there Herman smuggled him into Kobe, Japan. At Kobe he stayed a day or two with Taymoto. Taymoto was delighted to see him, especially when O'Banion handed him the $5,000 due him for obtaining the Japanese war plans. And then, in the boat previously purchased for Taymoto, he went on to China.

This boat was not only equipped with sails, giving it the innocent appearance of an ordinary fisherman's boat; it also had a high-powered engine. Being under twenty-five feet long, it could be cleared in any port without papers being shown. Taymoto was to be paid for taking this trip with O'Banion, so the two men started across the sea for China. It took them a few days to reach Amoy, a short run.

All plans had been previously made by Duke, and O'Banion knew, if he wished to arrive safely, he must follow these instructions to the letter. They came into the harbor at Amoy at night. And then, in disguise as a fisherman's boat, sailed up the river. They had only some fourteen miles to go. There were certain buildings that Duke had told O'Banion would serve as landmarks. Finally, they came to a rickety old shack. There were lights in it, as people lived here. Beyond this was a landing where some white flags were placed. The next landing, O'Banion knew, was where he was supposed to go.

They anchored the boat in the river, and Taymoto rowed

O'Banion ashore in a dory. Then he went back to the boat and waited. Following the map Duke had given him, O'Banion walked about half a mile inland. Here was the farm, and here Lum Sing and Quong Soo were waiting for him.

"At last!" exclaimed Lum Sing, saluting O'Banion.

"We haven't left this place in almost a week—not knowing just when you would get here," said Quong Soo.

"Well, here I am," said O'Banion, grinning.

He deposited his luggage and the two bundles and went back to the riverbank with Lum Sing. Lum had two bowls filled with coal oil, and a rag hanging over their sides. He lighted first one rag, and then the other. From the boat in the river Taymoto waved a lantern. This was the signal agreed upon.

Taymoto knew that O'Banion was safe and everything was in order. He was to go on home now. But on a certain date and certain hour, two months from now, he was to return to this spot and signal to O'Banion that he was waiting, ready to take him back to Japan.

Just exactly what O'Banion was doing here in China, Taymoto never knew. He was being paid to keep his mouth shut—and if a crazy American wanted to be put ashore in China and do a lot of signaling, that was his business!

The next morning O'Banion looked about him. The farmhouse was made of mud and straw. There were only three small rooms, furnished with homemade benches, a dirt floor—everything was very crude. It was a run-down house, poor and shabby. How could anyone in his right senses suspect this of being a hideout and a meeting place for revolutionists?

The wives of these two farmers were in Canton at this

time—sent there purposely. Women have a habit of asking too many questions. So O'Banion never met them.

Quong Soo had made some bunks in the room at the east, as they were expecting important visitors. It was a dismal, dingy spot—but the food was wonderful! Far better than two such "poor coolie farmers" could afford.

There was no fence around the house, and chickens, ducks, and pigs ran in and out. Near by were other poor farmhouses. There was nothing colorful or exciting about the spot.

O'Banion didn't mind the dirt or the inconveniences. His only worry was two old, mangy chow dogs. A Chinese chow is a one-man dog—and if given the chance will bite hell out of a stranger. O'Banion made friends as best he could with the dogs but managed to stay out of their way as much as possible.

Always, while he was here, either Lum Sing or Quong Soo remained with him. He never left the farm and avoided being seen by the neighbors. The money he kept hidden in the dirt floor under his bunk.

The first day after O'Banion's arrival, Lum Sing took a short trip. He went to meet the various brigand chieftains—and shortly after that they began to arrive, one at a time.

They came in disguise, dressed like coolies, wearing straw hats, black jackets, and the usual Chinese blue trousers. Most of them were barefooted, although occasionally one wore heavy, laced boots. They always came on foot. Anyone seeing them wandering about the countryside would not have given them a second thought. Just a poor farmer trudging along.

It didn't take too long to dispose of each visitor. Now and then there was a little haggling over the price agreed upon, but O'Banion invariably paid off as he was told. Usually the transaction took no more than two or three hours. Once the brigands received the money, they were just as anxious to get away as O'Banion was to have them go.

It must not be thought that the money went into their own pockets. Arms and ammunition were needed for their troops, and the soldiers must be prepared for the coming revolution and the day of liberation.

There was no written word of guarantee that they would fulfill their bargain. However, O'Banion had had enough experience with the Chinese to know that they would not have accepted the money if they had not fully expected to do their part when the time came. Many of them had known and trusted Homer Lea. It was only fair play, so they reasoned, that now Homer Lea should trust them.

With the Manchu Army officers, the procedure was the same. A few of these grumbled at first because they were not being paid in gold. But when the value of American currency was explained to them, and the rate of exchange made clear, they did not quibble.

Just how they made this exchange was no affair of O'Banion's. Probably through roundabout sources the money was turned over to merchants in the various towns. And since there was no Chinese equivalent of the FBI in those days, the matter was easily handled and suspicion was never aroused.

O'Banion also instructed the chieftains in what they were to do. First of all, they were to return to their hideouts in the hills and wait for orders. It might be several years before these would be coming along. Then, when the time came, the brigands were to swoop down upon the Manchu Army; kidnap a whole company, if necessary, but, in any event, take it over. The Manchu officers, already bought and paid for, would quickly surrender. If some Manchu had not as yet been convinced and was still loyal to the Empress Dowager, he was to be killed. But, as Homer Lea said, he didn't want any man shot unless it was absolutely necessary. Better to capture an army from within than from without.

When O'Banion's mission to China was accomplished successfully, it was time for him to return to the United States. On the day and the hour set for Taymoto to appear, O'Banion, together with Lum Sing and Quong Soo, sat on the riverbank waiting. An hour passed. Two hours. Taymoto did not appear. Lum Sing and Quong Soo were plainly worried.

What a nice fix he'd be in if the Japanese didn't arrive! It wasn't a thought O'Banion cared to contemplate. All during his stay in China he had never left the farmhouse. He had never once gone into town, and his only exercise was a walk around the farm late at night. The neighbors had not known of his presence. To be stranded in China would be embarrassing.

Finally, out in the river they saw a lantern being waved. Taymoto had come. The dory was rowed ashore. O'Banion said good-by to Lum Sing and Quong Soo and went back to Kobe. There he was picked up by a boat, all arrangements having been made by Herman Osterhaus. The rest was easy—from Kobe to Mazatlán, then on to San Diego, and finally back again to Los Angeles.

"That much is done," he told Homer Lea. "Everything worked out according to plan. And now for our second step—smuggling into China the soldiers we have been training in this country."

"I'm not going to ask you how it will be done, Captain," said Homer. "But I hope you'll be able to manage it. Good luck!"

It was again time, O'Banion felt, to enlist the help of Duke.

CHAPTER NINETEEN

The Art of Smuggling

BEFORE the soldiers were started on their way to China, several things had to be done. First of all, maneuvers were necessary to complete the training of the troops. Then boats must be obtained and professional smugglers hired to man them. It all took time.

Meanwhile, Homer Lea was writing his book *The Valor of Ignorance*. Westlake Park was only a few blocks from where he was living at the time. Almost every day, when it was bright and sunny, he took an Indian blanket and sat in the park to do his work. He spread out the maps O'Banion had brought him from Japan, studied them, and made notes.

His friends often joined him. They'd sit around asking questions and debating point after point with Homer Lea. It was quite a sight, really—this young lieutenant general in the Chinese Army discussing military tactics in a public park.

Several of his visitors were important men: General Harrison Gray Otis, owner of the *Los Angeles Times;* Marco Newmark, an old friend; various newspaper reporters, among them Harry Carr and Charlie Van Loan. Captain D. P. Quinlin of the United States Army also spent long hours chatting with him. And, following his retirement from the army, Lieutenant General Adna R. Chaffee, who was now living in Los Angeles, was more than ordinarily interested in what Homer Lea was doing.

Now and then, with O'Banion, General Lea took trips up and down the coast, checking on the information afforded him by the Japanese maps. There was yet another reason for these seemingly innocent fishing and hunting trips. Homer Lea was looking for suitable camps in the mountains where the soldiers could be taken for maneuvers. It was not to be done too openly, of course—and nobody was to know the real reason for these camps. First, find the ideal spot. Then on a week end, take along a few of the soldiers. Once established, the number of men could be increased without creating too much suspicion. In the beginning they looked like ordinary hunting parties.

And, on one occasion, it really was. Walter Pixley, O'Banion's old friend from Orange, had a summer home at Arch Beach. He had written to O'Banion saying that five whales were playing offshore from his cottage—and why not come down with a few friends for a week end and have some sport? So, one hot July day, Homer Lea and O'Banion went to the beach with a dozen of the Chinese soldiers. They took along their Mauser rifles. The whales made good targets.

The soldiers lined up in military precision and, in volleys of twelve shots at a time, fired at the whales when they came to the surface. It probably didn't hurt the whales much— but it did give the soldiers good rifle practice.

The first camp to be established was in the Malibu Mountains, back of Santa Monica. Being government land, there was no rent to be paid for it in those days. Once established, the troops would go for a week at a time. They'd leave Los Angeles in a tally-ho, some sixty in each group.

Now and then Duke went with them, and since he liked to cook, he was, with no grumbling on his part, put on permanent duty as mess sergeant. For KP there were always plenty of volunteers. Probably no other company of soldiers in the world have had as much fun on maneuvers as these Chinese.

But Duke had a problem or two of his own. One time, among the live chickens which they always brought along, there was a white rooster who was, as Duke said, "the devil himself!" He'd fight with the other chickens, chase them into the woods, and Duke had his troubles getting them back. Being a plump, fat rooster, Duke had decided to keep him until the final banquet, as a special treat for General Lea and Captain O'Banion. But how to do this was a question. Then Duke had an idea. It was based on an old Chinese custom.

In China, when a thief has been found guilty his hands were encased in a wooden block. So Duke got some melon rind, cut holes in two pieces, and stuck the rooster's feet through the holes. It worked. The rooster could walk all right, but he couldn't chase the hens. And having to drag the melon rind around with him, he became, in time, not only a very well-behaved rooster but fatter and plumper than ever.

Occasionally the soldiers would go on maneuvers to a small town near Los Angeles, called Hollywood. They rented some ground on Sunset Avenue, just north of Norton. In those days a wagon road passed by this property. It was near where the motion-picture studios are now located. There was yet another drill ground on that hilly land at the corner of Sunset and Vermont. Today on this corner is a billboard saying "Free India." But in 1906 the watchword was "Free China!"

In other cities where soldiers were training, there were the same setup and procedure as in Los Angeles. Whenever and wherever possible, maneuvers were held in the near-by countryside. When fully organized and running smoothly, there were in all 2,100 Chinese under arms in this country. But finally their training was completed.

Along in 1906, the first of the soldiers were "graduated" from the Western Military Academy. After three years of training, each soldier was adjudged a gentleman and made an officer in the Chinese Imperial Reform Army. From the day he received his commission he took orders only from General Lea.

The military training of these men had been thorough and efficient. They knew all the tricks and arts of warfare. They had their commissions as officers and also their secret orders. The time for active duty had come. This would be in China.

Over there, they were to enlist as buck privates in the Royal Manchu Army, sometimes as many as three or four in one outfit. And as privates, they were to serve until the day of the revolution came. Then they were to declare themselves for what they really were, come out in the open, and take command of the Royal Manchu Army as officers. When that happened, the Empress would find her army gone like a puff of smoke. She would have nothing with which to fight. Instead, she would be facing not her soldiers, but the Chinese Imperial Reform Army commanded by General Homer Lea.

It was not to be known these soldiers had been secretly trained in the United States. Back in China—once they got there of course—they were instructed to act and behave as if they had always lived in China, and never once were they to mention the fact that they had been in the United States. That was why they had to be smuggled out of this country and into China.

Now, smuggling one or two men in—or out—of the United States was a comparatively simple matter. But sending 2,100 soldiers secretly overseas to China was something else again.

Duke and O'Banion sat down and made their plans as carefully as possible. Nothing must go wrong once the scheme was in operation, or it might blow up in their faces and the revolution be delayed, if not lost entirely, even before it had actually begun. It took many a lengthy discussion but at last they arrived at a plan of action. They hoped it would work satisfactorily. Even then, there were many grave risks and dangers involved.

Boats were needed and also men to sail them—and who knew better than John Osterhaus how to get both boats and men? Fortunately, Duke and O'Banion had already been working, in a small way, through John and Herman Osterhaus. But they needed more help than these two men could give by themselves. However, as Charlie Lung often said, "If I am Potato King, the Osterhaus boys are kings of the smugglers."

It had been through Charlie Lung that O'Banion first met them. One of the favorite hangouts for John Osterhaus in San Francisco was O'Keefe's saloon, down by the Southern Pacific station. John Osterhaus was about seventy at the time, dressed well, a distinguished-looking man, really, and had a friendly and breezy manner. He was liberal and generous with his money. Easy come, easy go. And he was always helping out water-front bums who frequented O'Keefe's saloon. He was never averse to staking a man to a meal ticket or a place to stay and would hand him a $10 or $20 bill as easily as other men would give a dime or a quarter. In this manner, he had built up a big following among the drifters and the underworld characters. They were at hand to be used when he needed them, and they often spoke of him appreciatively as the Old Sea Wolf or the Old Gray Fox.

In time O'Banion, through John Osterhaus, became acquainted with every smuggler from British Columbia to Mexico. Now and then a stranger would come to see O'Banion. He'd say that John Osterhaus had sent him, and could O'Banion use him? He had been told by Osterhaus that O'Banion was to be trusted, and now he wanted to know if there was a job to be done.

O'Banion wasn't afraid these men would betray him or give away the secrets of the revolutionary movement—for one reason. He never told them anything. On every man who asked, he would check and double-check with Osterhaus. Learning that the man was all right, he would hire him—but never personally. He'd have someone else do this for him. Consequently, a lot of the men engaged in the smuggling of the Chinese out of this country never knew definitely of O'Banion's connection with it. Certainly they never knew the real purpose in sending these Chinese to China. In fact, they didn't even know their ultimate destination. Their job was to take the Chinese to Mexico; beyond that, they knew nothing. It is one of the unwritten laws of the underworld not to ask too many questions when paid for a specific job.

One of the first persons engaged for this business was Ed Hall, an officer in the Mexican Navy. Ed had formerly been a fireman in Los Angeles. His wife Ethel, being an enterprising woman, helped in her own way to contribute to the family fortunes. Like Charlie Lung and John Osterhaus, she had a title. She was known as the Queen of the Smugglers. But Ethel made a fatal mistake one day. She was caught, arrested, and sentenced to jail. Ed fled to Mexico and enlisted in the Mexican Navy. At this time the Mexican Navy had one boat—a patrol boat that sailed up and down the west coast for the sole purpose of preventing smuggling. And since Ed knew all the tricks, what a valuable man he was for this navy. He knew what to look for, and he also knew what not to see.

It was necessary to have a secret base in Mexico for the refueling of the boats for their return trip home. Herman Osterhaus made arrangements for this and had a talk with Ed Hall. Whenever the Mexican Navy, on the sharp lookout, came across this refueling, not a word was said. It wasn't even seen. Ed Hall could manage that easily with the $50 paid him each time. So the boats smuggling the Chinese into Mexico, and being refueled in Mexican waters, got by without trouble, and the Mexican government never suspected a thing amiss.

Another boat was needed to refuel in American waters and make contacts with John Osterhaus's boat. A number of boats had been rented from time to time, but O'Banion felt this was too dangerous. It might lead to betrayal. So they began to buy their own. Better to own a boat and hire someone to run it than to take the risk of renting one. The purchase of these boats was never handled by O'Banion.

Instead, Paul Beezoff, the young Russian helper of John Osterhaus, attended to the matter. O'Banion would give him the money, and Paul always paid cash for the boat purchased. The price paid was usually around $3,000. Now and then they had special things put into the boats, like extra tanks. In all, the revolutionary movement eventually came to own five boats.

Once something did go wrong with one of these boats. The boat was a beauty, new and seaworthy. To run this boat Paul engaged two young smugglers—let's call them Joe and Pete. The boat was loaded with oil and provisions to be sent to the secret base in Mexico. All that Joe and Pete knew was that they were to take this boat to a designated spot on the Mexican coast, unload, and then return to San Francisco.

The oil was got aboard in San Francisco Bay without any trouble, and Joe and Pete started off. At the Cliff House their engine went wrong. The boat started drifting toward shore. There was a heavy sea flowing, and any moment the boat was liable to go on the rocks. The two men did what they could to get the engine started, but to no avail. It looked as if the boat would be lost—and their lives with it.

The Coast Guard, always on the alert, saw their distress and came to the rescue.

"Do you need help?"

"We sure as hell do!" replied Pete.

So the Coast Guard stood by and managed to tow the boat to safety. In ordinary circumstances, everything would have been all right. But the Coast Guard saw two things not in order. First, the boat was loaded with drums of oil; and when they began to ask questions, they discovered that the boat was not registered. So Joe and Pete were taken off to headquarters.

"Where are you going?" was the first question asked.

"To San Pedro," replied Pete, who could lie with a straight face, and had been in jams like this before.

"Why?"

"To deliver the boat."

"To whom?"

"I don't know."

"What are those drums of oil aboard for?" the officer asked next.

"We don't know. The boat was loaded when we were hired. All we know is that we're supposed to take it to San Pedro."

"But who hired you?"

"We don't know."

"What's his name?"

"We didn't ask."

By this time the officer was becoming exasperated. "Don't know—you didn't ask! Tell me what happened, in your own words."

"Well," said Pete, "this guy comes up to us and says do we want to earn some money? And I says we sure do. So he says, 'Take this here boat to San Pedro, tie it up there to a certain place, and here's your money.' So he gave us $25 and return fare to Frisco—and that's how it happened."

That was their story and they stuck to it. It really sounded reasonable enough to the officer. He asked Joe and Pete their names and addresses. The men told him the truth. A quick checking by the Coast Guard proved they hadn't lied. Then, after three hours of questioning, they were let go.

But Joe and Pete had had sufficient experience on former occasions to know what would happen next. They would be followed, and their every move watched. They made it as easy for the Coast Guard as possible. Acting as if they had nothing to hide, they drifted into a bar and had a drink. For the rest of that day and into the early evening they re-

mained there, having a great deal of fun wearing out the
men trailing them.

There was nothing suspicious about their actions, and in
a day or two the Coast Guard, finding no evidence of anything wrong with these two young men, dropped the whole
matter. Immediately Joe got in touch with Paul Beezoff and
told him what had happened. Paul got in touch with
O'Banion.

"Pay 'em off just as if they had done the job, and then
forget about 'em," said O'Banion.

Paul did, and that's the last O'Banion ever heard of these
two men. He was grateful that he hadn't appeared in the
picture and hadn't hired Joe and Pete himself. Working
undercover, it was always best to act undercover. What became of the boat, he never knew or cared. And, obviously,
he never made any inquiries. The only thing to do was to
purchase another boat and go on as if nothing had happened.

Not one of the five boats purchased was ever owned by
O'Banion. He was only the paymaster, using the funds of
the Po Wong Wui. The members of this society did not
know exactly for what purpose the money was being used.
They did not care. They were interested only in results!

There was never a murmur or a question from the Chinese. Nor was the boat lost by Joe and Pete the only one
seized by the government. One of the boats, named the *May,*
was tied up at a dock in San Diego. The government agents
became suspicious and, not being able to discover the owner,
seized the boat. There was a long and baffling investigation,
but nothing definite was discovered. However, somewhere
along the line someone talked out of turn. Just who, O'Ban-

ion never knew. One day, however, Deputy United States
Marshal Dingle came to see him in Los Angeles.

"They've got that boat down there in San Diego and want
to give it back to you. The investigation is finished, and the
government is done with it."

O'Banion smelled a mouse of some sort or other. Was
Dingle trying to trap him?

He assumed an air of great surprise and innocence and
said, "Boat? What boat? I don't know anything about any
boats. I run a hay and feed market, I'm not a seafaring
man."

"The boat's yours if you want it," insisted Dingle.
"Thought you might like to use it now and then."

"Thanks, pal," said O'Banion. "But when I want to go
for a ride, I'll go on horseback—and on my own horse, too!"

"You're not so dumb," said Dingle, laughing, and confessed he had used this method in the hope of trapping him,
but it hadn't worked.

"Why should it?" answered O'Banion.

And so the matter was dropped. Later it annoyed O'Banion when the boat was sold at public auction in the United
States marshal's office—and Japanese bought it. They used
it to tow slop barges to a hog ranch on an island near San
Diego Bay!

As soon as all the boats needed were on hand and the
men hired to run them, the next step was taken. A well-
known Chinese merchant in Mazatlán was approached by
Duke. This merchant sent back word that he would be only
too glad to receive and entertain any visiting "cousins" who
might be coming his way from the United States. He would
see that they had a place to live, something to eat, and
would give them directions as to their next move.

"Just tell them to come see me immediately upon arrival in Mazatlán. I shall be most happy to greet them," he said. For a long time he had been paying his dues regularly to the Po Wong Wui.

Everything was now in order. The time had come for the secret "troop movement." It meant bringing across the continent the soldiers who had been trained in the East—New York, Boston, Philadelphia—and in all the other cities where there were companies. But they obviously could not cross the continent in a body. If the whole company came on one train, it would arouse suspicion. Nor could they all leave this country at one and the same time. They must be sent out in dribbles. Each boat could hold only around twenty-eight to thirty-two men. So, in all, nearly one hundred trips would have to be made. It would take several years.

But a plan was worked out, and it was the same scheme for every company in each city. All these soldiers—future officers in the Revolutionary Army, it was hoped—were intelligent young men. They knew their way around. They had passed every test and were in excellent physical condition. Of them all, only some forty failed to go. These men were sick or in failing health—and it was decided, anyway, that some few should remain here to serve as undercover contact men in case anything might go wrong.

The plan was this, and it worked beautifully: in small groups, three to eight at a time, from New York, for instance, the soldiers bought tickets to San Francisco. They were going there to visit relatives or friends, so they said. Others made it plain that they would engage in business in that city. The New York company would arrive thus in small groups; nor would they report at the Armory in San Francisco.

Scattered throughout the city were agents, the only men who knew who these soldiers really were and exactly why they were in San Francisco. Not even the soldiers in the city knew that these were soldiers from New York. It wasn't wise, O'Banion thought, to let your right hand know what your left hand was doing.

Immediately upon arrival, the soldiers would report to the agent. Then they would visit with friends and relatives. Should anyone ask what they were doing, it was the usual answer, "Here to visit."

"How long?"

"Week maybe. Two weeks maybe. Then back home again," would be the answer. "Home," in each instance, meant to the questioner the city he had come from—but to the soldiers it meant China. They did not, however, tell anyone their ultimate destination. And not a single one ever gave away the secret.

So they were dined and wined and entertained and had a good time "visiting." They didn't bother much about having a proper haircut, however. They knew well that by the time they arrived in China they would have to wear queues. But not for too long, they hoped.

In time, the full number for one boat load would be on hand. The agents had made their report that some thirty-two were here and accounted for. The day for their departure had arrived.

But they couldn't walk down to the docks in San Francisco Bay and board a smuggler's boat for Mexico. It couldn't be done as openly as all that.

The agent had his instructions. In groups of two and three the Chinese soldiers would leave San Francisco. Some would buy tickets to Pajaro, a small town near Watsonville, a seaport on the coast not far from San Francisco. Others would go by car. At Pajaro was a Chinese laundry.

It was more than a laundry, for in the back room were rows and rows of the poorest sort of Chinese clothes. The soldiers changed from their snappy new suits—often purchased especially for their visit to San Francisco—and donned these slovenly suits. From now on, until they finally put on the uniforms of the Royal Manchu Army, they were to dress and act like coolies. They were to show as little intelligence as possible, and the sloppier they appeared the better it would be. Too many well-clad Chinese arriving in Mexico from the United States might cause unnecessary questioning. They were even told to walk in Chinese fashion, shuffle along; if anyone spoke to them, "No speakee English," was to be the answer. It was a disguise of a sort—and a good one.

A necessary precaution, too. Suppose the boat they were on should be picked up by the Coast Guard, what then? The answer was simple. They were Chinese being smuggled into the United States—not out!

Dressed in this fashion, at a given time at night, they were to make their way to a certain cottage by the sea. One man was told to go first. If everything was in order, he returned to the others waiting in the shadows. They would then, one at a time, make their way to the cottage. And here they were told to wait.

It was rather easy to identify the right spot. Either O'Banion or Paul Beezoff was not far away. But once, with a boatload of soldiers on hand, they came very near being caught.

CHAPTER TWENTY

A Picnic on the Beach

IT HAD taken several months for O'Banion, in company with Paul Beezoff, to find this particular spot. In the back of his Studebaker car, he had a complete camping outfit. They traveled up and down the coast—ostensibly on an outing—but in reality searching for the exact spot to suit their needs. They found it on the beach near Port Watsonville.

It was ideal. Watsonville was a small town some ninety miles from San Francisco. A little streetcar ran once an hour, during the daytime only, between the town and the beach called Port Watsonville, about three miles away. If you missed the last car at night, you had to walk home. Therefore, at night, the beach was deserted. There were three small cottages here, two of them empty. The other was a small store located on the stub of a wharf that had been washed away during a storm.

The store was run by a redheaded man named Sandy— probably, O'Banion thought, the homeliest man he had ever seen. He had a wife and a small, freckled four-year-old daughter, who was no prize beauty, either. But she was susceptible to flattery. And when O'Banion told her how pretty she was, she'd giggle, blush, then run and hide behind her mother's skirts. Sandy's family lived in the back of the store— not much of a store, really. He sold fishing tackle, bait, soft drinks, cigars, and sometimes sandwiches to parties that came now and then to the beach for a picnic. But it wasn't a particularly popular spot. And at night, except for Sandy and his family, who went to bed early, there was nobody around. No lights even. So almost anything could go on here without fear of discovery. O'Banion rented one of the cottages and Paul the other. They wanted to be alone!

Sandy was an easy man to handle. He wasn't suspicious of anyone, except perhaps now and then a customer who tried to short-change him. When O'Banion wished to get him out of the way, he'd tell him some people in Watsonville wanted to buy clams—and into town Sandy would go, taking his whole family with him.

When the Chinese appeared, walking down the car tracks, they would vanish inside the cottage. They had been told to remain there, and not even to talk above a whisper. Nor were they to come out under any circumstances until told to do so. Outside the cottage, Paul Beezoff had a campfire and a big kettleful of stew, so the Chinese never went hungry. Sandy became so accustomed to the sight of the kettle always on the fire, that he never gave it another thought.

Everything, of course, must work on schedule. The soldiers must arrive at a certain time—and the boat, coming from San Francisco, must be there on time, also. Had anyone seen the boat offshore he would have thought it a fisherman's boat and let it go at that. The skipper of the boat would signal his presence to O'Banion by flashing a lantern. To let him know everything was in readiness, O'Banion would light a beach fire. The wood was always piled up and waiting.

Seeing the beach fire, the skipper would come in as close to shore as he could and drop anchor just outside the breakers. Then a dory with one man rowing would come ashore and beach the boat.

From the cottage, single file, would come the Chinese. A few at a time, while the others stood waiting, would get into the dory. Paul would help it through the breakers, and the dory would transfer the men to the boat and come back for another load. When all were aboard, the boat would start off for Mexico—and another group of officers in the Chinese Reform Army were on their way to China to become privates in the army of the hated Empress Dowager.

Nor were there ever any telltale footprints left in the sand on the beach. O'Banion made what he called a Holligan's pup. This was two pieces of wood fashioned in the form of a T, four feet long and four feet wide, the crosspiece driven full of spikes. It worked like a cultivator, and when the Chinese started down the beach, the last man would drag Holligan's pup behind him to cover their tracks.

The use of this beach at Watsonville was really something of a necessity. One of the boats was tied near a laundry in South San Francisco. That spot obviously couldn't be used for loading Chinese. Another boat was anchored near the coal bunkers at the foot of Franklin Street. Too much activity there would arouse suspicion. But on the deserted beach near Port Watsonville, Chinese soldiers could go aboard a boat without anyone's being the wiser.

However, one evening O'Banion and Paul were waiting for a group of soldiers from St. Louis, Mo., to report for shipment. Paul was cooking supper on the campfire back of the cottage—and getting the large kettle of stew ready for the expected men.

From the top of the sand dunes, near an old, tumble-down once-upon-a-time dance pavilion came a "Ho-Ho" in a woman's voice.

The two men, startled, looked up. There stood a young woman waving to them.

"Hello, down there! What are you doing? That coffee smells good," she said.

Paul looked at O'Banion with apprehension.

But O'Banion replied, trying to sound as casual as possible, "Come on down and have a cup!"

"Wait until I get my gang," she answered.

Soon three women and a small boy appeared. It didn't take long for O'Banion to find out who they were. The two younger women were nurses from a hospital in San Francisco, here in Watsonville having a vacation visiting their aunt. This woman was the mother of the boy, a sickly lad about nine years old, and she also was, so she proudly informed O'Banion, the wife of the mayor of Watsonville!

They were out here for the day, having a picnic on the beach.

"We didn't see you around," said Paul.

"We didn't know you were here, either," said the mayor's wife.

Then they told O'Banion they were going to catch the last car back to town.

"What's your hurry?" said O'Banion. "Have a cup of coffee. To heck with the streetcar. I'll drive you home in my automobile."

Better to pretend they didn't want to get rid of them than to arouse suspicion, he thought. And, too, knowing the mayor's wife might be of advantage.

"You boys have a lot of stew cooking there," said one of the nurses.

"Yeah," replied Paul. "We're heavy eaters."

"Have some," said O'Banion.

So they shared their simple supper with these women and about eight o'clock O'Banion drove them to town.

"We'll be back again tomorrow!" they said.

O'Banion groaned inwardly. But there was nothing he could do about it. The visiting nurses were lonely. Also, they had seen Paul Beezoff—and what they saw they liked. He was a very handsome young Russian, tanned and weather-beaten by the sea. Happy-go-lucky and bighearted, he was popular with the ladies. Well educated, too.

As they sat around eating their supper, he sang some old Russian folk songs. The nurses and the mayor's wife were enchanted. He could yodel a bit, as well. That, also, went over big!

So the next day they were back. In the meantime, the Chinese had arrived and were hidden in the cottage. The boat would not put in an appearance for a couple of days. It was up to O'Banion and Paul to entertain the visiting nurses from San Francisco. Had it been an ordinary outing, they would have enjoyed it. But there was too much on their minds to relax and indulge in romantic adventures. The nurses had nothing to do but enjoy themselves. And they thought Paul sang beautifully. He should go on the stage!

They came down to the cottage and shared their picnic lunch with Paul and O'Banion. They all went for a swim together—with the mayor's wife acting as chaperon. All the time they were playing around the beach, the Chinese from St. Louis were hidden in the cottage. But, properly, O'Banion never invited the ladies inside.

That night both O'Banion and Paul drove the girls and the mayor's wife back home. The mayor asked them in. They accepted and had a good time.

The mayor was a jolly fellow. He offered the boys drinks,

but Paul and O'Banion declined. They said they didn't touch the stuff. That made a hit with the mayor. He politely inquired about their business, of course. Paul said he worked in a hardware store in San Diego, and O'Banion replied that he was a buyer for a sporting goods store in Los Angeles. They told the mayor this was their vacation—and they liked camping out. He thought it was a fine idea, said he knew the girls were in good hands, and for them to show his nieces a nice time!

"We'll do our best, sir," replied Paul, politely.

Then he yodeled a bit for the mayor. The mayor enjoyed it. He said when he was younger he used to play the accordion, but in the last few years he had been so busy he didn't have time to practice any more.

One of the nurses asked Paul if he had ever been to San Francisco.

"Now and then," replied Paul.

"The next time you are there, look us up," said the nurse. "We'll take you two boys to Chinatown for chop suey."

Paul made a wry face. "I never eat the stuff," he said.

O'Banion confessed he didn't like it, either. He also said he didn't like the Chinese and certainly never wanted to do business with them.

This brought on quite a discussion. But O'Banion stuck to his guns and didn't have a favorable word to say about the Chinese. He had to admit, however, that he had never known any personally. Paul kept a straight face.

When it came time to go home, the girls said, happily, "See you again tomorrow!"

"Yeah, sure," said Paul, and gave a yodel as a farewell gesture.

When they got back to the beach the first thing Paul and

O'Banion did was have a good stiff drink. They needed it! Especially since tomorrow the boat was due from San Francisco!

The next morning, being the last day of their vacation, the nurses and the mayor's wife arrived on the beach early.

"Let's go clam hunting," suggested Paul. He knew a good spot, so he said, way up the beach.

But O'Banion said he wasn't feeling up to snuff and didn't want to go along. After all, someone had to remain near the cottage and see to it that the Chinese were fed. So, off went Paul with the women. He had previously promised O'Banion not to yodel until such time as they were headed in the direction of the cottage.

The mayor's wife wanted to leave her boy behind with O'Banion. She called the lad her little sick kitten, and while the others romped around the beach she would spread out a blanket for him, and he'd lie down.

But the boy, to O'Banion's delight, didn't want to be left behind and began to cry. It was the first and the last time in his life O'Banion was really pleased to see a weeping child. But he wiped away the boy's tears and told him to run along with his mother. He said that two sick men would be poor company for each other.

This was one of those days when he told Sandy that people in town wanted clams, so he had the place to himself. Knowing that the trip to Mexico was a hard one, he kept the stew cooking all day long. The Chinese had so much to eat that they were ready to burst. But it was a wise precaution. They wouldn't have hot food again until their arrival in Mexico.

That night the girls didn't want to go home as early as formerly. After all, it was their last evening together; and even though they had managed to make Paul promise to visit them in San Francisco someday, they didn't want to leave too early. One of the girls spotted the beach fire, all ready to be lighted—the signal for the dory to come in to shore for the Chinese.

"Paul," she cried, "how nice of you! Look, auntie, a beach fire—all fixed!"

Looking out to sea, O'Banion saw a lantern being waved. The boat had arrived and was waiting for the signal to put the dory ashore. To light the beach fire would mean they were ready to send the Chinese aboard.

Before Paul could stop her, one of the nurses had touched a match to the pile of wood. It burst into flame. There was no way now to prevent the skipper from bringing in the dory.

O'Banion looked at Paul and shrugged his shoulders in dismay. Paul gave a halfhearted grin.

It wasn't long until they heard the sound of a dory being pulled up on the sands. The skipper strolled up.

"Hello, stranger?" said O'Banion, looking at him as if he had never seen him before.

The skipper took his cue immediately. Seeing the women, he sensed immediately that something was wrong.

"What you folks doing here?" he asked.

"Just having a little picnic," replied O'Banion. "Come join us?"

"Don't mind if I do," replied the skipper.

"What you doing here?" asked O'Banion.

"Just a little night fishing."

"Caught any?"

"Not yet!"

"Maybe the fish are scared of these women and afraid to come out," said O'Banion.

Paul let out a loud guffaw. The women protested jokingly that they wouldn't frighten anybody. But the skipper got the idea.

Finally, as it was growing late, the women said it was time to go on home. Without a moment's hesitation, O'Banion gallantly offered as usual to drive them in. They wanted Paul to come along, too. But Paul, to O'Banion's delight and satisfaction, suddenly discovered he had a bad headache and thought he'd better remain behind rather than make it worse by a ride over the rough road to Watsonville.

"Don't forget, now," said one of the nurses when they were making their good-bys, "that you've a date with us in Frisco."

"I won't forget," said Paul.

"We'll take you fellows to dinner in Chinatown—have chop suey—and I bet you'll learn to like it."

"At least I can try," grinned Paul.

On the way into town O'Banion admitted to the girls that he was just as happy that Paul did remain behind.

"I didn't quite like the looks of that fisherman," he said. "If both of us had come in town, he might have swiped some of our camping stuff."

"I didn't quite like his looks, either," admitted the mayor's wife. "You can't be too careful these days. Never know who you're liable to meet up with."

"Ain't it the truth," grinned O'Banion.

When he got back Paul was sitting quietly smoking—and the Chinese were gone. It had been a close shave.

"How's your headache now?" he asked Paul.

"I really got one," replied Paul. "Two good-looking gals —and what a time! Never before in my life have I wanted so badly to get rid of a couple of women. If it hadn't been for those Chinese— Oh, what the hell!"

When the girls got back to San Francisco they wrote to Paul. But Paul never answered, and in time he lost track of them. However, he and O'Banion did go to Chinatown often for dinner. They had real Chinese food, too, not chop suey—but they never took the girls.

Following this episode, O'Banion and Paul decided it would be best to try to find another spot. So they walked down to Moss's Landing, two or three miles below. Here they found a most desirable place—and also met up with a couple of Mexican girls. One of them, named Esperanza, had had an unfortunate love affair with a soldier. When her baby arrived, her family completely disowned her. But she didn't care any more. There were plenty of other men in the world besides the soldier who had gone AWOL on her. And Paul was a handsome chap.

She did, however, have a job as housekeeper with the sheriff in Salinas. So Paul cultivated her acquaintance, and Esperanza told him a great deal about the sheriff and his family. She also told Paul that Moss's Landing was under suspicion as being a spot where smugglers unloaded their goods and that the sheriff had two men watching the place. She thought Paul and O'Banion were those two men!

They quickly decided to have nothing to do with Moss's Landing and continued using the beach at Port Watsonville. They were not there all the time, of course—but now and then came for a camping trip. And so, slowly but surely, the soldiers were sent to China.

They were taken, first of all, to Mazatlán in Mexico.

Since there was a large Chinese colony there, and it was quite a big seaport, a few strange Chinese walking the streets aroused no comment. From Mazatlán, Herman Osterhaus took the men to Kobe, where Taymoto was waiting to do his part. Osterhaus knew all sorts of beachcombers in Kobe who were willing to help him get the Chinese off the boats. Then it was up to Taymoto to escort the soldiers to Amoy.

The farmhouse at Amoy was their first point of contact in China. From here, Lum Sing and Quong Soo sent them on to their destinations—all carefully worked out in advance. Under no circumstances must the spies of the Empress Dowager know that these men had been trained as soldiers in the United States. Therefore, slowly and carefully, one by one, the men scattered over China and enlisted as quickly as they could in the Royal Manchu Army.

Some went into the hills and joined the brigands. Some few others were used as go-betweens, messengers, to contact by devious ways the soldiers serving under the flag of the enemy. It was a vast and intricate system—but there it was, a secret army within an army waiting patiently for the day when they could rise up and free China.

And then in November of 1908, overnight, the whole picture changed. The revolutionary movement was in a turmoil. Startling news had come from China. The Boy Emperor was dead.

CHAPTER TWENTY-ONE

Music for the Brigands

DURING the years that followed Homer Lea's return to this country from China he had been in constant communication with Kuang Hsu, the Boy Emperor. One of the secret agents whom Homer Lea had planted at the court of the Empress Dowager was Kuang Hsu's personal doctor. He could come and go as he pleased, even though the Boy Emperor was a prisoner in his own palace. During the summer of 1908, through this doctor, had come disturbing messages from Kuang Hsu.

He was troubled and frightened. Rumors had reached him that the Empress Dowager was plotting to get rid of him. He didn't know how or when the blow would fall. He wrote frantically to Homer Lea and Kang Yu-wei, begging them to hurry and release him. The time was growing shorter.

Then news came in September that the Empress Dowager was seriously ill. Should she die, Kuang Hsu would be restored to his throne. But the Empress Dowager, even on her deathbed, had other plans. Had she made a secret treaty with Japan? Who knows exactly? But it fitted in nicely with her schemes that Kuang Hsu should die before she did. He passed away early in November of 1908. Rumor has it that the Empress Dowager had him poisoned by her favorite eunuch, Li Lien-ying.

Immediately, as was the custom with the Manchu Dynasty,

the Empress Dowager named as her successor the five-year-old boy, Prince Pu Yi, the son of Kuang Hsu's brother, Prince Chun. He was brought to the palace at midnight, a crying, shy, frightened youngster, and crowned Emperor of China. A few days later the Empress Dowager Tsu Hsi died.

(Today Henry Pu Yi, as he is known to the world, is the Puppet Emperor of the Manchu Dynasty. He lives at the present moment in Manchuria, under the protection of the Japanese flag. The only nation that recognizes him as the rightful and legal ruler of China is Japan! Should the Army of the Republic of China under the leadership of Generalissimo Chiang Kai-shek be defeated and lose this present war, Henry Pu Yi will return to Peiping and ascend the Dragon Throne, and the Manchu Dynasty, under the dictatorship of Japan, will again rule all China. It is not necessary to tell the Chinese soldiers today what they are fighting for. They know! Preserve the Republic of China and continue to build and ultimately achieve a truly democratic form of government for the Chinese people.)

But in 1908 the revolution had not yet occurred, and the Manchus were still in power. However, upon the death of the Empress Dowager, the internal affairs of the Manchu Dynasty were in a turmoil. There was no strong, forceful, outstanding leader. The Emperor was a lad of five, under the supervision of regents.

Even in America, among the revolutionists, there was doubt and indecision. The motto of the Po Wong Wui—"Liberate the Boy Emperor"—no longer had meaning. With the death of Kuang Hsu, Kang Yu-wei considered himself not only the leader of the revolutionary movement, but also the head of the coming government in China. Among his political opponents there was a whispering campaign that

Kang Yu-wei was personally ambitious, and if he had the opportunity would make himself the ruler of China. But it was no secret that he was openly in favor of continuing the Manchu Dynasty in power with a constitutional monarchy as the government of China.

However, his popularity with the members of the Po Wong Wui was waning. More and more, the Chinese in America were flocking to the support of Dr. Sun Yat-sen.

Dr. Sun wanted only to free China. He had no personal ambitions, wanted nothing for himself, but devoted his life to what he felt was right—the liberation of his people from centuries of oppression. Who would head the government? It didn't matter so long as it was someone who would be acceptable to the Chinese as a whole. In America he had seen at first hand the workings of a people's government. That was what Dr. Sun wanted for China.

He would often say, "The political tendency of this age is toward democracy. The struggle for democracy began with the American War for Independence. . . . One hundred and fifty years ago the American colonies freed themselves from Britain, and set up a republican form of government which has been one of the most valuable political experiments in human history. . . . Ever since that time the struggle for democracy and liberty has taken place all over the world. In spite of its many difficulties and drawbacks, the democratic movement has been preeminently successful. Inasmuch as democracy is the political tendency of the day, China also should advance toward it."

It was that sort of political philosophy which Dr. Sun Yat-sen preached as he went about the world—often in disguise and with a price on his head—to wherever there were Chinese. There is no doubt he was often in this country, unknown to Homer Lea and O'Banion, talking to the members of the Po Wong Wui and attempting to swing them over to his point of view.

That was, therefore, the situation in 1908 when the Boy Emperor died. There was no question but that the present Manchu government would ultimately fall. What form of government would take its place? Kang Yu-wei wanted a constitutional monarchy. Dr. Sun Yat-sen wanted a republic.

Homer Lea, in the very center of this life-and-death struggle, felt that, unless these two men got together and agreed, the whole revolutionary movement might fail. Two opposing forces working against each other in a revolution might completely wreck every plan made and every achievement so far completed. He had but one purpose—to do what he could to make Kang Yu-wei and Dr. Sun see this thing eye to eye. And it meant that one of the two men must step out of the picture.

Homer Lea was, however, on the side of Dr. Sun and had been from the very first. He foresaw a republic for China— the day of emperors and kings was drawing to a close. Yet he knew that in the beginning, as Dr. Sun had advised him, it would be necessary to proceed cautiously. First implant in men's minds the necessity for a revolution; make them see what it meant to be a free people. Organize the revolutionary movement—then use it for the founding of a republic.

Kang Yu-wei was, of course, quite aware of the ideas of Dr. Sun. He also knew what was happening in this country, where the Chinese had seen for themselves the benefits to be derived from a democratic form of government. Like Dr. Sun, he paid several secret visits here. And on the death of the Boy Emperor he came once again.

Many discussions and arguments took place in Homer Lea's home near Westlake Park. One night O'Banion received a telephone call to come over. It was long after midnight, but O'Banion went. When he arrived, Kang Yu-wei and Homer Lea were in the midst of a violent argument.

"Dr. Sun's following is growing by leaps and bounds!" said Homer Lea. "Yours is diminishing. The right thing for you to do is to get together and pull in the same direction. Sun is willing to do everything possible. He says he's tired of this delay and dillydallying—and God knows there's been lots of it!"

But Kang Yu-wei beat his chest and exclaimed that he was the only leader of the revolutionary movement. He was opposed to a republic for China. Dr. Sun was a madman. A democracy in China? It would never succeed. The Chinese people would not accept it.

The argument went on until morning, with Homer Lea winding up by saying, "If you don't throw in your lot with Dr. Sun, we'll never get anywhere. Already we are delayed."

But Kang Yu-wei was adamant. He didn't quite believe or accept the real truth of the matter. He still had his following, he felt—royalists, who believed as he did.

During this visit, Kang Yu-wei often addressed the troops. He spoke to them as his army. The soldiers responded in typical Chinese fashion: listened politely, applauded—and then went about minding their own sweet business. On the surface they seemed to agree with Kang Yu-wei, but in reality they did not. They received all their orders from Homer Lea, and accepted them gladly. What Kang Yu-wei did not know or suspect was that the soldiers were all loyal followers of Dr. Sun and in their hearts acknowledged him as the real leader of the revolution.

One night, after Kang Yu-wei had left Los Angeles, there was a ring on Homer Lea's doorbell. When he answered it, there stood Dr. Sun Yat-sen—alone. He had come to this country to confer with Homer Lea in private. The only Chinese who knew he was here was Duke, who had again smuggled him in. This time there were no banquets in his honor, and he made no appearances in Chinatown. During this visit he remained quietly at Homer Lea's home. They lived at Long Beach, where they knew they would not be disturbed.

In the conferences that were held, a great deal was accomplished. It was at this time that the final plans for the coming revolution were perfected. But while no Chinese visitors came and went, several important men came to meet and talk with Dr. Sun, among them Lieutenant General Adna R. Chaffee and Major General J. P. Story. These generals often gave their advice, but most of the conferences were between Dr. Sun and Homer Lea.

All day long they pored over maps. Maps were everywhere—on the tables, pinned to the walls. With colored pins, Homer Lea checked and rechecked troop movements. Dr. Sun's eyes twinkled, and he agreed.

As Homer Lea moved a pin from this point to that, he told Dr. Sun of the soldiers already planted in the Royal Manchu Army, and where others would be placed as soon as they reached China. He showed how the triangle from Nanking to Hankow to Shanghai would collapse like a balloon when the revolution occurred.

It was to start at Hankow, the narrow point of the triangle. As the narrow point moved in, with the enemy armies in front, their forces would diminish fast. As the armies were taken over by the revolutionists, the distances to be covered would grow less and less. It was the pincer movement—like the two arms of a pincers squeezing until the whole thing gave way.

But Dr. Sun was worried about one point. Were all the men needed in this area taken care of? Were there others, besides those already planted, who should be bought over? Also, what about the followers of Kang Yu-wei in China? Shouldn't something be done about them? There were certain viceroys who would be helpful—and certain others, once persuaded, who could be won over to this cause. Also, some of these viceroys had sons who were eager to do their part in the coming revolution and wanted military experience. Could they be brought to this country and trained here?

"Can it be done?" Homer Lea asked O'Banion.

O'Banion tightened his belt. "Smuggling men out of this country is one thing. The government doesn't care too much. But bringing men in is another matter. However, I don't see why not. It may mean I'll have to take another trip to China to make arrangements."

On this second trip O'Banion didn't go alone, nor did he spend all his time at the farm near Amoy. He took with him a Chinese brass band from Los Angeles. And they played—not in the towns and cities—but in the mountain hideouts of the brigand chieftains. Hearing the latest popular song hits from America played by a brass band in the Chinese manner was a new and novel experience for the brigands.

It was Homer Lea's idea. Knowing how the Chinese love music, he felt it would be a wonderful morale builder if the band went with O'Banion. It would go a long way toward showing the Chinese in China what was being done in this country and would add a note of gaiety and freshness to the grim plotting of a revolution. There were sixteen musicians in all—and good ones. Whenever they had appeared in public in Los Angeles, they had always made a great hit.

Homer Lea wanted all sixteen to go to China, but O'Banion felt that would be too many musicians to manage conveniently and comfortably. Four were all he thought he could handle. However, they finally compromised on eight. And then trouble started. Which eight of the sixteen should go? Each musician wanted to be included. It took all the tact and diplomacy O'Banion possessed to settle the matter amicably.

The musicians wanted to draw straws to decide. But that wouldn't do. There was the tuba player, for example. Now, as everyone knows, the tuba is a big brass instrument, heavy and unwieldy. It gives a deep and hearty tum-tum-tum in accompaniment to the melody. Homer Lea felt certain the tuba would make a great impression on brigands who had never seen one. However, as O'Banion suggested, smuggling men out of this country and into China was enough of a problem; why complicate matters by lugging along—of all things—a tuba?

No; the only way to decide who should go would be by the size of the instrument to be carried, and not by the ability of the player. And that's how the matter was settled. The tuba player was disappointed, of course. He blamed himself for lacking foresight. He said he should have been smart enough and wise enough in the beginning to take up the flute or the cornet.

So into Mazatlán, Mexico, went O'Banion with eight Chinese musicians, concealing their instruments as best they could, tagging along after him. Herman Osterhaus got them all on the same boat for Kobe—but O'Banion, once on board, never spoke to them or had any contact with them on the way over.

They remained long enough at the farm near Amoy for Lum Sing to get in touch with a brigand chieftain who was somewhat dubious about joining the army of the revolution. Then one night, O'Banion and the band, guided by Lum Sing, went into the mountains to the hideout of this brigand chieftain. They remained there two or three days. The brigands had never seen American musical instruments. They marveled at them and, since the band could play Chinese classical music as well as the latest American song hit, the chieftain was much impressed. There was one cornetist who was something of a clown. He would make a great show of hitting a high note, bending far over on one foot— and then rising up as the clear, sweet note burst forth. The brigand chieftain no longer had any doubts. The music pleased him and the cornetist amused him.

His entire, ragged army was placed at the disposal of the revolutionists. Homer Lea had been right. Convincing soldiers to join a revolutionary party by playing music to them —only the Chinese would do things that way. Taking the brass band to China proved a good investment. Quite a number of brigand chieftains were won over in this manner.

There was constant trouble in China between the soldiers of these brigand chieftains and the Manchu Army. Often the brigands would swoop down upon a village, rob and loot it. It was the way they made their living. The soldiers were not paid a regular wage but shared with their chieftain in the loot. The Manchu Army did their best to put a stop to this practice and there were numerous skirmishes between the two forces. Whenever possible, the Manchus arrested the brigands.

Each viceroy in the city had his own army, of course, paid for by the Empress. What Dr. Sun chiefly wanted O'Banion to do on this second visit was to bring the bandit chieftains and the armies of the viceroys together, unite them in a common cause, so that when the revolution broke they would all be fighting on the same side.

O'Banion began buying up the viceroys. They came to the farm at Amoy, disguised as coolies. The list of those to be approached had been furnished O'Banion by Dr. Sun. The agents of the revolutionary party in China had already made certain that these men were in favor of the coming revolution. O'Banion's task was to furnish them with money. The price varied, according to the standing of the viceroy. Some received as high as $5,000.

Nor was that all O'Banion was supposed to do. Dr. Sun had promised some of these viceroys that their sons could receive training as soldiers in the United States. He had given O'Banion the list of names. In all, there was some 250 sons. And it was up to O'Banion to see that they were smuggled into the United States. It was a tough assignment.

O'Banion proceeded with great care. To each viceroy he gave the name of a Chinese merchant in Mazatlán.

"Tell your son to go to Mazatlán and contact this merchant," he said. "Arriving there, he will be told what to do next. There will be many hardships."

"My son understands that."

"He will have to do exactly as he is instructed all along the line."

"My son has been well-trained in obedience."

"He will have to cut his queue."

"He will gladly make that sacrifice!"

"How he will manage to get to Mexico is none of my business."

"It can be arranged," smiled the viceroy.

And it was. Coming back on the boat to Mexico with O'Banion were some sixty Chinese lads. But none of them acknowledged him. They were regular passengers on the boat, their papers in order—their purpose apparent. This trip to Mexico was purely an educational tour of wealthy and well-bred young Chinese gentlemen.

The boat docked at Mazatlán, and O'Banion, picked up in the launch by John Osterhaus, came on home to Los Angeles by the backdoor of Neely's store in San Diego. The Chinese viceroys' sons were to follow later.

Plans for bringing them into the United States had been carefully worked out in advance. Duke had had a long conference with Herman Osterhaus, who knew all the tricks of smuggling men and goods into California from Mexico. The two of them made the arrangements.

As Duke said to O'Banion, "You told me some sixty on the boat with you landed in Mazatlán on their strictly educational tour of Mexico. Now, sixty can't come into the United States in a body, nor can they walk across the border without being seen. What they must do first of all is disappear. But that's easy."

He outlined the entire scheme to O'Banion, step by step. First of all, he had left instructions with the Chinese merchant in Mazatlán to tell these young tourists to move on to their next station in groups of two, three, or five; never more than that. They were to go straight to Ensenada, a small town some eighty miles south of San Diego.

How they got there was their own affair. Some walked.

Some rented Mexican carts and were driven to Ensenada in style. On arrival, they were to go into a small store, where they would be fed, given a rest, and then sent on to their next stop.

This was a Chinese farm some nine miles away. It was called the China Camp and had been set up for just such a purpose as this. For years it had been used by Mexicans smuggling men and goods into the United States. Some Chinese made a pretense of farming it. They raised vegetables, it's true—but it didn't matter whether they ever sold their produce or not. There was always plenty to eat, though the buildings were hovels. But the viceroys' sons never complained of the poor quarters. No sacrifice was too great for them to make for the cause, and they were prepared for the many hardships that awaited them.

A guide led the way to this farm, not far from Todos Santos Bay. They were to remain here until the next move would be explained to them. In the meantime, they helped around the farm; if any passer-by wished to take a second look, all he saw were Chinese farmers, barefooted, with trousers rolled up to their knees, hoeing vegetables. It was a new experience for the viceroys' sons—accustomed to luxuries and being waited upon—but the healthy out-of-door life did them good.

When around thirty men had arrived, the agent in Ensenada sent a list of these men—in Chinese—to Duke. O'Banion was then told the number now waiting at the border. And a boat, which had been lying at anchor in San Francisco Bay, would start its voyage south to get the men and bring them into this country. These boats, purchased for the purpose, had been especially fitted up to hold thirty men. Since the boats were only some twenty-five feet long, crowding the men in required a certain ingenuity.

They were packed like sardines. In the bottom of the boat, cleats were put in and boards placed on top. Row after row, as close together as possible. In loading a boat the last row would get in first, sit down, then the board in front of them put into place, and so on until the seating capacity was reached. There was no possibility for anyone to change his seat, once he had taken it.

While the boat was anchored in the San Francisco Bay, incidentally, the boards were never left in place. They were stored at the produce market run by Charlie Lung. When orders came to set sail, one of his potato boats would take the boards on board just before the boat lifted anchor. The boat itself was never near the produce market, and consequently no questions were ever asked.

It was an uncomfortable way to travel up the coast from Mexico to San Francisco, but it had to be done that way. The boats posed as fishermen's boats; and, since they were small, no one would suspect they were loaded to the brim with Chinese being smuggled into the United States. Hoeing vegetables on the farm was easy compared with this hardship. It took about a week from the time of sailing to arrival —and the Chinese were supposed not to move from their seats. Food and water were passed down to them. It was a tough way of living for a week, but not once did a single one complain.

Landing in San Francisco was one problem. Seeing that the boat arrived safe and on time was another. Everything had to work according to schedule. If something went wrong with the timing, discovery might follow—and what a stir that would cause. It wouldn't be only the United States government that would investigate, but the Manchu government might ask questions, and also the viceroys would be more than merely disturbed. They would say that Dr. Sun had failed them—and the whole revolutionary movement might collapse from within.

Once the boat was loaded, as per schedule, it started up the coast. It was then O'Banion's duty to signal that everything was ready for their arrival in San Francisco and that the boat could proceed to its destination.

Now at Arch Beach, not far from Laguna Beach in Southern California, there was an art colony. Boats could come in close to shore at this point, but they couldn't land. And often when a boat was on its way north, O'Banion would go there for a beach party. As he told people, combining pleasure with a certain amount of business, he fished for lobsters. Into the water he'd drop a wire pot with a hunk of beef in it. There was a good stout rope on the end of this lobster pot. When the curious and hungry lobsters had crawled into the pot, he'd raise it, take out the lobsters— and sometimes prepare a stew. Now fishing for lobsters requires patience. The lobsters are slow; so the only thing to do is to sit and wait, sometimes for hours. But it was a perfect blind.

Often, people joined him, and O'Banion proved a popular host at lobster parties. And, of course, his guests never once guessed that what he was really doing was waiting for boats to appear from Mexico loaded with Chinese.

He always knew, obviously, just which boat it was. The boat would come up close to shore—sometimes so close O'Banion could have talked to those on board had he so wished. On the boat was posted a man fishing. If everything was in order and the boat could—and should—proceed immediately to San Francisco, O'Banion gave the go-ahead sign. He'd pretend he was weary of sitting on the beach so long, waiting for the lobsters. He'd stand up and do some setting-up exercises.

There were two places to unload the men in San Francisco Bay: one in South San Francisco and the other in Oakland. If the boat was to proceed to Oakland, O'Banion's setting-up exercise consisted of stretching and bending over; arms extended straight above head, then, without bending his knees, he would lean over and touch his toes. To do this twice meant to proceed to Oakland. If he wanted to warn the fisherman to be cagey and take every precaution, he'd merely stretch but not bend over. Then he'd stand up straight, hold his arms out at his sides and drop them. He'd turn around, do the same thing over again. And so it went, through the whole system of prearranged signals.

To the casual observer he was merely stretching himself. But to the fisherman on the boat, it all meant something else. Once the fisherman got the signal, he'd pretend fishing was no good at this spot, take up his line, and sail away.

As soon as he possibly could, without appearing to be unduly hasty, O'Banion would draw up the lobster pot, call it a day's work, jump into his car and drive to San Francisco. He always arrived ahead of the boat. Now came the ticklish job of unloading the men.

There were two places: One was in South San Francisco, not far from a most convenient laundry. When the boat came into the bay, O'Banion was at this Chinese laundry waiting. The skipper of the boat would so time himself that he managed to come in at dusk with the regular fishing fleet. The fleet would go to their regular wharves, where they would tie up for the night. But, once in the bay, the

smuggler's boat would swing around and go up San Pueblo
Bay, or sometimes up what was called Mud Creek. When
everything was clear, he would then manage to reach a place
to anchor down by the laundry.

The next step was for the skipper to get into a dory and
begin to paint the boat. This was a signal for O'Banion that
everything was in order. Probably no other boats in the
bay were ever painted as much as these. The job was never
really completed, either. Seeing the painting being done,
O'Banion would signal from shore and the skipper would
row in and get him.

He'd go aboard the boat and then tell the Chinese they
were in San Francisco and would soon be put ashore. All
the way up the coast they had seen the lights of the towns
they were passing and always wanted to know just where they
were. But the skipper never told them. Or, if he did give
an answer, it would always be wrong. The Chinese never
really knew just where they were to be landed. And it was
better that they didn't know. They had been instructed in
Mexico not to ask too many questions. It was wiser not to
know in case anything went wrong. But when O'Banion
put in an appearance, he told them that now they were at
the end of their journey.

That night, when the coast was clear, five at a time the
men were rowed ashore in the dory. The laundry was
pointed out to them, and singly or in pairs the men went
quickly to the laundry, opened the door, and walked in.

The owner of this laundry worked hand in glove with
Duke. Preparations for each man's accommodations had
been made in advance. Duke had the list of names of the
young men coming in, and he had previously spoken to
friends or relatives of these men. Now from the laundry

they were to be delivered to their hosts. For this purpose, guides were waiting at the laundry. These had been planted here especially by Duke. During the day they posed as laundry helpers. For each man the guides delivered they were paid $5.

The overseas Chinese, of course, spoke no English. Nor were they, upon their arrival, dressed in conventional American clothes. Chinese dress, quite naturally. They all, also, had queues.

Immediately upon their arrival at the laundry they were given a bath, some good hot food—and then Duke cut their queues. O'Banion once asked him why that wasn't done at the farm in Mexico. But Duke replied, with a twinkle in his eye, "Better upon their landing in the United States. Make a ceremony of it! Let them feel they are not free men until they arrive in the Land of Freedom. Every time I cut a queue I give a little speech."

The men were given a suit of American clothes, shoes, socks, shirt, tie, and hat, and all that goes with it. They usually kept this suit for a week or so until they had time to purchase clothes of their own. The borrowed suit was returned to the laundry to be ready for the next viceroy's son who was coming in. The thirty suits of clothes kept at this laundry, locked in a back room, sometimes caused Duke to refer to this place as the Chinese-American Clothing and Queue Cutting Store!

Once properly attired, the charge would be taken in tow by the guide, and off they'd go. They might have walked the streets in their Chinese dress. It was often done in those days, and it was no strange sight to see a Chinese shuffling along in a Chinese gown and slippers. Yet any immigration officers could detect at a glance dirty garments that had been worn on a boat coming from overseas and had not been cleaned and stored away on these shores in a teakwood chest. So, the safest thing to do with these men was to dress them up quickly in American clothes.

Then, too, while waiting in Mexico, they had been given certain instructions; particularly in how to walk properly on the streets: Don't shuffle along in the Chinese manner—but keep head up, eyes front, pick up your feet—and don't "rubberneck" around too much for the first few days in America. "Watch your step," in short, and behave as if you have been here a long time.

And in going to the new home, there were certain things to be done. This was to follow the guide and do exactly as he did. If he stopped, they were to stop. If he boarded a streetcar and dropped a coin into the conductor's hand, they were to do the same. When the guide got up to get off—they were to stand up, too. They were to keep their distance, follow the guide—and if they got lost, that would just be too bad!

Their arrival, of course, at the homes of friends and relatives had all been prepared for. When a guide rapped on a door and walked in, they were to rap and walk in, too. Then the banquets and feasting and ceremonies of welcome to a visitor from overseas were in order. These young men were all from wealthy families and were well supplied with spending money. They had not, however, brought in money on their persons from China to Mexico and then to the United States. But everything had been arranged in the Chinese manner.

Through friends, relatives, or family connections, the viceroys had made contact with Chinese businessmen in this country. To them were entrusted funds to be placed at the disposal of their sons. So the money was already here when the boys arrived.

They consequently never did any work while in this country, but spent their entire time either attending school or training with the troops. The idea at first was for each one to remain here for three years. But some proved such apt students and worked so hard that they were sent back to China before the three-year period was over.

Nor did they all remain in San Francisco. Many went on to New York, Boston, and Philadelphia. St. Louis was a favorite place at this time, and a great many were trained in the company there.

Returning them to China simply meant reversing the process. From this country they were taken to Todos Santos Bay, and from there, by way of the farm again, to Mazatlán and then on back to China.

Among all the viceroys' sons who came to the United States, only one failed to return. He was among a boatload that landed at Oakland.

In those days Chinatown in Oakland was about a block from the water front. At the foot of Franklin Street were the coal bunkers, where the seagoing ships were loaded. Tugs and small boats of all descriptions came and went freely. It was an ideal spot for landing men.

About half a block from the wharves was an old store building. Here an agent was planted. He posed as a cigar manufacturer, a one-man factory. Outside his door was a small green light. During the day, anyone looking through the windows of his little shop could see him busy at work. He made a special rate to sailors, but he never urged them to buy. He had to sell a few cigars, of course, to keep up a front. Always when O'Banion came around he would have a box of cigars ready for him.

"With my compliments," he would say, smiling. "Someone must smoke my cigars."

These were good cigars, and O'Banion always had a pocketful. Everything connected with the store was paid for: the rent, the tobacco, and so forth. Whatever the Chinese agent made from sales now and then he kept for himself.

This spot in Oakland was where the majority of men were landed. The cigar store served the same purpose as the laundry in South San Francisco. Duke would be waiting for the men to arrive, and would then send them on to their destination.

On the day when O'Banion knew a boat was coming in, he would ramble around the docks and look things over. If there was too much activity and it wouldn't be safe to land, he'd signal the boat to go on to South San Francisco. Or, as sometimes happened, he'd signal for them to wait until he let them know that everything was safe. Now and then, a boat remained at anchor in the bay for as long as twenty-four hours.

Once a boat was held up even longer. There was a dead youth on board.

He was the son of an important viceroy. When he arrived in Mazatlán—a quiet, studious lad—he was ill. According to the doctor, he had tuberculosis. Now the trip from Mexico was a hard one. Only the men in the best physical condition could survive. Should a man be ill when he arrived at the farm at Ensenada, he was not brought into America until he was in good health again. The risk of bringing in a frail, half-sick man was too great. Some were even sent back home from Mexico.

The Chinese merchant in Mazatlán wrote to Duke and strongly advised that this particular boy be returned to China. But the boy didn't want to go. He refused to budge, even when Duke told him he was not in favor of bringing him into this country. The boy wrote a letter home to his father. Several months went by.

In China, through the underground, the viceroy made contact with Dr. Sun. Sun wrote to Homer Lea and urged that, because of the father's political importance, the boy be smuggled in. Neither the father nor the son wished to be left out of the coming revolution. They both wanted to do their part and were willing to take any risk, even if their lives were at stake. So Homer Lea told O'Banion to do what could best be done under the circumstances. The boy was sent to the farm, where he stayed some time gaining strength. And finally they all felt he was well enough to be brought in. At least they would risk it. But the boy died on the boat, two days before arriving in San Francisco.

Ordinarily, he would have been buried at sea. But in this case it could not be done. His bones must some day be returned to China to rest forever in the tomb of his ancestors.

When Duke and O'Banion were informed by the skipper what had happened, they shook their heads in dismay. They had felt all along it was the wrong thing to do; but, after all, they were soldiers and were only carrying out orders. Nobody really could be blamed. No revolution is fought without casualties.

They sent the boat with the body on board to Acid Point on San Pueblo Bay. Then they went to San Francisco to discuss the matter with the man posing as the boy's uncle. Finally a decision was reached. A cock-and-bull story to be told the police was carefully rehearsed.

The plan was to strip the body of all clothes and place it

naked on the beach. Carrying out this unpleasant task fell
to the lot of Paul Beezoff. The nude body was put into a
rowboat and taken ashore at Hunter's Point. Near by was an
acid factory. As Paul was placing the body on the shore he
saw the night watchman, an old man, coming toward him
with a lantern.

Quickly Paul stepped up to him and grabbed the lantern.
He put it out. Everything happened so swiftly that the old
man was taken by complete surprise. And before he knew
it, Paul had also seized his gun and dropped it into his
pocket. Now Paul always carried with him, for any emergency that might arise, two or three $100 bills.

"Listen, Pop," he said, and thrust a bill into the old man's
hand. "Look at this when you have time. If it's worth your
while, go on home and forever after keep your mouth shut!"

The old man knew it was money. That was certain. Paul
gave him back his gun, after removing the shells. Then he
marched the old man up the beach and stood there until
he vanished behind the corner of the factory. Obviously,
Pop had a decision to make. And he made it when he saw
the size of the bill. He did as he was told—put the money in
his pocket, kept his mouth shut, and forgot all about it. A
poorly paid night watchman doesn't get one hundred dollars
every night in the year. Certainly, in the investigation that
followed, there was no peep of any sort from Pop.

The body was left on the beach and Paul went back to
San Francisco. That much had been successfully accomplished. Meanwhile the boy's uncle had carried out his part
of the scheme. That same morning he had gone to the
police station and reported that his nephew was missing.
The uncle said he was deeply worried, for the boy had been
ill for some time, both physically and mentally. Because of

his ill-health he had been brooding and had spoken of suicide. And now he had vanished. The uncle was afraid he had killed himself. Would the police help him find the boy—and bring him back safe?

The police promised they would do what they could. Late the next day they informed the uncle that a body had been found at Hunter's Point—and would he come and identify the boy?

The uncle had never seen him, of course, but he went to the morgue and claimed the body as that of his nephew. An autopsy was held, and the coroner's report said that the boy had died of natural causes. But the police were puzzled about the naked body. Nor could they find the boy's clothes anywhere.

But the uncle stuck to his story that at times the boy had been unbalanced, had acted peculiarly, and had even said he wanted to go to Hunter's Point to swim. And since he had in his previous visit to the police stressed the boy's brooding nature and his unnatural behavior, the police accepted the coroner's verdict and, as far as they were concerned, the matter was closed.

The uncle made the proper display of mourning and buried his nephew with a truly magnificent Chinese funeral. It was a fitting tribute to a soldier who had given his life for the cause he was serving.

Some ten years later, the uncle told O'Banion that this boy, too, had gone home to China as had the other sons of the viceroys. At the Feast of the Dead his bones were taken up, polished carefully, placed in a box especially prepared for them, and shipped overseas to his father.

CHAPTER TWENTY-TWO

Came the Revolution

THE day came, of course, when the training in this country was over, and the soldiers had all been sent to China, where they were serving, disguised as privates, in the Royal Manchu Army.

There was no longer any need for the boats. Certainly neither Duke nor O'Banion wanted them. They had served their purpose, so they were given to the skippers. One or two of them put their boats to good use and hired them out to fishing parties for a cruising holiday around the bay. Other skippers returned to their former occupation of conventional smuggling. Ultimately, John Osterhaus was caught and sent to prison. But he had made a small fortune out of all this—some $16,000.

The time had now come to set a date for the revolution. Quite openly, in 1910, Dr. Sun came to this country. Kang Yu-wei was already here. Now it must be decided, once and for all, who was to be the acknowledged leader of the revolution.

In Los Angeles a banquet was given in honor of Dr. Sun at the Po Wong Wui Hall. This was located on the upper floor of a two-story building at 409 Apablasa Street, and was called the Sun Building. By this time, the majority of Chinese in the United States were in favor of Dr. Sun and his principles.

In his speech at this banquet, he publicly declared that,

should the revolution succeed, he had no ambitions to become president of China. He promised his undying loyalty to the republic and said he would devote the rest of his life to working for a truly democratic form of government.

Following the banquet, Dr. Sun and Homer Lea, together with O'Banion, who acted as bodyguard, went on to New York. Kang Yu-wei was there, living in style at the old Waldorf-Astoria Hotel on the corner of Fifth Avenue and 34th Street. He had a magnificent suite of several rooms, especially furnished by the hotel with rare antiques. Among them was an inlaid table, a museum piece, said to be worth at least $4,000.

Behind this table Kang Yu-wei sat when he received visitors. And many people came to see him. He was posing as the head of the Reform party in China and was only too glad to discuss the possibilities of granting concessions to the prominent bankers and businessmen who had money to invest. Many of them had been unable to make satisfactory arrangements with the Manchu government. But Kang Yu-wei was eager to make promises.

Then Dr. Sun Yat-sen and General Homer Lea appeared on the scene. The three men sat at the conference table in the Waldorf-Astoria suite. Homer Lea knew that, if these two men did not agree at this time, all the work and plans of years would be lost. It was impossible to proceed with this deadlock.

And so the old arguments continued. Dr. Sun, gentle, mild and calm, but absolutely fearless, proclaimed his belief in a republic for China. Kang Yu-wei blustered and thumped his chest and wanted his form of government, a constitutional monarchy. Between them sat young Homer Lea, wearing the uniform of a general in the Chinese Reform Army and carrying the sword given him by Kuang Hsu, the Boy Emperor.

Had a stenographer taken down in shorthand their conversations, he would have recorded a sound and important discussion of opposing political theories. Both men advanced well-founded opinions in support of their ideas. And there was right on both sides.

The polite, courteous, philosophical discussions continued in the approved Chinese manner, day after day. But one morning the matter was finally decided, following an outburst of Yankee anger on the part of Homer Lea.

As he said afterward to O'Banion, "Look at my sword. See those three nicks. It was the first time I've drawn this sword. Kang Yu-wei almost jumped out of his chair. I think he thought I was going to behead him on the spot. But I banged my sword on the table.

"I told Kang Yu-wei that he was standing in the way of the revolution, and it was up to him—if he loved China, as he said he did—to step aside. I gave as my reason the simple fact that Dr. Sun had greater support and more followers than he—not only in America but also in China. I told him that by popular vote the members of the Po Wong Wui sided now with Dr. Sun.

"I banged the table again and told him the soldiers we had trained were loyal only to Dr. Sun. Then I whacked the table once more and told him that, because of all this, Dr. Sun was the logical leader of the revolution and should be acknowledged as such.

"I practically ruined the table!"

General Lea carried his point. Kang Yu-wei, who knew all this to be true, proved himself the great man he really was and bowed out of the picture. He acknowledged Dr.

Sun as the accepted leader. And with the typical politeness and courtesy of a genuine Chinese gentleman, he paid out of his own pocket for the damage done the table.

Final plans were now made and a date set for the outbreak of the revolution. It was planned for some time in 1912—only Dr. Sun and General Lea knew the exact date.

O'Banion went back to Los Angeles. There was nothing much for him to do now but wait. Later, he would be given further orders. Following the successful conclusion of the revolution, he was to go to China. There he would take the men he had trained in this country and with these officers as a nucleus build up the Chinese Revolutionary Army—the army that would support the new government.

One morning in October of 1911, O'Banion was at home when the telephone rang. It was a long-distance call from San Francisco. On the other end of the line he heard the excited voice of Duke.

"Hurrah for us, Captain. It's started!" said Duke.

"What's started?" asked the surprised O'Banion.

"The revolution! It will be in the papers in a day or so. This is advance information. Wait!"

And so O'Banion waited. The news spread around Chinatown. But there were no celebrations, no banquets. Everyone went about his business as usual. Final word as to the success had not yet come through, and the outbreak of the revolution had been premature.

What happened was this: On Oct. 9, some powder, which had been stored in a house in the Russian Concession at Hankow, accidentally exploded. It revealed to the officials the existence of a revolutionary plot. Immediately the Viceroy of Wuchang ordered thirty arrests. He sent a wire to the

Regent saying that the rebellion had been suppressed and everything was under control. But he had jumped too hastily to this conclusion.

On Oct. 10, in the evening, the garrison at Wuchang revolted. The viceroy suddenly found himself without soldiers to defend the government. By the evening of the next day, Oct. 11, in the three cities of Wuchang, Hankow, and Hanyang, the Royal Manchu Army was taken over by the revolutionists. Commanding the army were officers trained for this very purpose in America. The plan had worked!

Dr. Sun was in Denver, Colo., at the time, and not aware of what was happening in far-off China. The night before, tired and worn out from a long day's traveling, he had gone to bed early, hoping to get a good night's rest. He slept until eleven o'clock the next morning. On his way to a restaurant for breakfast he bought a newspaper.

"Wuchang occupied by the revolutionists!" said the headlines.

Dr. Sun was amazed and surprised. He had previously received cablegrams from China telling him that the troops were becoming impatient. He had been worried and distressed. But now it had happened.

He noticed the date, Oct. 10—the Tenth Day of the Tenth Month. Should the revolution succeed, this day would be for China what the Fourth of July was to liberty-loving Americans—their Independence Day. And so it has become, and ever since then the Chinese have taken this date as their Fourth of July—the day on which their Liberty Bell rang in China. Yearly it is celebrated by the Chinese and known now as Double Ten, the day China became a republic.

From that Oct. 10 in 1911, events in China moved swiftly. After the outbreak of the revolution unexpectedly in

Wuchang, there were uprisings all over China. In less than three weeks after the explosion of the gunpowder, ten provinces had been won over by the revolutionists. Even the troops that the Manchu government sent to suppress the rebellion were unsuccessful—and for a reason we well know.

The Manchu government saw that its regime was tottering, and the centuries of their supremacy in China were over. They declared an armistice. In the negotiations that followed, they agreed to transform China into a constitutional monarchy. But the revolutionists refused.

They insisted on the abdication of the Manchus and the founding of a republic. In Nanking, the revolutionists set up a Provisional Reform government and asked Dr. Sun Yat-sen to become its head.

For this humble doctor who had fled around the world in disguise with a price on his head, there was a triumphal return to China. Knowing that the Republic of China would have the support of foreign powers, he went from Denver to Washington, and then on to London. There he was joined by General Homer Lea and his wife and secretary, Mrs. Ethel Powers Lea. From London to Paris and other capitals of the world, they traveled. And then, by way of India, they went on to Shanghai, where they arrived on Christmas Eve, 1911.

The rest is history. On Jan. 1, 1912, Dr. Sun Yat-sen was proclaimed provisional president of the Chinese Republic. On Feb. 12, the Manchus abdicated.

Then, on Feb. 15, an imposing ceremony took place just outside Nanking—at the tomb of Chu Yuan-chang, the founder of the Ming Dynasty.

Dr. Sun, escorted by the members of his cabinet, officials of the newly formed government, and a large escort of soldiers commanded by General Lea, visited the tomb. It was a gesture of courtesy and politeness from the new government to the former ruler of a free China. On this occasion, it was only fitting that Dr. Sun should be the spokesman for the people.

He said in conclusion, "I have heard that in the past many would-be deliverers of their country have ascended this lofty mound wherein is your sepulcher. It has served them as a holy inspiration. As they looked down upon the surrounding rivers and upward to the hills, under alien sway, they wept in the bitterness of their hearts, but today their sorrow is turned to joy. The spiritual influences of your grave at Nanking have come once more into their own. The dragon crouches in majesty as of old, and the tiger surveys his domain and his ancient capital. Everywhere reigns a beautiful repose. Your legions line the approaches to the sepulcher; a noble host stands expectant. Your people have come here today to inform Your Majesty of the final victory. May this lofty shrine wherein you rest gain fresh luster from today's event and may your fine example inspire your descendants in the times which are to come. Spirit, accept this offering!"

That same day an election was held and Yuan Shi-kai was named Dr. Sun's successor, and the President of the Republic. Dr. Sun was sincere when he had said that he did not wish anything for himself; he only wanted to serve China. He could be a better patriot as a private citizen than as a president. The republic had been born. There would be turbulent years ahead. The Republic of China must be firmly established. He felt that he could work to better advantage to achieve his ideals if he remained in the background. His work, he felt, had in reality only begun.

What has happened in China since 1912 is another story

GENERAL HOMER LEA IN CHINESE COSTUME

and does not concern us here. It is the story of China's efforts to make Dr. Sun's ideal of a democracy come true. And the struggle still goes on. It took the United States many years after 1776, and the Revolutionary War, to establish firmly our form of government. We are still working toward a true democracy—and so is China. The struggle will continue, for no revolution is ever finally finished until all men everywhere are free.

During the months that Dr. Sun and General Lea were in China, O'Banion sat waiting in Los Angeles. He knew that the American end of it was over. So he began to make plans and arrange his affairs to go to China and take over the army under the command of General Lea.

Then one day word came through the Chinese in San Francisco that Homer Lea was ill and dying and was being brought back to this country. O'Banion went to San Francisco to receive him. General Lea arrived here in May of 1912, accompanied by his wife. He had to be taken off the boat in a wheel chair. While in Nanking he had suffered a stroke, and his left side was paralyzed.

Mrs. Lea had written to O'Banion saying that the general wished his arrival to be as quiet as possible. The strain and excitement of any public demonstration, she felt, would be too much for him. There were no reporters present; not even Homer Lea's Chinese friends had been told.

His first words to O'Banion were, "Don't let this worry you, Captain. I'll fool them yet. No man can die until his work is finished."

In the days that followed, there was little discussion of the revolution. Both O'Banion and Mrs. Lea avoided mentioning all that had happened, for fear General Lea might have another stroke.

But one day he did say to O'Banion, "I'm sorry you weren't with us in China, Captain. There wasn't a single hitch in any of our plans. They all worked—just as we had hoped they would. And it was—I am happy to say—for a revolution a comparatively bloodless one. Only such a friendly, peace-loving people as the Chinese could have managed it that way."

One morning he sent word for O'Banion to come to see him. Delayed because of business in Los Angeles, it was two days before O'Banion could get away.

When he arrived, General Lea said, "I'm sorry, Captain, you weren't here on Thursday. I've made all my funeral arrangements, and I want you to know about them."

"You're not giving up, certainly," said O'Banion.

"It won't be long now," smiled Homer Lea. "And please stand by. I don't want to have a horse-drawn hearse and go poking along to the cemetery. I know automobiles aren't popular for funerals, but I want to be taken in an automobile, and no slow driving, either. Just go right along. And I want only my family and closest personal friends— and as few as possible. Please, no fuss. When a man's work is done, let's ring down the curtain quickly."

There wasn't much that O'Banion could say. He didn't know this was the last time he would see General Lea. A few days later, at three o'clock in the morning, Mrs. Lea telephoned O'Banion that General Lea had passed away in his sleep.

The funeral was a quiet one, as he had wished it. Only members of his family, his sister Hersha, Captain and Mrs. O'Banion, and one newspaper reporter were present.

When the word was made public, there were newspaper stories all over the country and a great deal of speculation on the career and life of this somewhat mysterious man, General Homer Lea of the Chinese Reform Army.

Among the many letters and telegrams of condolence Mrs. Lea received was one she highly treasured. It said:

Accept our sincere regrets in your bereavement as we the Chinese Free Masons feel that your loss is our loss; your esteemed husband and our tried and true friend. We accept the same with heads bowed down as we know it is the wish of our Creator.

Authorized by the Chinese Free Mason Society,

Loo Qwong, President

Quom Sim, Secretary.

Two weeks after the funeral Mrs. Lea asked O'Banion to come to Santa Monica.

"I've been thinking of disposing of Homer's personal effects," she said. "His uniform and his sword and the decorations he received, I shall always keep. But the papers, the maps, and the documents, what shall we do with them?"

In China, as they both knew, the republic was having birth pains. The struggle for a democratic form of government was still in progress, and would continue for years. Among the papers were the names of the revolutionists. In the right hands, they would be of value. But what damage they could cause if they fell into the possession of the wrong people!

"We've kept it a secret during the years we were working together," said O'Banion. "Perhaps it had better remain that way, at least for the present."

So they carried out to the back yard great packages of papers: letters, maps, drawings, lists of names, and so forth —and burned them.

Following the death of General Lea, O'Banion knew that now he would never again go to China. So he, too, rang down the curtain. He wound up his business affairs in Chinatown as gracefully and as quietly as he could. He withdrew gradually and as time went on even stopped going to Chinatown. He kept only one contact among his Chinese friends, and that was with Duke.

Yet his part in the Chinese Revolution was not completely over. There remained one more thing he had to do. It came about most unexpectedly and was quite unforeseen.

One of the men engaged in the smuggling of soldiers in and out of this country talked out of turn. Not knowing the real truth of what was behind it all, he told a garbled story. Rumors of this reached the ears of certain Federal officials. And O'Banion was accused of smuggling Chinese into the United States.

An indictment was returned in 1912. O'Banion, of course, could at this time have told the truth in the matter and probably nothing would have been done. But it was too soon, and the whole story was still a secret to be kept and closely guarded. If he spoke, he would betray the trust the soldiers had placed in him, the memories of the confidence and respect of Homer Lea, and the ideals Dr. Sun had for a free China.

Looking at the evidence today, it is all too plain that it was exactly what Duke said at the time, "The right man, but the wrong case."

However, O'Banion, like a true soldier, loyal to his oath of silence, accepted the judgment of the court.

In 1916, when, as far as he was concerned, it was finally over, he came to Sierra Madre to live. And here his home has been ever since. Today he is proud of the fact that he remained silent at the time and said nothing that might have jeopardized the success of the revolution and the lives of those he knew had been connected with it here in America.

One day in 1918, after the First World War was over and the Armistice had been declared, Paul Beezoff came to see him. He was one of the few men connected with all this who knew where O'Banion lived. The two men had dinner together and then sat and talked over old times.

"I've made quite a bit of money," said Paul. "I've put some of it aside. There's a revolution going on in Russia, among my own people. Plenty doing over there. I want to be in on it. So I'm off, Captain. This isn't good-by—if all goes well, you'll be hearing from me again one of these days!"

Paul went to Russia. And that is the last O'Banion ever heard from him.

The next person to bid O'Banion good-by was Duke. He said he was going to China to spend the rest of his life there. Years passed, and then one day, before the present war, O'Banion received a message from a Chinese in San Francisco. He said that Duke had written him and wanted O'Banion to know he was living quietly in Canton, enjoying life, writing poetry, and was now a grandfather. What happened to Duke after the Japanese captured Canton, O'Banion does not know. Perhaps when the war is over, he'll be hearing from Duke again.

In the spring of 1942, when Mme Chiang Kai-shek was in Los Angeles, a reception was given in her honor. Mr. Chang, the Chinese Consul, sent Captain O'Banion an invitation.

When he met Mr. Chang at the reception he asked, "How did you know where to find me?"

"How do you think?"

O'Banion had one more question to ask.

"Why did you invite me?"

Mr. Chang smiled again, and said, "Why not?"

As Captain O'Banion passed down the receiving line, he bowed gravely to Mme Chiang. She smiled and, with a small graceful gesture, lifted her hand in greeting. That was all.

One afternoon, a short time after this, the doorbell of O'Banion's home gave a merry tinkle. Standing on the door-step was a young Chinese, a stranger to O'Banion, wearing the uniform of a lieutenant in the United States Army Air Force.

"Excuse me, sir," he said. "Are you the Captain O'Banion who drilled the Chinese troops back in 1903?"

"The same," replied O'Banion.

"Do you remember the little Wong girl who used to come around occasionally?"

"I most certainly do!"

"I'm her eldest son!" said the lieutenant, proudly.

"Come on in!" exclaimed O'Banion, holding the door wide open. When they were seated, the young lieutenant said, "Soon I shall be overseas, I hope. My mother wanted me to come to see you. She sends her regards and says she will never forget the old days."

"Nor will I," said O'Banion, soberly. "There aren't so many of us left now. Dr. Sun Yat-sen died in 1925. He's buried at Nanking."

"Yes, I know," said the lieutenant softly.

"Kang Yu-wei passed on about the same time—in Shang-hai, so I've been told. Of all those closely connected with what went on here in America, I'm one of the few old-timers still around."

"So my mother said. She also wanted me to tell you she always regretted she was a girl and couldn't be a soldier. But she says—unworthy as I am—she is very proud to see her son wearing the uniform of the United States. She says we're fighting the same battle. And she asked me if you would please accept this simple gift—as a remembrance—after all these years."

It was a brass ruler with a Chinese tassel on it, and incased in a gold, red, and blue Chinese box.

"My mother says this ruler reminds her of you. You always stood so straight and were so straight in everything you did!"

The lieutenant rose to go.

"One of these days I hope to be in China," he said, soberly. "Nanking—where is the tomb of Dr. Sun Yat-sen—is in the hands of Japan. But I want to assure you, Captain—and I'm speaking not only for myself, but also for the sons and grandsons of all the Chinese you have known, who are now fighting again for China—we shall not surrender. We shall not rest until we all shall stand before the tomb of Dr. Sun and tell him, as he told the Mings, that China is once again free!"

He saluted and was gone.

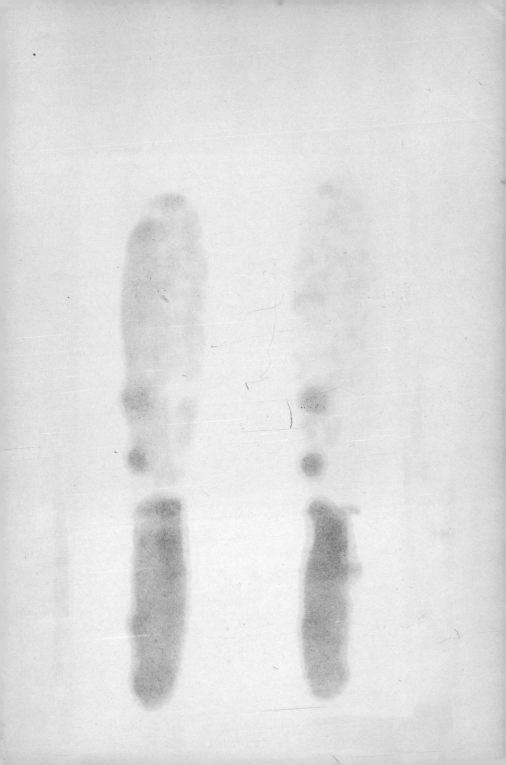

DATE DUE	